Learning BASIC Programming:
A Systematic Approach

Brooks/Cole Series in Computer Science

Program Design with Pseudocode
T. E. Bailey and K. A. Lundgaard

BASIC: An Introduction to Computer Programming with the Apple
Robert J. Bent and George C. Sethares

BASIC: An Introduction to Computer Programming, Second Edition
Robert J. Bent and George C. Sethares

Business BASIC
Robert J. Bent and George C. Sethares

FORTRAN with Problem Solving: A Structured Approach
Robert J. Bent and George C. Sethares

Beginning BASIC
Keith Carver

Beginning Structured COBOL
Keith Carver

Structured COBOL for Microcomputers
Keith Carver

Learning Basic Programming: A Systematic Approach
Howard Dachslager, Masato Hayashi, and Richard Zucker

Problem Solving and Structured Programming with FORTRAN 77
Martin O. Holoien and Ali Behforooz

Basic Business BASIC: Using Microcomputers
Peter Mears and Louis Raho

Brooks/Cole Series in Computer Education

An Apple for the Teacher: Fundamentals of Instructional Computing
George Culp and Herbert Nickles

RUN: Computer Education
Dennis O. Harper and James H. Stewart

Learning BASIC Programming: A Systematic Approach

Howard Dachslager
Masato Hayashi
Richard Zucker
Saddleback Community College, North Campus

Brooks/Cole Publishing Co.
Monterey, California

Dedicated to
Frankie, Gayle, and Connie
with love

Brooks/Cole Publishing Company
A Division of Wadsworth, Inc.

Photo Credits: Chapter 1—Brunswick Corporation, Chapter
2—Stanley Rice, Chapter 3—LEGO® Systems, Inc., Chapter
4—Stanley Rice, Chapter 5—Stanley Rice, Chapter 6—The
Metropolitan Museum of Art, Gift of Thomas F. Ryan, 1910,
Chapter 7—Knott's Berry Farm, Chapter 8—Stanley Rice,
Chapter 9—Stanley Rice, Chapter 10—Stanley Rice, Chapter
11—Stanley Rice, Chapter 12—Jamie Pettengill

Printed in the United States of America

10 9 8 7 6 5 4 3

Library of Congress Cataloging in Publication Data

Dachslager, Howard.
   Learning BASIC programming.

   (Brooks/Cole series in computer science)
   Includes index.
   1. Basic (Computer program language) I. Hayashi,
Masato. II. Zucker, Richard. III. Title. IV. Series.
QA76.73.B3D33   1983   001.64'24   83-2519
ISBN 0-534-01422-4

Apple, Apple II, Apple II Plus, and APPLESOFT II are registered
trademarks of Apple Computer Inc with regard to any computer
product.

Subject Editor: Michael Needham
Manuscript Editor: Jennifer DeJong
Production Coordination: Cobb/Dunlop Publisher Services
Production Editor: Maureen P. Conway
Interior Design: Otto Spec
Cover Design: Stan Rice
Typesetting: Graphic Typesetting Service

Preface

Our concern about the lack of a simple, systematic method for teaching BASIC was the motivation for writing this book. Over the years we have experienced some frustration in our attempts to teach students to write programs beyond an elementary level. This led us to reexamine the traditional methods of teaching programming and to search for a fresh approach to the subject. This book is the result of our endeavors.

In step with the increasing popularity of microcomputers, we have chosen to use Applesoft II BASIC, the standard language of the popular Apple II Plus computer. Our intention, however, is to present as many universal aspects of BASIC as is possible. With that in mind, the features of Applesoft which are strictly unique to the Apple II Plus computer have been left to the last chapter. What remains is the essence of Applesoft, which is remarkably similar to the versions of BASIC found on many other microcomputers.

Four features of this book set it apart from other BASIC programming texts. They are the Box Diagram, hands-on laboratory assignments, a discussion of algorithms and modules, and an entire chapter devoted to the special "extras" found in Applesoft BASIC. What follows is a short description of each of these noteworthy highlights.

THE BOX DIAGRAM

The Box Diagram is like a window into the memory of the computer. Students can see how variables are stored and how data changes. The usually abstract ideas of data storage and sequential program flow are visualized, so learning becomes conceptual rather than rote. An especially good example of the value of the Box Diagram can be found on pages 9 and 10, where it is used to demonstrate the technique of exchanging the contents of two variables. The Box Diagram is present throughout the book, making visible the effect that BASIC instructions have on variables.

HANDS-ON LABS

At the end of each of the first ten chapters are lab assignments which cover the important topics of the chapter. These labs are meant to be done "hands-on" with a computer. We believe that a real experience with a computer accelerates learning, and the labs do just that. Each lab is a structured "do this, do that" kind of activity with questions that force students to analyze the computer's responses. Answers and explanations immediately follow the questions posed in the labs, so that students are never left to wonder for too long. The labs have been a boon to our students. Many of them tell us that the labs have both eliminated their fear of the computer and increased their comprehension of BASIC.

ALGORITHMS AND MODULES

We feel that an early introduction to writing programs using modules is important in developing good programming skills. In Chapter 3 we introduce the A.C.O. method which gives students a way of structuring simple programs into modules. Later we bring up the subject again by introducing the notion of an algorithm. Students learn to "piece" together algorithms to form modules. From these modules programs are born. (See Chapter 10.) This technique has helped our students learn to "divide and conquer" large problems by breaking them into smaller ones. The module approach also establishes good programming habits.

SPECIAL FEATURES OF APPLESOFT BASIC

The last chapter of the book presents some exciting features of the Applesoft language. It is a well-deserved reward for the student who has endeavored to the book's end. Here you will find topics such as prettyprinting, peeks and pokes, high and low resolution graphics, speaker and game paddle control, and much more. We believe you will be delighted with these topics and in our opinion gain a greater appreciation for the wonderful power of the Apple II Plus.

NOTES TO THE INSTRUCTOR

We refer you to the table of contents for a complete list of the topics and the order in which they appear. In addition, however, we offer the following remarks for your consideration.

1. The study of BASIC in Chapter 1 is done in the immediate mode. This allows students to get right onto a computer without having to learn the more difficult concepts involved with the deferred mode. Using the LET and PRINT statements only, students learn about variables, assignment, and arithmetic. Avoid the temptation to pass lightly over this material. A good understanding of this chapter will pay off later when more difficult concepts are introduced.

2. Chapter 2 deals with BASIC functions. Such an early treatment of functions is definitely a break from tradition, but we feel students should work with functions as soon as possible in order to gain an appreciation for the built-in power of the computer. This chapter can be skipped if functions are taken up by the instructor on an as-needed basis.

3. While the Box Diagram is used throughout the book, it is especially useful in Chapters 6, 7, and 8 when the IF-THEN and FOR-NEXT instructions and arrays are discussed. In Chapter 6, students can "see" how the contents of variables affect the outcome of a decision statement. In Chapter 7, with the topic of looping (which students commonly find difficult), the Box Diagram clearly shows how the index and other variables change during the looping process. And in Chapter 8, the Box Diagram is a natural technique for conveying the concept of arrays and subscripted variables.

4. Chapter 9 takes up the subject of concatenation. Section 9.3 discusses how concatenation is used to build records from fixed length fields. The importance of this section cannot be overstated. The subject of fields and records plays a primary role in Chapters 10 and 11, to say nothing of business applications in "real life."

5. Chapter 10 takes up structured programming (i.e., using algorithms to build modules to build programs), subroutines, and the notion of a menu. It is advisable to spend enough time in this chapter to emphasize to students that good programming means much more than writing programs that simply work.

6. Reading and writing sequential and random access data files is not always the subject of a first course in BASIC programming. Chapter 11 approaches

the subject in a conservative way by treating sequential file processing only. This chapter may be skipped without loss of continuity if time is short.

7. A section entitled "Projects" has been included in each chapter except Chapter 12. The projects were designed to enhance the students' understanding of material in each chapter and to give them additional applications for what they have learned. Solutions to the projects will be available in the instructor's guide.

8. The appendices should not be overlooked. Their relationship to the chapters is shown in the chart below.

CHAPTER SEQUENCE

A dashed line indicates an optional path.

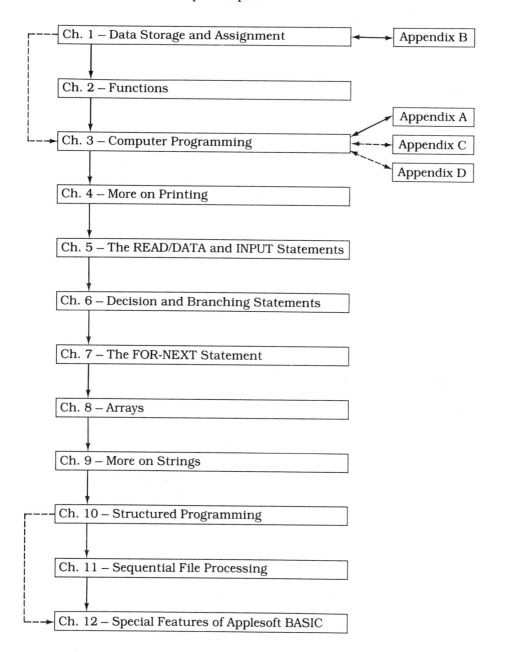

ACKNOWLEDGMENTS

We would like to thank those people who helped make this book a reality.

Thanks for the valuable critical analysis and suggestions of Professor Susan Anderson of Illinois Wesleyan University, Professor David Hansen of Monterey Peninsula College, Professor Leon Pearce of Drake University, Dr. Tom Richard of Bemidji State University, Professor Peter Simis of California State University, Fresno, and Professor Kenneth Trester of Golden West College.

Special thanks to Mr. Gerard Walsh for his many hours on the computer checking for errors in the example programs.

Also thanks to Mr. Gordon McDonald for his several interesting projects, to Mr. Albert Murtz for his assistance in editing the book, to Ms. Maureen Conway who, despite the miserable weekends she made for us was an invaluable help, and to our students who endured.

Last but not least to our loving wives without whose patience and encouragement this book could never have been written.

Howard Dachslager
Masato Hayashi
Richard Zucker

Saddleback College, North Campus
5500 Irvine Center Dr.
Irvine, California 92714

Contents

Chapter 3 Computer Programming

Chapter 4 More on Printing

Chapter 5 The READ/DATA and INPUT Statements

Chapter 6 Decision and Branching Statements

Chapter 7 The FOR-NEXT Statement

Chapter 8 Arrays

Chapter 9 More on Strings

Chapter 10 Structured Programming

Chapter **11** Sequential File Processing

Chapter **12** Special Features of Applesoft BASIC

1

Data Storage and Assignment

1.1 Computer data

Computers work with data. There are two types of data used in BASIC, *numeric* and *string*.

Numeric data are standard decimal numerals, including decimal points and negative signs when necessary. (Numeric data may also be expressed in scientific notation. See Lab 1.2 for examples.) The positive sign (+) is optional when expressing positive numbers.

Examples of Numeric Data

| 2.38 | 5 | 92714 | −0.567 | +406.5 | 0.06 |

A STRING is any collection of letters, digits, spaces, and symbols, all of which are simply known as "characters."*

Examples of Strings

| 10SNE1? | I LOVE MILK | HI HO SILVER, AWAY! |
| 92714 | !#$!&%##! | AN "ACUTE" ANGLE |

Data such as 92714 can be stored in the computer's memory either as a number or as a string. When 92714 is stored as numeric data, it can be used for calculations. As string data it is better suited for applications that do not involve arithmetic. For example, if 92714 is the population of Irvine, California, then storing this number as numeric data allows us to use it in census calculations. But, when 92714 is used as the zip code for Irvine, it is stored as string data and can be used in string applications, such as printing mailing labels.

EXERCISES 1.1

1. Which of these expressions are numeric data in BASIC?

   (a) 2.34   (b) 2 + 3   (c) −56.43

   (d) 4082 PLEASANT ST.   (e) $3.45   (f) +0.08

*In some versions of BASIC, the quotation mark (") is not permitted as a character within a string. Applesoft BASIC does allow the quotation mark, although certain restrictions apply, as we will discuss later.

2. Which of the following expressions are strings?

   (a) −2.34   (b) $45.00   (c) A STITCH IN TIME

   (d) THE WORD 'ENIGMA' IS VERY PUZZLING.

   (e) "RUN FASTER"! HE SAID SWIFTLY   (f) SAVES N-I-N-E

3. Count the number of characters in the following strings.

   (a) THE RAIN IN SPAIN   (b) HI HO SILVER, AWAY!

   (c) −23.34 + 47.93   (d) ANTIDISESTABLISHMENTARIANISM

1.2 The Box Diagram

Data has to be stored in computer memory. A simple way to visualize this is to assume that the computer places data into memory boxes designated by special names, such as X1, Z$, G3, and Y4$.

This box symbol ☐ stands for a storage location in memory.

Examples of the Box Diagram

X1	Z$	G3	Y4$
7.8	SING A SONG	−45.45	HI THERE

We shall refer to the data within a box as the value or contents of the box. The names of these boxes are called variables. There are two types of boxes: those that hold numeric data and those that hold string data. They are named by NUMERIC VARIABLES and STRING VARIABLES, respectively.

1.3 Numeric variables

Numeric variables can only contain numeric data.

Examples

X	Y	K1
345	−.00465	10

Numeric variable names are made from the letters A through Z and the digits 0 through 9 under the following rules:

RULES FOR NUMERIC VARIABLE NAMES

1. All numeric variables must begin with a letter and may be followed by from zero to 237 letters and digits.
2. Only the first two characters of the variable name are recognized by the computer. Therefore AMOUNT and AMBIDEXTROUS name the same box in the computer's memory.
3. No numeric variable name may contain a "reserved word." A reserved word is a word that is used by the computer in a special way. The words TO, AND, FOR, and AT are all reserved words. So TOTAL, SANDY, FORTITUDE, and COATS are all invalid variable names because they each contain a reserved word. A complete list of Applesoft reserved words appears in Appendix B.

These rules apply to Applesoft BASIC. In many versions of BASIC, numeric variable names must be one letter or a single letter followed by one digit only. Longer variable names, like those in Applesoft, allow variables to be descriptive, such as SALARY and GPA instead of S and G.

Examples of
Valid Numeric
Variable
Names
     X   X1   GOLFTALLY   K9   X15   SUM

Examples of
Invalid
Numeric
Variable
Names

4U	(cannot start with a digit)
RATE	(contains a reserved word)
BRANDX	(contains a reserved word)
FILE#3	('#' is not a letter or a digit)
D$	('$' is not a letter or a digit)

Example   The Box Diagram at the right is not correct since X is a numeric variable and can only contain numeric data.

X
LOVE

EXERCISES
1.3

1. Which Box Diagrams are possible?

   (a)   Y2   (b)   Q3   (c)   V   (d)   T1

     | −2.44 | | 23.4 | | 4.6 | | BILLY |

has to have $ sign

2. Which of the following are correct numeric variable names?

   (a) Y4   (b) G$ (c) T45   (d) R0   (e) GRANDTOTAL

   (f) SOCKIT2ME   (g) 7YEARITCH   (h) TAXES

1.4 String variables

String variables can only contain strings. A string variable in Applesoft can hold any string up to 255 characters long. (The number of characters a string variable can hold depends on the version of BASIC being used.)

Examples   X$ Q$ T$

     | HI HO | | SILVER | | 23.6 |

The names of string variables are made from letters, digits, and the symbol "$" under the following simple rule:

RULE FOR STRING VARIABLE NAMES

All string variable names are formed by putting a $ at the end of any valid numeric variable name. So IDENTITY$ is a valid string variable because IDENTITY is a valid numeric variable.

EXERCISES
1.4

1. Which Box Diagrams are possible?

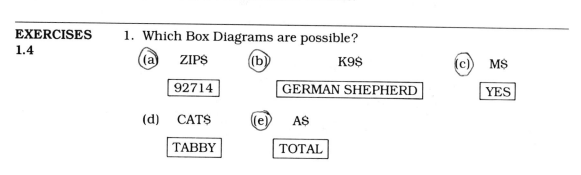

2. Which of these are valid string variable names?

(a) Q$ (b) TT$ (c) 7T$ (d) "Y$"   (e) FORM$

(f) ADDRESS$ (g) ZIPCODE

1.5 The LET instruction

LET is an instruction that assigns values to numeric and string variables. It is one of four kinds of so-called "assignment" instructions.

Examples   LET X = 2
LET Y1 = 456
LET Q$ = "ROMEO OH ROMEO"

In the LET command,

LET X1 = 7.2

the numeric value 7.2 is placed into the box named X1. The Box Diagram looks like the following:

	X1	
	0	before the LET command
LET X1 = 7.2	7.2	after the LET command

Note that the box named X1 has zero in it before the execution of the LET command. This is true in most versions of BASIC. However, when it is necessary that a variable contain a zero, never assume that the zero is already there. Assign the zero to the variable with a LET instruction.

In the LET command,

LET M$ = "WELCOME TO BASIC"

the string WELCOME TO BASIC is placed in the box named M$. The Box Diagram looks like this:

	M$	
LET M$ = "WELCOME TO BASIC"	WELCOME TO BASIC	(no quotes!)

Note that the box named M$ is blank before the LET command is given.

IMPORTANT RULES ABOUT ASSIGNING STRING DATA

1. Whenever a string is assigned to a string variable using a LET instruction, the string must be enclosed in quotation marks. The quotation marks are not considered part of the string and are not stored.
2. Since quotation marks are used to enclose the string, quotation marks within the string are not permitted.

Example　correct

LET X$ = "BASIC"

LET X$ = "AN 'ACUTE' ANGLE"

incorrect

LET X$ = BASIC

LET X$ = "AN "ACUTE" ANGLE"

Suppose the following LET commands are typed into the computer:

LET Z = 2

LET T = 5.46

LET K$ = "HI THERE"

LET Z = T

The Box Diagrams for these BASIC instructions look like the following:

	Z	T	K$	
	0	0		(before execution of LET Z = 2)
LET Z = 2	2	0		(after execution of LET Z = 2)
LET T = 5.46	2	5.46		(after execution of LET T = 5.46)
LET K$ = "HI THERE"	2	5.46	HI THERE	(after execution of LET K$ = "HI THERE")
LET Z = T	5.46	5.46	HI THERE	(after execution of LET Z = T)

EXPLANATION

After the execution of the first command, LET Z = 2, the number 2 will be placed in the box named Z.

After the second command, LET T = 5.46, the number 5.46 will be placed in the box named T.

After the third command, LET K$ = "HI THERE", the string HI THERE will be placed in the box named K$.

Finally after the last command, LET Z = T, the number in box T (5.6) will be placed into the box named Z.

IMPORTANT: The LET Z = T destroyed the value 2 in Z during the transfer but kept the value 5.46 in box T. This is called "destructive read-in" and "nondestructive read-out."

All of the important aspects of the LET instruction are discussed in the following five rules. Know them well.

FIVE RULES FOR THE LET INSTRUCTION

Rule 1:

A numeric or string variable name must always appear on the LEFT side of the "=" sign.

Example　LET X1 = 34.5

LET Q5$ = "WHERE WERE YOU LAST NIGHT?"

Rule 2:

Assignment ALWAYS takes place from RIGHT TO LEFT across the "=" sign. Whatever value is on the right of the "=" sign is placed into the box named at the left.

Rule 3:

Data transferred into the left-hand variable ALWAYS destroys the previous data assigned to that variable. After a value has been assigned to a variable it remains there until a new value is assigned to that variable (or until the NEW or CLEAR command is typed in—more on that in Chapter 3).

Example

	X	Q$
	0	
LET X = 2	2	
LET X = −67.89	−67.89	
LET Q$ = "HI"	−67.89	HI
LET Q$ = "LO"	−67.89	LO

Rule 4:

If a variable is on the right side of the "=" sign, the LET instruction transfers a COPY of the value from the right side into the variable of the left side. The assignment is destructive to the contents of the variable on the left and nondestructive to the variable on the right.

Example

	X$	Y$
LET X$ = "ME"	ME	
LET Y$ = "MINE"	ME	MINE
LET X$ = Y$	MINE	MINE

Example

	Q	K
	0	0
LET Q = 6	6	0
LET K = −7.2	6	−7.2
LET K = Q	6	6

Rule 5:

A numeric variable can only be assigned numeric data. A string variable can only be assigned string data. String data must be enclosed in quotation marks, and no quotation marks can be part of the string data itself.

Example   LET X1$ = "TO BE OR NOT TO BE"
LET K2 = 6.7897
LET T = −7
LET Q2$ = "SAID HAMLET"
LET R$ = "EINSTEIN SAID, 'E = M∗C^2'"

EXERCISES 1.5

1. Which LET commands are incorrect? Explain why.

   (a) LET Q\$ = "45*56"   (b) LET E\$ = S

   (c) LET 4X = 45   (d) LET T\$ = "THE BEATLES"

   (e) LET V2 = 34   (f) LET T = "WEE"

   (g) LET X = Y   (h) LET M\$ = Y

   (i) LET F = K\$

2. Complete the Box Diagram.

	T	R	R\$	Q\$	T\$
LET T = 45	45				
LET R = 22.22		22.2			
LET T\$ = "MICHELLE"					Michelle
LET Q\$ = "WROTE"				wrote	
LET R\$ = "BEATLES"			Beatles		

3. Complete the Box Diagram.

	A	B	C
LET A = 3			
LET B = 5			
LET C = A			
LET A = B			
LET B = C			

1.6 Exchanging the contents of variables

In the last exercise (1.5.3), the numbers 3 and 5 started out in the variables A and B, but they ended up changing places. We say that the contents of A and B were exchanged or switched. The ability to exchange the values of two variables is critical in developing programming skills.

Let's set up the variables X and Y with some values:

	X	Y	Z
	0	0	0
LET X = 2	2	0	0
LET Y = 7	2	7	0

Our goal here is to switch the positions of the 2 and 7. To do this we require a third variable for temporary storage. Let's use Z.

The following LET commands will exchange the values in X and Y. NOTICE THAT NUMBERS ARE NOT USED ON THE RIGHT SIDE OF THE "=" SIGN.

	X	Y	Z
LET Z = X	2	7	2
LET X = Y	7	7	2
LET Y = Z	7	2	2

Done! Here's an example which first assigns values to K1$ and Q$, and then exchanges them.

Example

	K1$	Q$	P$
LET K1$ = "HI"	HI		
LET Q$ = "LOW SCORE"	HI	LOW SCORE	
LET P$ = Q$	HI	LOW SCORE	LOW SCORE
LET Q$ = K1$	HI	HI	LOW SCORE
LET K1$ = P$	LOW SCORE	HI	LOW SCORE

EXERCISES 1.6

1. Complete this Box Diagram which exchanges the contents of F and G.

	F	G	X
	0	0	0
LET F = 3	3	0	0
LET G = 8	3	8	0
LET X = F	3	8	3
LET F = G	8	8	3
LET G = X	8	3	3

2. Complete this sequence of LET commands and the adjoining Box Diagram to exchange the contents of T and P. Don't refer to problem 1 unless you have to.

	T	P	Z
	0	0	0
LET T = 7	7	0	0
LET P = 9	7	9	0

3. Complete the Box Diagram for

	X$	Y$	Z1$	K$	P$
LET X$ = "SWEET"					
LET Y$ = "GOOD"					
LET Z1$ = "PRINCE"					

	X$	Y$	Z1$	K$	P$
LET K$ = "NIGHT"					
LET P$ = X$					
LET X$ = Y$					
LET Y$ = K$					
LET K$ = Z1$					
LET Z1$ = P$					
LET P$ = "!"					

In the exercise 1.6.3 above, you exchanged the contents of more than two variables. Here is an example which does that again.

Example Here we want to "rotate" each of the values in A, B, and C one box to the left. We use a temporary storage variable like always.

	A	B	C	R
	0	0	0	0
LET A = 3	3	0	0	0
LET B = 1	3	1	0	0
LET C = 2	3	1	2	0
NOW ROTATE				
LET R = A	3	1	2	3
LET A = B	1	1	2	3
LET B = C	1	2	2	3
LET C = R	1	2	3	3

Example Let's see if we can write some Shakespeare. Start with this Box Diagram:

	A$	Q$	R$	V$	G1$	A2$
LET A$ = "OR"	OR					
LET V$ = "TO"	OR			TO		
LET A2$ = "NOT"	OR			TO		NOT
LET G1$ = "BE"	OR			TO	BE	NOT

Now write a sequence of LET commands to finish with a row of boxes which reads "TO BE OR NOT TO BE." Do it only by copying and interchanging the contents of variables. Try it before you read on.

Here's one solution:

	A$	Q$	R$	V$	G1$	A2$
LET R$ = A$	OR		OR	TO	BE	NOT
LET Q$ = G1$	OR	BE	OR	TO	BE	NOT
LET A$ = V$	TO	BE	OR	TO	BE	NOT
LET V$ = A2$	TO	BE	OR	NOT	BE	NOT
LET A2$ = G1$	TO	BE	OR	NOT	BE	BE
LET G1$ = A$	TO	BE	OR	NOT	TO	BE

4. Notice that this Box Diagram "rotates" the contents of A, B, and C to the right. But some of the diagram is missing. Supply the missing values and the appropriate LET commands.

A	B	C	D
0	0	0	0
5	0	0	0
5	4	0	0
5	4	3	0
3	5	4	3

5. Given these three LET commands

LET R$ = "MARY"

LET Q$ = "JOHN"

LET T$ = "LOVES"

use a fourth variable and a sequence of LET commands so that the last line of the Box Diagram will look like this:

R$	Q$	T$
JOHN	LOVES	MARY

1.7 The PRINT instruction

The PRINT instruction is used to write information to the CRT. (CRT means *Cathode Ray Tube*, which is a fancy way to say video screen.)

Example

```
                        CRT
PRINT "HELLO"         (HELLO)
PRINT 8                 (8)
PRINT "6+2"            (6+2)
```

Here the symbol ◯ is our way of picturing the data printed on the screen.

One important function of the PRINT command is to display on the screen the contents of variables.

Example

	X	K$	CRT
	0		
LET X = 2	2		
PRINT X	2		(2)
LET K$ = "BEATLES"	2	BEATLES	
PRINT K$	2	BEATLES	(BEATLES)
PRINT "GOT IT!"	2	BEATLES	(GOT IT!)

Note that PRINT "GOT IT!" affects the screen but does not affect the variables!

RULES FOR THE PRINT INSTRUCTION

1. The PRINT instruction can print strings and numeric data onto the screen directly, without storing them first in variables. All string data must be enclosed within quotation marks, and no quotation marks can be part of the string data itself.
2. The PRINT instruction can print the contents of numeric and string variables onto the screen.
3. The PRINT instruction never changes the contents of a variable, i.e. it is nondestructive to variables.

Example

	M$	S	CRT	
		0		
LET M$ = "PLAY"	PLAY	0		
LET S = 556	PLAY	556		
PRINT "PLAY"	PLAY	556	(PLAY)	Rule 1
PRINT M$	PLAY	556	(PLAY)	Rule 2
PRINT 556	PLAY	556	(556)	Rule 1
PRINT S	PLAY	556	(556)	Rule 2

EXERCISE 1.7

1. Fill in the Box Diagram from the LET and PRINT commands below.

	V	S	R$	CRT
	0	0		
PRINT V				◯
LET V = 17				
PRINT V				◯
LET S = 42				
PRINT S				◯
LET V = S				
PRINT "V IS NOW"				◯
PRINT V				◯
LET R$ = "THAT'S FUN"				
PRINT R$				◯
PRINT "THE END"				◯

1.8 Doing arithmetic

The usual arithmetic operations are permitted in BASIC. Listed below are the symbols used for doing arithmetic on the computer:

^	Exponentiation	–	Subtraction
*	Multiplication	+	Addition
/	Division		

Exponentiation means "raising to a power." That is, 5^3 means 5 raised to the 3rd power, or 5*5*5. So 5^3 equals 125.

Arithmetic operations are used with many BASIC commands. Most commonly, arithmetic is done in a LET command.

Example

X

| 0 |

LET X = 2 + 3 | 5 |

The computer performs the arithmetic operation 2 + 3, and then assigns the answer to the box named X.

Example

	X	R	U
	0	0	0
(a) LET X = 1 + 1	2	0	0
(b) LET R = X*3	2	6	0
(c) LET U = R/X	2	6	3

Lines (b) and (c) in this Box Diagram are very important. They show that arithmetic can be done on the data inside of a box BY USING THE BOX'S NAME IN THE ARITHMETIC PROBLEM. Line (b) multiplies the contents of X by 3 and assigns the answer to box R. Line (c) uses the numbers found in boxes R and X to do a division problem. The answer 3 is assigned to box U.

Now pay attention! You are about to learn something very important. IT IS POSSIBLE TO HAVE THE SAME VARIABLE APPEAR ON BOTH SIDES OF THE " = " SIGN. Consider this Box Diagram:

X

| 0 |

LET X = 5 | 5 |

LET X = X + 7 | 12 |

A mathematician might faint at LET X = X + 7, but to the computer it is very meaningful. First, the value 5 is placed in X. Then, the value in X (namely, 5) is added to 7 for an answer of 12. The answer is then put BACK INTO THE BOX X, which destroys the 5 that was there. Remember RULE 2 for the LET instruction: ASSIGNMENT ALWAYS TAKES PLACE FROM RIGHT TO LEFT. That should help you understand why the same variable can be on both sides.

Example

	X	Y
	0	0
LET X = 4	4	0
LET Y = X^3	4	64
LET X = Y/X	16	64
LET Y = Y − X	16	48

EXERCISES 1.8

1. Complete the following Box Diagram

	X	A	C3
	0	0	0
LET X = 4			
LET A = X − 2			
LET C3 = A*X			
LET X = C3^A			

2. Complete the following Box Diagram.

	E	F
	0	0
LET E = 3		
LET F = E*E		
LET F = F − E		
LET F = F − E		
LET E = F^E		

What value should X be assigned in this LET instruction?

LET X = 8 − 4 + 2

If the computer subtracts 4 from 8 and then adds 2 the answer is 6. But, if the computer adds 4 and 2 and then subtracts the result from 8, the answer comes out 2! Ambiguous, eh? Well it would be if it weren't for a standard set of rules called . . .

THE ORDER OF ARITHMETIC OPERATIONS

The computer performs arithmetic operations in the following order:

1. Arithmetic inside of parentheses is done first.
2. Positive (+) and negative (−) signs apply before any arithmetic is done. So −2^4 is the same as (−2)^4, or 16.
3. Exponentiation is done before all other operations.
4. Multiplication and division are done next, from left to right.
5. Addition and subtraction are done last, from left to right.

Examples

W

$$\boxed{0}$$

LET W = 10 − 4 + 5 $\boxed{11}$

LET W = 10 − (4 + 5) $\boxed{1}$

LET W = 20 + 3 ∗ 4 $\boxed{32}$

LET W = (20 + 3) ∗ 4 $\boxed{92}$

LET W = 4ˆ3 − 1 + 8/2 $\boxed{67}$

LET W = (5ˆ3 + 25)/15 ∗ 10 $\boxed{100}$

(If your answer to the last example is 1, you multiplied before you divided.)

Finally, it should be said that arithmetic operations may also appear in a PRINT command. This allows you to do arithmetic problems directly, without having to assign values to variables first.

Example

CRT

PRINT 2∗5 + 8/4   (12)

**EXERCISES
1.8 contd.**

3. Fill in this Box Diagram.

A   CRT

$$\boxed{0}$$

LET A = 6 $\square$

PRINT A∗3 + 2 $\square$ ◯

PRINT A/3∗2 $\square$ ◯

LET A = (A − 4) ˙ 2 $\square$

PRINT A − A/4 $\square$ ◯

PRINT (A − A)/4 $\square$ ◯

LET A = A∗A − A + A/A $\square$

PRINT "A∗A − A + A/A" $\square$ ◯

4. To the left of each line of the Box Diagram below, write an appropriate LET or PRINT command. In each LET or PRINT command, however, use only the numeric data already stored in the variables. There may be more than one answer for each line in the diagram. Choose the "simplest." The command LET X = K/K has been given to you as an example.

	X	K	F	CRT
	0	0	0	
LET K = 5	0	5	0	
LET X = K/K	1	5	0	
	1	5	4	

1	5	4	(9)
10	5	4	
10	0.2	4	
10	0.2	4	(98)

Example   The formula for the total return on a one-year investment at a given simple interest rate is

A = P*(1 + R)

where

P = Amount of dollars originally invested

R = Annual interest rate

A = Total return on investment in one year

Application Example   Assume Mr. Smith invests $2,500 in a savings account paying 15% interest a year. Write a sequence of LET and PRINT commands to compute and print A, the total return.

Solution

```
LET P = 2500
LET R = .15
LET A = P*(1 + R)
PRINT A
```

EXERCISES 1.8 contd.

5. Complete a Box Diagram for the application example above.

6. The formula for the return on an investment when interest is compounded annually for N years is

A = P*(1 + R)^N

Write a sequence of LET and PRINT commands to compute the return on Mr. Smith's money after 5 years. Use the values of R and P in the example above.

Example   In mathematics, the *factorial* of a counting number N (denoted by N!) is the product of all the counting numbers less than and equal to N. (The counting numbers are 1, 2, 3, etc.) For example,

```
1! = 1
2! = 2*1 = 2
3! = 3*2*1 = 6
4! = 4*3*2*1 = 24
5! = 5*4*3*2*1 = 120
```

Here is one way in which the factorial numbers up to 5! can be computed and printed:

```
LET X1 = 1
LET X2 = 2*X1
LET X3 = 3*X2
LET X4 = 4*X3
LET X5 = 5*X4
PRINT X1
PRINT X2
PRINT X3
PRINT X4
PRINT X5
```

**EXERCISES
1.8   contd.**

7. Complete a Box Diagram for the factorial example above.

8. Discover the pattern in the Box Diagram below. The diagram shows another way to generate the factorial numbers, but it uses only two variables and the number 1. Complete the sequence of LET and PRINT commands to generate and print the factorial numbers up to 5!.

	X	Y	CRT
	0	0	
LET X = 1	1	0	
LET Y = 1	1	1	
PRINT X	1	1	1
LET Y = Y + 1	1	2	
LET X = X*Y	2	2	
PRINT X	2	2	2
LET Y = Y + 1	2	3	
LET X = X*Y	6	3	
PRINT X	6	3	6

Example   Mrs. Jones purchased 250 shares of IBM at $76.25 a share and later sold the shares at $81.50 a share. Write a sequence of LET commands and PRINT commands to compute and print her total investment and her net profit.

Solution

```
LET S = 250
LET C1 = 76.25
LET T1 = S*C1
PRINT T1
```

```
LET C2 = 81.5
LET T2 = S * C2
LET P = T2 - T1
PRINT P
```

**EXERCISES
1.8 contd.**

9. Complete a Box Diagram for the example above.

10. Assume Mrs. Jones received dividends of $4.50 a share while she owned the stock. Modify the above sequence so that her total dividends will be computed into her net profit.

11. Along with her dividends, she paid a 5% commission to purchase the stocks and a 7% commission when she sold her stocks. Modify the sequence in problem 10 to reflect these costs in her net profit.

1.9 Projects

1. Mrs. Smith purchased 134 shares of IBM stock at $75.50 a share. She received $2.50 a share dividends and later sold the 134 shares of IBM at $88.75 a share.

   Write a sequence of LET and PRINT commands that will compute and print the TOTAL PURCHASE PRICE, THE TOTAL DIVIDENDS RECEIVED, THE TOTAL SALE PRICE, and NET PROFITS RECEIVED, where

   TOTAL PURCHASE PRICE = # SHARES PURCHASED * PURCHASE PRICE PER SHARE

   TOTAL DIVIDENDS = # SHARES PURCHASED * DIVIDENDS RECEIVED PER SHARE

   TOTAL SALE PRICE = # SHARES PURCHASED * SALE PRICE PER SHARE

   NET PROFITS = TOTAL SALE PRICE + TOTAL DIVIDENDS - TOTAL PURCHASE PRICE

2. Mr. Smith purchased a new automobile for $10,000. He paid $1,000 down and financed the remainder at 1½% a month with monthly payments of $200. The following explains how INTEREST PAYMENTS, EQUITY PAYMENTS, and BALANCE DUE are computed for the first two months.

   PURCHASED PRICE OF AUTOMOBILE = $10,000
   BALANCED TO BE FINANCED = $10,000 - $1,000 = $9,000
   MONTHLY PAYMENTS = $200

   END OF FIRST MONTH:

   INTEREST PAYMENT = $9000 * .015 = $135.00
   EQUITY PAYMENT = $200 - $135 = $65.00
   BALANCE DUE = $9000 - $65.00 = $8935

END OF SECOND MONTH:
INTEREST PAYMENT = $8935 * .015 = $134.03
EQUITY PAYMENT = $200 − $134.03 = $65.97
BALANCE DUE = $8935 − $65.97 = $8869.03

Write a sequence of LET and PRINT commands which will compute and print the INTEREST PAYMENT, EQUITY PAYMENT, and BALANCE DUE for three months. Compare your answers for the first two months to the numbers above.

3. Billy deposited $1,500 into a savings account that pays 15% per year. He decides to leave the $1,500 and all interest earned in the account until his account has at least $2,500. The method for computing compound interest is as follows:

END OF FIRST YEAR:
INTEREST PAID TO ACCOUNT = $1500 * .15 = $225
TOTAL AMOUNT IN ACCOUNT = $1500 + $225 = $1725

END OF SECOND YEAR:
INTEREST PAID TO ACCOUNT = $1725 * .15 = $258.75
TOTAL AMOUNT IN ACCOUNT = $1725 + $258.75 = $1983.75

Write a sequence of LET and PRINT commands that will compute and print

a) Interest paid to the account for each year

b) Total amount in account each year until at least $2,500 is in the account.

4. π is an important number in mathematics. One of the interesting facts about π is that it has a nonrepeating infinite decimal expansion:

π = 3.1415926 . . .

The following sequence of sums can approximate π as accurately as desired:

4 − 4/3,
4 − 4/3 + 4/5,
4 − 4/3 + 4/5 − 4/7,
4 − 4/3 + 4/5 − 4/7 + 4/9 . . .

Write a sequence of LET and PRINT commands which will give 3.1 as an approximation to π. This requires at least nineteen terms. To get 3.14 requires 119 terms! Accuracy to the fifth decimal place requires over 200,000 terms. It looks like we'll need to learn a bit more before we can tackle that!

LAB 1-1   The LET instruction

Type in the command: NEW

After you have typed in a command, be sure to press the RETURN key.

The LET instruction gives you the ability to assign data into the memory of the computer.

Type in the command: LET X = 4

> Be sure to press the RETURN key after you have typed in this command.
>
> When the computer executes this command it assigns the numeric data 4 to the box named X. Thus, the number 4 is now stored in the box named X.

Type in the command: LET 3 = X

What is the response of the computer? _____

> The computer is programmed to give the response ?SYNTAX ERROR whenever it tries to execute an instruction with a mistake in syntax.
>
> A ?SYNTAX ERROR was caused in this case because in a LET instruction, only a variable may appear to the left of the equals sign.

Type in the command: LET X = 7

What is now in the box named X? _____ 7 _____

> You should have written 7. The LET instruction assigns and stores data into the memory of the computer. When the computer executed the command LET X = 7, the number 4 was replaced by the number 7 in the box named X. This is called "destructive read-in," because the number 4 was erased when the value 7 was assigned to X. Only one value can be stored in a variable at any one time.

Type in the command: LET Y = 25

What is contained in the box named Y? _____

Type in the command: LET Y = X

What is contained in the box named Y? _____

> You should have written 7. When the computer executed the command LET Y = X, it first made an electronic copy of the number stored in the box named X. This is called "nondestructive read-out," because the number 7 is not erased from the X box. Next, the computer assigned this electronic copy, the number 7, to the Y box.

What is contained in the box named X? _____

> If you said "7" then you understand! The command LET Y = X simply copies the value of X into Y, but does not destroy the contents of X.
>
> Remember this always: The LET instruction assigns the value on the right of the equals sign to the variable on the left.

LAB 1-2 The PRINT instruction

Type in the command: NEW

> After you have typed in any command, be sure to press the RETURN key.
>
> The PRINT instruction creates "output" which usually goes to a printer or the CRT (cathode ray tube), and makes it possible to see computer data.
>
> The PRINT instruction can be used to display numeric data.

Type in the command: PRINT 4

Don't forget to press the RETURN key after your have typed in this command.

What is the output of the computer? _____ *4* _____

You should see the number 4 displayed below the command PRINT 4 on your screen.

String data can also be displayed using the PRINT instruction.

Type in the command: PRINT "HI THERE"

What is the output of the computer? _____ *Hi There* _____

The computer displays HI THERE without the quotation marks. A "string" is any collection of characters. To display a string, you must enclose the string in quotation marks following the PRINT instruction. Thus, the quotation mark cannot be enclosed in quotation marks.

What command must be typed into the computer for the computer to display the string BASIC PROGRAMMING?

_____

You should have written: PRINT "BASIC PROGRAMMING".

Let's return to numeric data.

Type in the command: PRINT 123456789

What is the output of the computer? _____

It should be no surprise that the computer displayed the number 123456789.

Type in the command: PRINT 1234567890

What is the output of the computer? _____

The output $1.23456789E+09$ is called scientific notation. It means 1.23456789 times 10 raised to the 9th power, which in fact is 1234567890. The BASIC language uses scientific notation to express very big or very small numbers.

Type in the command: PRINT .01

What is the output of the computer? _____ *.01* _____

Type in the command: PRINT .009

What is the output of the computer? _____ *9E-03* _____

In the second case the output is in scientific notation. Numbers larger than 999999999 or less than .01 are displayed in scientific notation, with no more than nine significant digits showing.

Type in the commands: LET X = 7
                    PRINT X

What is the output of the computer? _____ *7* _____

You should see the number 7 displayed below the command PRINT X. When the computer executes the command PRINT X, it takes a copy of the contents of the box named X and displays this copy on the CRT. It must be understood that the command, PRINT X, does not remove or destroy the contents of X (nondestructive read-out).

LAB 1-3 Numeric and string variables

Type in the command: NEW

> Don't forget to press the RETURN key after you have typed in a command.

> A variable is the name of a "box" or storage area in the computer's memory. There are two types of variables used in BASIC. They are NUMERIC and STRING variables. Both types of variables have names that are combinations of letters and digits, but they must start with a letter. In addition, string variable names must end with a dollar sign ($). For example, X and TAX82 are numeric variables and store numeric data. Examples of string variables are X$ and TAX82$, which would be used to store string data.

> The "default" value for a numeric variable is zero (0). This means that if a numeric variable has not been assigned a value, it will contain zero.

Type in the command: PRINT X

What is the output of the computer? _____ 0 _____

> Since no value has been assigned to X, the computer assigned the value 0 to it, by default.

> The default value for a string variable is a string of no characters, called the "null string."

Type in the command: PRINT X$

What is the output of the computer? _____

> You are looking at the null string, which is why you don't see any output at all!

> A string is any collection of characters. To assign a string to a string variable with a LET instruction, you must enclose the string in quotation marks.

Type in the commands: LET X$ = "HELLO"
                          PRINT X$

What is the output of the computer? _____ Nella _____

> Note that the quotation marks are not printed. This is because the quotation marks are used by the computer to identify the beginning and the end of a string. Since quotation marks are used for this special purpose they cannot be used as characters within the string when using a LET instruction.

Type in the command: LET X = "5"

What is the response of the computer? _____

> X is a numeric variable and will only accept numeric data. The "5" is a string. The computer will not store a string in a numeric variable. A TYPE MISMATCH ERROR occurs, as you have seen.

Type in the commands: LET X = 5
                    PRINT X

What is the output of the computer? _____ 5 _____

Since the 5 is not enclosed in quotes, the computer looks at this 5 as numeric data.

As mentioned at the beginning of this lab, variable names can be several characters long (up to 238 in fact!). Most combinations of letters and digits can represent a variable. However there are reserved words that you may not use within variable names.

Type in the command: LET TOTAL = 345

What is the response of the computer? _____

The word TO is a reserved word. You cannot have TO anywhere in a variable name. Thus, the response ?SYNTAX ERROR. A complete list of reserved words can be found in Appendix B of the text.

Type in the commands: LET PAY = 345
                    PRINT PAY

What value is stored in the variable PAY? ____ 345 _____

Type in the command: PRINT PAYMENT

What is the output of the computer? ____ 345 _____

Surprised? Both of the variables PAY and PAYMENT have the same value, yet the variable PAYMENT was not assigned the value 345. Applesoft BASIC recognizes only the first two characters of the variable name. Since both PAY and PAYMENT have the same first two characters, the computer looks at both as the same variable.

Type in the command: PRINT PA
Explain why the output of the computer is 345. ___ has same Charater ___

_____

Type in the commands: LET NAME$ = "JOE COOL"
                    PRINT NA$

What is the output of the computer? ____ Joe Cool _____

Type in the command: PRINT NA

What is the output of the computer? ____ 0 _____
Explain why the computer printed a 0 instead of JOE COOL. _____

_____

_____

_____

LAB 1-4 Switching

Type in the command: NEW

Many computer applications require that the contents of two different variables be interchanged. In sorting a list of numbers, for example, it might be necessary to move what is stored in X into Y and what is stored in Y into X. We call this switching the data of the two variables.

Type in the commands: LET X = 5
LET Y = 2

What value is stored in the variable X? ___ 5 ___

What value is stored in the variable Y? ___ 2 ___

The number 5 is stored in the variable X and the number 2 is stored in the variable Y. Let's assume that we don't know what data are stored in X and Y. Switching the data of X and Y, therefore, must not depend on any prior knowledge of what those data are. To do the switching, we require a third variable which we will call P.

Type in the commands: LET P = X
LET X = Y
LET Y = P

The first command, LET P = X assigns to P a copy of the data in X. The second command, LET X = Y destroys the data in X by replacing it with a copy of the data in Y. The third command, LET Y = P assigns to Y the data in P. But remember, the data stored in P is the original data of X. So Y becomes X and X becomes Y. A perfect switch!

Suppose a student types in the following sequence of commands to switch the contents of X and Y.

LET X = 8
LET Y = 3
LET X = Y
LET Y = X

Explain why this particular sequence of commands will not switch the contents of X and Y. _____

_____

The third command, LET X = Y, will replace the contents of X with a copy of the contents of Y. At this point, both X and Y contain a 3. Think about it! There is no more 8 to be found. The fourth step does nothing more than reassign 3 to Y. Thus, both X and Y will have the data 3.

Type in the commands: LET X$ = "HELLO"
LET Y$ = "THERE"

What sequence of commands needs to be typed into the computer to switch the contents of X$ and Y$ using only variables on both sides of the equal sign? _____

_____

Type in the commands you have written. Then print X$ and Y$ to see if you succeeded in switching them.

Here are two possible ways to do it.

1) LET Z$=X$ 2) LET Z$=Y$
    LET X$=Y$ LET Y$=X$
    LET Y$=Z$ LET X$=Z$

There is nothing sacred about using Z$ as the third variable. Any string variable different from X$ and Y$ will do.

LAB 1-5 Arithmetic operations

Type in the command: NEW

There are five arithmetic operations in BASIC. They are Addition (+), Subtraction (−), Multiplication (*), Division (/), and Exponentiation (ˆ).

Type in the commands: PRINT 2+3
LET C=5*9
PRINT C

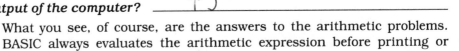

What is the output of the computer? _____45_____

What you see, of course, are the answers to the arithmetic problems. BASIC always evaluates the arithmetic expression before printing or assigning it.

The order in which the operations in an arithmetic expression are carried out follows these rules:

1. Operations within parentheses are done first.
2. Exponentiation is done before the other four arithmetic operations.
3. Multiplication and Division operations are done before Addition and Subtraction operations.

On most keyboards the exponentiation symbol (ˆ) is the SHIFT-N. That is press the SHIFT key and the N key simultaneously.

Type in the command: PRINT 5+3*4ˆ2

What is the output of the computer? _____

Use the order of operations rules to explain why the answer is 53. _____

How the computer arrived at 53 can be shown by the following steps:

Step 1 $5+3*16$ Exponentiation is done before multiplication or addition.

Step 2 $5+48$ Multiplication is done before addition.

Step 3   53   Sum of 5 and 48.

Type in the command: PRINT $(3+5)\hat{}2$

What is the output of the computer? _____

Explain how the computer came to an answer of 64.

The following steps show how the computer arrived at 64 as the computed value of the expression $(3+5)\hat{}2$.

Step 1 $8\hat{}2$ Operation within the parentheses is done first.

Step 2   64   Exponentiation of $8\hat{}2$. $8\hat{}2$ means $8*8$.

Type in the command: LET $X = 2*(3+1)\hat{}2/(9-1)+7$

What is the value stored in the variable X? _____

Type in the command: PRINT X

Explain the following steps which show how the computer arrived at 11.

Step 1: $2*4\hat{}2/8+7$ _____

Step 2: $2*16/8+7$ _____

Step 3: $4+7$ _____

Step 4:   11   _____

In step 1, operations within the parentheses are done first. Step 2, exponentiation of $4\hat{}2$. Step 3, the product and quotient of $2*16/8$. And step 4 the sum of 4 and 7.

Type in the command: LET $X = 2(4-1)$

What is the response of the computer? _____

Every arithmetic operation needs a symbol. In this case the multiplication symbol ($*$) is missing between the 2 and $(4-1)$. Hence the syntax error.

2

Functions

2.0 Introduction

Functions may be thought of as built-in instructions which accomplish specific tasks. Functions fall into two categories: arithmetic and string. Arithmetic functions extend the computer's power of computation beyond the simple operations we studied in Chapter 1. But, while many people think of the computer as just an expensive calculator, its ability to process string data is just as important. That is what string functions are for.

All functions are constructed in the same way. (Computer programmers like to say that they have the same general "syntax.") Every function has a name, such as SQR, which suggests its purpose, in this case taking a SQuare Root. The name is always followed by a set of parentheses, as in SQR(X). What goes inside the parentheses is called the *argument* of the function. An arithmetic function operates on its argument and returns numeric data. A string function operates on its argument and returns either numeric or string data.

The following built-in functions are available in Applesoft BASIC. Those marked with an asterisk are discussed in Chapter 12.

ARITHMETIC FUNCTIONS	STRING FUNCTIONS
ABS(X)	* ASC(X$)
ATN(X)	* CHR$(X)
COS(X)	LEFT$(X$,N)
EXP(X)	LEN(X$)
INT(X)	MID$(X$,J,K)
LOG(X)	RIGHT$(X$,N)
* PDL (X)	STR$(X)
* PEEK(X)	VAL(X$)
RND(X)	
SGN(X)	
SIN(X)	
SQR(X)	
TAN(X)	

2.1 Arithmetic functions

The arguments of arithmetic functions are always numeric values, numeric variables, or arithmetic expressions.

Example   Here are some valid function arguments.

VALID ARGUMENTS	VALID EXPRESSIONS
3 is a numeric value	SQR(3)
X is a numeric variable	ABS(X)
4*3+2 is an arithmetic expression	LOG(4*3+2)
X^2+5 is an arithmetic expression	INT(X^2+5)

A. THE SQUARE ROOT FUNCTION, SQR(X)

Many applications call for the square root of a number. The expression SQR(X), when used in a BASIC program actually becomes the square root of the argument. The function SQR(X) can be used just like a number. It can be used in arithmetic operations, in PRINT and LET instructions, and anywhere else numeric data are permitted.

Examples

	X	Y	CRT
PRINT SQR(49)	0	0	7
LET X=4	4	0	
LET Y=3	4	3	
PRINT SQR(X*X+Y*Y)	4	3	5
LET Y=(SQR(X)+20)/11	4	2	
PRINT SQR(Y)	4	2	1.41421356
PRINT SQR(SQR(X))	4	2	1.41421356

As the last line shows, the argument of a function may contain another function.

**EXERCISES
2.1**

1. Assume: LET X=3 and LET Y=4

   Write appropriate BASIC instructions to compute the square roots of

   (a) X+Y   (b) X*Y   (c) X+SQR((X+4*Y)/3)   (d) X−Y

   Use a computer to find the answers. Can you explain the result you got for (d)?

2. In mathematics, equations of the form

   $X^2 - K = 0$

   where K is a positive number, have two solutions given by

   X1 =   SQR(K)
   X2 = −SQR(K)

Write appropriate BASIC instructions to compute and print the solutions to the following equations:

$X^2 - 3.4 = 0$

$X^2 - 7 = 0$

$X^2 - 150 = 0$

3. Miss Moneypenny will be going to college in two years. Her tuition will be $1300, but at the moment she has only $1000. If she wants to put her money in an account that compounds interest annually, what interest rate should she choose? The formula for the interest rate, R, is

R = SQR(A/P) − 1

where A is the amount to be returned in two years and P is the amount invested. Write a sequence of LET and PRINT commands which will find the interest rate she needs to turn $1000 into $1300.

4. Equations of the form

$AX^2 + BX + C = 0$

where A > 0 and C < 0

have the following two solutions:

X1 = (−B + SQR(B^2 − 4*A*C))/(2*A)
X2 = (−B − SQR(B^2 − 4*A*C))/(2*A)

Write appropriate BASIC instructions to compute and print the solutions to the following equations:

$X^2 - 7X - 11 = 0$

$5X^2 - X - 5 = 0$

$14X^2 + 111X - 2 = 0$

B. THE ABSOLUTE VALUE FUNCTION, ABS(X)

We can change a negative number into a positive number by taking its "absolute value." The absolute value of −8 is 8, and the absolute value of −23 is 23. The absolute value of a nonnegative number is just the number itself, e.g., the absolute value of 47 is 47, and the absolute value of 0 is 0. The built-in function in BASIC which determines the absolute value of a number X is ABS(X). Like all arithmetic functions, it is used just like a number wherever it is needed.

Example

	X	Y	CRT
	0	0	
PRINT ABS(−234)	0	0	234
LET X = −5	−5	0	
LET Y = 1	−5	1	
PRINT ABS(X−Y)	−5	1	6
LET X = SQR(ABS(X+Y))	2	1	

Example   The difference, D, in elevation between two cities is given by

LET D = ABS(E1 − E2)

where E1 and E2 are the elevations of the two cities. It doesn't matter which elevation is greater; the difference will always be measured as a positive number.

Example   The command

LET L = (X + Y + ABS(X − Y)) / 2

always assigns to L the larger of the two numbers X and Y.

EXERCISES   5. Write a LET command which assigns to S the smaller of two numbers
2.1   contd.   X and Y. Study the example above, and make a few adjustments.

C. THE INTEGER FUNCTION, INT(X)

This function returns the largest integer less than or equal to X.

Example

X	INT(X)
2.5	2
15.62	15
78	78
0.23	0
−4.2	−5
−35	−35

It seems from these examples that the INT(X) function behaves differently for positive numbers than negative numbers. But remember that, for example, −5 is the greatest integer less than −4.2. For positive numbers the INT(X) function truncates the decimal part.

By itself, the INT(X) function does not round off decimal numbers. However, there is a method which uses INT(X) to round off long decimal numbers to as many places after the decimal point as desired. (See Lab 2-1.) The following will round off the number 9.6872 to the number 9.69.

A

| 0 |

LET A = 9.6872	9.6872
LET A = 100*A	968.72
LET A = A + .5	969.22
LET A = INT(A)	969
LET A = A/100	9.69

The procedure can be simplified to just one instruction:

LET A = INT(100*A + .5)/100

Changing the number 100 to 1000 will round A to three decimal places, and so on.

---

6. Write a LET command which rounds numbers to one decimal place after the decimal point.

7. Write a LET command which rounds numbers to the hundreds placevalue. (That is, 35874 would become 35900.)

D. THE RANDOM NUMBER FUNCTION, RND(X)

Games of chance usually require a random process such as the roll of dice or the flip of a coin. It is easy to get random numbers from the computer using the RND(X) function. The RND(X) function will compute a random number greater than or equal to zero but less than one. The argument of the function may be any number, but the range of random numbers will always be from zero to one. Therefore, since it is irrelevant, we will use an argument of one. (A negative or zero argument, however, does have a special effect on the RND function. See Lab 2-2 for examples.)

Example   The following will compute three random numbers:

$$X$$
$$\boxed{0}$$

LET X = RND(1)	$\boxed{.21167342}$
LET X = RND(1)	$\boxed{.89321343}$
LET X = RND(1)	$\boxed{.00553125}$

In many applications, integer random numbers are needed. The sequence of LET commands below shows how a random integer between 1 and 6 can be created. (See also Lab 2-2).

$$X$$
$$\boxed{0}$$

LET X = RND(1)	$\boxed{.432431}$	X is between 0 and 1, (not including 1).
LET X = 6*X	$\boxed{2.594586}$	X is now between 0 and 6, (not including 6).
LET X = INT(X)	$\boxed{2}$	X is now an integer from 0 to 5.
LET X = X + 1	$\boxed{3}$	X is now a random integer from 1 to 6.

The whole sequence can be written in one LET command:

LET X = INT(6*RND(1)) + 1

8. Write a sequence of BASIC commands to compute and print five random integers between 1 and 20.

9. Write a sequence of BASIC commands to compute and print five random integers between 6 and 15. Hint: There are ten numbers from 6 to 15, so use INT(10*RND(1)), and then add an appropriate number.

E. OTHER ARITHMETIC FUNCTIONS (OPTIONAL)*

Some advanced mathematical functions are also built into the BASIC language. They are

SIN(X)   the sine of X radians,

COS(X)   the cosine of X radians,

TAN(X)   the tangent of X radians,

ATN(X)   the arctangent of X,

LOG(X)   the natural log of X,

EXP(X)   e to the power of X, where
              e equals 2.71828183.

SGN(X)   returns a +1 if X is positive,
              returns a −1 is X is negative,
              returns a   0 if X is zero.

Example A mathematical model for population growth for a country is given by the formula

Q = P1 * EXP(K*T1)

where P1 is the initial population, Q is the population T1 years later, and K is the "growth constant." The constant K can be found if the population of the country is known at another point in time. The formula for K is

K =(LOG(P2) − LOG(P1))/T2

where P2 is the population at a different time, and T2 is the number of years elapsed between the populations P1 and P2.

The population of Uganda in 1969 was 9.5 million. In 1977 the population was 12.3 million. Compute the expected population in 1985.

The following BASIC commands will compute and print the estimated population in 1985.

```
LET P1 = 9500000
LET P2 = 12300000
LET T2 = 1977−1969
LET K = (LOG(P2) − LOG(P1))/T2
LET T1 = 1985−1969
LET Q = P1 * EXP(K*T1)
PRINT Q
```

*This section may be skipped without loss of continuity. Students with a good understanding of algebra and trigonometry may find the topics interesting.

**EXERCISES
2.1 contd.**

10. The population of the United States in 1960 was 179 million and 203 million in 1970. Write appropriate BASIC instructions that will predict the population in the year 2000.

Example Assume we have a triangle with sides of lengths A, B, and C, and corresponding opposite angles A1, B1, and C1. The Law of Cosines can be used to compute side A if the other sides and the opposite angle A1 are known:

$$A = \sqrt{B^2 + C^2 - 2BC\,COS(A1)}$$

The following set of BASIC instructions will compute side A when B = 24, C = 32, and A1 = 2 (in radians).

```
LET B = 24
LET C = 32
LET A1 = 2
LET A = SQR(B^2 + C^2 - 2*B*C*COS(A1))
PRINT A
```

**EXERCISES,
2.1 contd.**

11. A rearrangement of the Law of Cosines gives us this interesting formula for finding the cosine of the angle A1 of a triangle:

$$\text{Cosine of A1} = \frac{B^2 + C^2 - A^2}{2BC}$$

Assume we have a triangle with sides A = 1.732, B = 1, and C = 2. Write a set of BASIC instructions which compute and print the cosine of the angle A1.

As you have no doubt gathered from earlier examples, functions may be used within expressions that do arithmetic. FUNCTIONS ALWAYS TAKE PRECEDENCE OVER ^, *, /, +, AND −. You may want to write this fact into the ORDER OF ARITHMETIC OPERATIONS chart in Section 1.8.

Example In the instruction

```
LET A = SQR(B^2 + C^2 - 2*B*C*COS(A1))
```

the first quantity evaluated is COS(A1), because it takes precedence. Then the exponentiation is done, followed by the multiplication, followed by the addition, followed by the subtraction, and finally the SQR function is performed. The SQR function came last in this example because its argument had to be evaluated first. Remember, the computer always evaluates expressions within parentheses first.

2.2 String functions

With much talk lately of "word processing," most people realize that computers can process string data as well as numeric data. The built-in functions in BASIC which do this are called string functions.

A. THE LENGTH FUNCTION, LEN(X$)

The length of X$ is the number of characters in the string stored in X$. The LEN(X$) function gives this length.

Example

	X$	A	CRT
LET X$ = "HELLO"	HELLO	0	
LET A = LEN(X$)	HELLO	5	
PRINT A	HELLO	5	5
PRINT LEN("MARK UP")	HELLO	5	7

It is important to note that ALL characters of the string are counted in the length. In the above example, LEN("MARK UP") is equal to 7 since the space is also counted as a character.

B. THE VALUE FUNCTION, VAL(X$)

The command

LET X$ = "54.23"

assigns the string 54.23 to the variable X$. But 54.23 is a number you say! Inside the computer, the string 54.23 is stored quite differently than a number. Sometimes it is necessary to change such a string into the number it resembles. This is the purpose of the VAL(X$) function. The command

LET A = VAL (X$)

changes the string into numeric data and assigns it to A. Chapters 9, 10, and 11 will bring out important applications of the VAL(X$) function.

Example

	Q$	P
		0
LET Q$ = "65.2"	65.2	0
LET P = VAL(Q$)	65.2	65.2
LET P = P + VAL("22.4")	65.2	87.6

C. THE STRING FUNCTION, STR$(X)

The STR$(X) function is the opposite of the VAL(X$) function. STR$(X) converts a number into a string.

Example

	T	L$
	0	
LET T = 27.82	27.82	
LET L$ = STR$(T)	27.82	27.82

Again, we shall later see interesting applications of the STR$(X) function.

D. SUBSTRING FUNCTIONS

Riddle: What is the longest word in the English language?
Answer: SMILES, because there's a MILE between the two S's!

The riddle demonstrates the notion of a "substring" of a string. MILE is a substring of SMILES. There are three functions in Applesoft which extract substrings. They are the MID$, RIGHT$, and LEFT$ functions.

(1) MID$(X$,J,K)

The MID$(X$,J,K) function makes it possible to extract any length substring from anywhere within a string. In the MID$(X$,J,K) expression, the J is the starting position in X$, and the K counts the number of characters to be included in the substring. If the number K is left out, as in MID$(X$,J), then the substring starts at the Jth character in X$ and goes to the end of the string.

Example

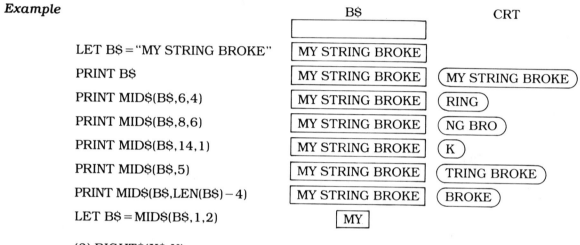

	B$	CRT
LET B$ = "MY STRING BROKE"	MY STRING BROKE	
PRINT B$	MY STRING BROKE	MY STRING BROKE
PRINT MID$(B$,6,4)	MY STRING BROKE	RING
PRINT MID$(B$,8,6)	MY STRING BROKE	NG BRO
PRINT MID$(B$,14,1)	MY STRING BROKE	K
PRINT MID$(B$,5)	MY STRING BROKE	TRING BROKE
PRINT MID$(B$,LEN(B$)−4)	MY STRING BROKE	BROKE
LET B$ = MID$(B$,1,2)	MY	

(2) RIGHT$(X$,N)

The RIGHT$(X$,N) function returns the substring made up of the N rightmost characters from the end of X$.

Example

	B$	CRT
LET B$ = "BEATLES"	BEATLES	
PRINT RIGHT$(B$,3)	BEATLES	LES
LET B$ = RIGHT$(B$,5)	ATLES	
PRINT RIGHT$(B$,1)	ATLES	S

The RIGHT$(X$,N) function can be replaced by MID$(X$,LEN(X$)−N+1), which does the same thing. But, it is more convenient to use RIGHT$.

(3) LEFT$(X$,N)

The LEFT$(X$,N) function returns the substring made up of the N leftmost characters from the beginning of X$.

Example

	Y1$	CRT
LET Y1$ = LEFT$("HEART",4)	HEAR	
PRINT LEFT$(Y1$,1)	HEAR	H

Notice that LEFT$(X$,N) is equivalent to MID$(X$,1,N). So the LEFT$ function, like RIGHT$, is a luxury.

EXERCISES 2.2

1. Without using a computer, determine the output of the following PRINT commands:

   LET A$ = "STRING ALONG WITH MID"

   (a) PRINT LEN(A$)

   (b) PRINT MID$(A$,3,4)

   (c) PRINT MID$(A$,9,1)

   (d) PRINT MID$(A$,15)

   (e) PRINT LEN(MID$(A$,15))

   (f) PRINT RIGHT$(A$,3)

   (g) PRINT LEFT$(A$,3)

   (h) PRINT MID$(RIGHT$(A$,8),3,2)

   (i) PRINT RIGHT$(LEFT$(A$,5),1)

2. What errors have been made in writing the following functions?

   (a) MID(X$,2,1)

   (b) STR$("THREE")

   (c) LEN(43.2)

   (d) LEFT$(X$,0)

   (e) MID$(DOUGHNUT,3,2)

   (f) LEN(X$,3,2)

2.3 Projects

1. (For the mathminded.) Many of the mathematical functions described in this chapter have Taylor Series expansions. A Taylor Series is an "infinite polynomial" whose value at X is the same as the function's value at X. Here are some Taylor Series for a few of the functions we have seen.

$$EXP(X) = 1 + X + \frac{X^2}{2} + \frac{X^3}{6} + \frac{X^4}{24} + \ldots$$

$$LOG(1+X) = X - \frac{X^2}{2} + \frac{X^3}{3} - \frac{X^4}{4} + \ldots$$

$$COS(X) = 1 - \frac{X^2}{2} + \frac{X^4}{24} + \ldots$$

$$SIN(X) = X - \frac{X^3}{6} + \frac{X^5}{120} + \ldots$$

The first few terms of a Taylor Series can be used to approximate the actual value of the function at X.

   (a) Use the terms given in the Taylor Series to find the approximate value of each of the functions when X equals 2.
   (b) Compare the answers you got in part (a) to the answers you would get by using the computer's built-in functions.

2. The Ajax Advertising Agency accepts classified advertising. The cost of running a classified ad is $1.25 per line, where one line is 55 characters (including spaces). A portion of a line is charged as a whole line.

The following ad will appear next month:

   Local retail store is looking for a hard-working man or woman to enter into the exciting field of retail management. Applicants must have at least one year of college education. Contact Mr. Davis at 555-1423.

Write appropriate BASIC instructions that will compute the total cost of the ad.

LAB 2-1 The INT function

Type in the command: NEW

An integer is a whole number or the negative of a whole number. For example, 5, 0, and −3 are all integers. The INT(X) function generates the greatest integer which is less than or equal to the argument X, where X stands for any expression which evaluates to a number.

If we picture X as a number on a number line, then INT(X) is equal to the first integer to the left of X, if X is not already an integer. If X is an integer, then INT(X) is equal to X.

Type in the command: PRINT INT(4.9)

What is the output of the computer? _____

The number 4 is the greatest integer less than or equal to 4.9. Note that 4 is the first integer to the left of 4.9 on a number line.

Type in the command: PRINT INT(−3.1)

What is the output of the computer? _____

Did you think you would get −3 as the output? Remember that on the number line the number −4 is the first integer to the left of −3.1. The number −4 is the greatest integer less than or equal to −3.1.

Type in the command: PRINT INT(2.9 + 6.5)

What is the output of the computer? _____

The arithmetic expression 2.9 + 6.5 evaluates to 9.4 and is the argument of the INT function. The computer will always evaluate the arithmetic expression in the argument first.

The INT function can be very useful for rounding off numbers to a designated placevalue. For example, the numbers 158 and 153 rounded off to the nearest tens placevalue are 160 and 150, respectively.

The table below shows what formula to use to round off the number N to a given placevalue.

When the number is rounded off to this place value:	The formula to use is:
Thousandths	INT(1000*N + .5)/1000
Hundredths	INT(100*N + .5)/100
Tenths	INT(10*N + .5)/10
Ones	INT(N + .5)
Tens	INT(.1*N + .5)/.1
Hundreds	INT(.01*N + .5)/.01
Thousands	INT(.001*N + .5)/.001

Write the PRINT command that will display the number 352.7461 rounded off to the nearest hundredths.

You should have written PRINT INT(100*352.7461 + .5)/100

Type in the above command.

The formula for rounding off any number is

INT(R*N+.5)/R

where N is the number and R is the reciprocal of the placevalue to which the number is going to be rounded. For example, to round off the number 352.7461 to the hundredths place value, set R = 1/.01 and N = 352.7461.

Type in the commands: LET N = 352.7461
                            LET R = 1/.01
                            PRINT INT(R*N +.5)/R

What is the output of the computer? _____

Write a sequence of commands that will print the number 216738 rounded off to the nearest ten-thousand.

You should have written: LET N = 216738
                            LET R = 1/10000
                            PRINT INT(R*N+.5)/R

Type in the above sequence of commands.

What is the output of the computer? _____

In summary, the INT function will always generate the greatest integer less than or equal to its argument. The computer will do any necessary arithmetic in the argument first, before generating the integer.

LAB 2-2 The RND function

Type in the command: NEW

The RND function generates a random number greater than or equal to zero and less than one. Applesoft BASIC requires a number for the argument of the RND function.

Type in the command: PRINT RND(1)
                          PRINT RND(1)

What are the outputs of the computer? _____

Note that the two numbers printed are different. Whenever the argument of the RND function is a positive number, the RND function will generate a new random number between zero and one every time it is executed.

Type in the command: PRINT RND(0)

What is the output of the computer? _____

You should see the same number that was last generated by the RND function. Whenever the argument of the RND function is 0, RND(0) will return the last random number generated.

Type in the commands: PRINT RND(2)
PRINT RND(0)

Explain why the computer printed the same number twice.

_____

Type in the command: PRINT RND(− 1)
PRINT RND(− 1)
PRINT RND(− 1)

What is the output of the computer? _____

Are all the values the same? _____

Your answer should be YES. If another negative number is used for the argument, the RND function will generate a different random number.

Type in the command: PRINT RND(− 2)
PRINT RND(− 2)
PRINT RND(− 2)

What is the output of the computer? _____

Type in the commands: PRINT RND(− 1)
PRINT RND(− 2)

Compare the results with the previous outputs.

Type in the commands: PRINT 6∗RND(1)
PRINT 6∗RND(1)
PRINT 6∗RND(1)

What are the outputs? _____

_____

_____

You should see random numbers greater than or equal to zero but less than six.

What command prints random numbers greater than or equal to zero but less than 10?

_____

You should have written PRINT 10*RND(1).

We can also generate random integers.

Type in the commands: PRINT INT(6*RND(1))
PRINT INT(6*RND(1))
PRINT INT(6*RND(1))

What are the outputs of the computer? _____

_____

_____

The numbers which appear are random integers from zero to five.

Type in the commands: PRINT INT(6*RND(1)) + 1
PRINT INT(6*RND(1)) + 1
PRINT INT(6*RND(1)) + 1

What are the outputs of the computer? _____

_____

_____

The numbers you are looking at are random integers from 1 to 6. This illustrates how the RND function can be used to simulate the toss of a die.

The formula for generating a random integer bounded between two integers including the upper and lower bounds, is

INT (D*RND(1)) + L

where D is the difference of the upper and lower bounds plus one, and L is the lower bound.

For example, to generate a random integer bounded between 3 and 7, set D = 5 (7 − 3 + 1 = 5) and L = 3.

Type in the command: PRINT INT(5*RND(1)) + 3

What is the output of the computer? _____

Write a command that will print a random integer bounded between 4 and 9.

_____

You should have written: PRINT INT(6*RND(1)) + 4

In summary, the RND function will generate different random numbers between 0 and 1 when the argument is a positive number. The RND function will generate the last generated random number if the argument is 0. And if the argument of the RND function is negative, it will generate the same random number.

LAB 2-3 The LEN function

Type in the command: NEW

> The LEN function returns a number equal to the number of characters in a string. The argument of the LEN function can be a string enclosed in quotation marks, a string variable, or a string expression.

Type in the command: PRINT LEN("HELLO")

What is the output of the computer? _____

> Since the string HELLO has five characters, the output is 5.

Type in the commands: LET X$ = "HELLO"
> PRINT LEN(X$)

What is the output of the computer? _____

> Note that the argument of the LEN function is a string variable. The output is 5, the number of characters stored in the string variable X$.

Type in the command: PRINT LEN("JOE COOL")

What is the output of the computer? _____

> Although the string JOE COOL has only seven letters, the output is 8. This is due to the space character between the words JOE and COOL.

Type in the commands: LET B$ = "   " (*Three spaces between quotes*)
> PRINT LEN(B$)

What is the output of the computer? _____

Type in the commands: LET C$ = "" (*No spaces*)
> PRINT LEN(C$)

What is the output of the computer? _____

> While B$ really contains three spaces characters, C$ is the string containing no characters. It is called the "null string."

Does B$ contain the null string? _____

> You should have answered NO. B$ contains a string of length three, but the null string has length zero.

LAB 2-4 The VAL function

Type in the command: NEW

> There are two types of data used in BASIC, numeric and string. The VAL function is used to convert string data into numeric data.

Type in the commands: LET X$ = "123"
> LET A = VAL(X$)
> PRINT A

What is the output of the computer? _____

> Note that 123 is a string stored in X$. When the computer executed the command LET A = VAL(X$), the VAL function transformed the string 123 into numeric data and assigned it to the numeric variable A.

Type in the commands: LET X$ = "4.5 AND 6.7"
> LET A = VAL(X$)
> PRINT A

What is the output of the computer? _____

> The VAL function attempts to interpret its argument as a number. It starts at the beginning of the string, and when it reaches a character that no longer makes sense as a number, it stops. Spaces, however, are simply ignored. In the case of "4.5 AND 6.7," it returned 4.5 because it stopped when it reached the letter A.

Type in the commands: LET X$ = "FOUR"
> LET A = VAL(X$)
> PRINT A

What is the output of the computer? _____

> The first character of the string FOUR is F, which does not makes sense as a number. So the VAL function stops there and returns a value of zero.

Type in the commands: LET X$ = "12 45"
> LET A = VAL(X$)
> PRINT A

What is the output of the computer? _____

> Remember, the VAL function will scan the string from the beginning, ignoring spaces, and stopping only when it reaches a character that cannot be part of a number. The output is 1245, since the space is ignored.

___

LAB 2-5 The STR$ function

Type in the command: NEW

> There are two types of data used in BASIC, numeric and string. The STR$ function is used to convert numeric data into string data.

Type in the commands: LET X = 123
> LET A$ = STR$(X)
> PRINT A$

What is the output of the computer? _____

> First, the numeric data 123 is stored in X. When the computer executed the command LET A$ = STR$(X), the STR$ function transformed the number 123 stored in X into a string and assigned it to the string variable A$.

Type in the commands: LET X = 4
> LET A$ = STR$(X + 5)
> PRINT A$

What is the output of the computer? _____

> The computer will always evaluate the expression in the argument first. Thus, the number 9 was transformed into a string and assigned to A$.

LAB 2-6 The MID$ function

Type in the command: NEW

> A *substring* is a part of a string. To extract a substring from a string, the MID$ function is used.

Type in the command: PRINT MID$("COMPUTER",4,3)

What is the output of the computer? _____

> The argument of the MID$ function consists of three parts, separated by commas. The first part can be a string enclosed in quotation marks, a string variable, or a string expression.

In the command above, what is the string from which the substring will be extracted? _____

> Your answer should be COMPUTER.
>
> The second part of the argument must be an expression which evaluates to a positive integer. This integer gives the character position in the string which is the first character of the substring.

In the command above, what character position in COMPUTER is the first character of the substring? _____

> Your answer should be 4. This means that the fourth character in COMPUTER is to be the first character of the substring that will be extracted.
>
> The third part of the argument must be an expression which evaluates to a positive integer or zero. This integer gives the number of characters the substring will have.

In the command above, how many characters will the substring have? _____

> Your answer should be 3. The substring PUT starts at the fourth character position in the string COMPUTER and is three characters long.

Type in the commands: LET X$ = "BASIC PROGRAMMING"
> PRINT MID$(X$,10,4)

What is the output of the computer? _____

> The tenth character of the string stored in X$ is the letter G. Remember, a space is counted as a character. Taking four characters beginning with G gives us GRAM, which you have already seen on the screen.
>
> There is one other form of the MID$ function.

Type in the command: PRINT MID$ (X$,10)

What is the output of the computer? _____

> The computer displays GRAMMING. In this special form of the MID$ func-

tion, there is only one number in the argument. It tells what character position to begin with in the string. The function then returns the rest of the string from that position to the end.

LAB 2-7 The RIGHT$ function

Type in the command: NEW

The RIGHT$ function gives us a handy way of extracting the rightmost characters of a string.

Type in the command: PRINT RIGHT$("COMPUTER",3)

What is the output of the computer? _____

The argument of the RIGHT$ function consists of two parts separated by a comma. The first part can be either a string enclosed in quotation marks, a string variable, or a string expression.

In the command above, what is the string from which the substring will be extracted? _____

Your answer should be COMPUTER.

The second part of the argument must be an expression which evaluates to a positive integer. This gives the number of characters the substring will have.

In the command above how many characters will the substring have? _____

Your answer should be 3. As you saw above, the substring printed is TER. The three characters of this substring are the last three characters of COMPUTER.

Type in the command: LET X$ = "BASIC PROGRAMMING"
                         PRINT RIGHT$(X$,7)

What is the output of the computer? _____

The seventh character from the right in the string BASIC PROGRAMMING is the letter R. Thus, the output is RAMMING. The last seven characters of the string BASIC PROGRAMMING form the substring RAMMING.

LAB 2-8 The LEFT$ function

Type in the command: NEW

The LEFT$ function gives us a handy way of extracting the leftmost characters of a string.

Type in the command: PRINT LEFT$("COMPUTER",3)

What is the output of the computer? _____

The argument of the LEFT$ function consists of two parts separated by a comma. The first part can be either a string enclosed in quotation marks, a string variable, or a string expression.

In the command above, what is the string from which the substring will be extracted? _____

> Your answer should be COMPUTER.

> The second part of the argument must be an expression which evaluates to a positive integer. This gives the number of characters the substring will have.

In the command above how many characters will the substring have? _____

> Your answer should be 3. As you have already seen on the screen, the output for the command above is COM. The three characters of this substring are the first three characters of COMPUTER.

Type in the command: LET X$ = "BASIC PROGRAMMING"
                              PRINT LEFT$(X$,5)

What is the output of the computer? _____

> The first five characters of the string BASIC PROGRAMMING form the substring BASIC.

3

Computer Programming

3.0 Introduction

To an actor, how is doing live theater different than making a movie? The answer is that in a movie, the actor's performance is stored on film or tape to be edited and viewed later, but live theater is here and now. Once an actor utters his lines, that moment becomes history. This theater-movie comparison is meant to give you an understanding of the two modes in which a computer can operate. In *immediate mode*, instructions to the computer are performed "live." To be performed again, they must be typed into the computer again. This has been the mode you have been using in Chapters 1 and 2. (Hopefully you have been working with a computer all along and have seen the "immediate" results.) But in *deferred mode*, the computer saves the instructions it receives so that they may be executed later, at your command. A list of statements entered in the deferred mode is called a *program*. The statements in a program can be run and rerun just like a movie. And just as a movie can be edited after it is filmed, a program can be edited after it has been typed. The real power of a computer is its ability to operate in the deferred mode.

It is a good idea to read Appendix A at this time. Appendix A will teach you about the Disk Operating System, so that you can save the programs that you write.

3.1 Line numbers and the RUN command

There are no switches to throw or knobs to turn to put the computer into deferred mode. So how do we get there? The answer is *line numbers*. If we type

10 PRINT 2+3

the line number 10 informs the computer that this PRINT statement is

NOT to be executed now but is to be stored for later use. (The statement is saved in computer memory, but not exactly in the same way data is stored in variables.)

The command which tells the computer to execute the statements in memory is RUN. It is typed in WITHOUT a line number so that its effect is immediate. This is how the screen would look:

10 PRINT 2 + 3

```
]RUN
5
```

When several statements are typed into the computer in deferred mode, their line numbers must be different. When the RUN command is given, the computer will begin executing the statements IN NUMERICAL ORDER. Like this:

10 PRINT "READY"
20 PRINT "SET"
30 PRINT "GO!"

```
]RUN
READY
SET
GO!
```

Even if the statements had been typed in like this:

30 PRINT "GO!"
10 PRINT "READY"
20 PRINT "SET"

the output would have been the same as before. The computer executes the instructions in numerical order. The line numbers tell the computer in what order the statements are to be executed when the RUN command is typed.

RULES ON LINE NUMBERS

1. Line numbers may be any whole numbers from 0 to 63999 in Applesoft. (1 to 9999 in many other BASICs.)
2. Line numbers determine the order in which the statements are to be executed: lowest line number to highest.
3. It is recommended that line numbers have a large gap between them, such as 10, 20, 30, etc. This is to allow other lines to be inserted between existing lines when the program is edited later.

Let's take a look at another program. This time its Box Diagram is shown along with it:

X	Y	Z	CRT
0	0	0	

10 LET X = 2

| 0 | 0 | 0 | |

	X	Y	Z	CRT
20 LET Y = 5	0	0	0	
30 LET Z = (X + Y)*X	0	0	0	
40 PRINT Z	0	0	0	

]RUN

	X	Y	Z		
	2	0	0		(LINE 10)
	2	5	0		(LINE 20)
	2	5	14		(LINE 30)
14	2	5	14	(14)	(LINE 40)

Notice that the boxes X, Y, and Z are unchanged until the RUN command is typed. Then the computer processes the statements sequentially, as the Box Diagram shows. From now on, however, whenever a Box Diagram is given next to a program, the effect of each program line will be shown simultaneously in the boxes. Continue to bear in mind, of course, that the real effect on the boxes doesn't take place until the command RUN is typed. The program above could therefore be diagrammed this way:

	X	Y	Z	CRT
	0	0	0	
10 LET X = 2	2	0	0	
20 LET Y = 5	2	5	0	
30 LET Z = (X + Y)*X	2	5	14	
40 PRINT Z	2	5	14	(14)

3.2 The END statement

The END statement is an instruction in BASIC which signals the computer to stop executing instructions in the deferred mode. In Applesoft, processing of deferred mode statements will stop automatically when the last statement is reached. For this reason an END statement as the last line of a program is optional. (Some versions of BASIC, however, require that a program terminate with an END statement.) We recommend that every BASIC program end with an END statement even though it is optional. The reason will be made clear when you read about the LIST command to follow.

Example   The three programs in the last section could (and should, by our recommendation) be written this way:

```
10 PRINT 2 + 3        10 PRINT "READY"        10 LET X = 2
20 END                20 PRINT "SET"          20 LET Y = 5
                      30 PRINT "GO!"          30 LET Z = (X + Y)*X
                      40 END                  40 PRINT Z
                                              50 END
```

3.3 The LIST command and editing

Typing LIST as an immediate mode command (that is, without a line number) causes the computer to display all the line numbered statements that have been stored in memory. LIST always displays the statements in a program in numerical order, even if the statements are typed in out of order.

Suppose you have typed the program

```
10 PRINT "THREE"
20 PRINT "TWO"
30 PRINT "BLASTOFF"
40 END
```

and forgot to include PRINT "ONE". Simply type

```
25 PRINT "ONE"
```

to insert the line, and then type LIST to see that it has been done:

```
]LIST
10 PRINT "THREE"
20 PRINT "TWO"
25 PRINT "ONE"
30 PRINT "BLASTOFF!"
40 END
```

Now you see why we want to have gaps between line numbers. There would have been no way to insert a line between two statements numbered 2 and 3.

IMPORTANT: To replace a line, just retype the line. For instance, if we want line 30 to say PRINT "GO!" we need only to retype it.

```
]30 PRINT "GO!"
]LIST
10 PRINT "THREE"
20 PRINT "TWO"
25 PRINT "ONE"
30 PRINT "GO!"
40 END
```

(Lines can also be edited without being completely retyped. However, the technique is somewhat complicated. See Appendix D.)

To remove a line completely from a program, just type the line number alone and press the return key, like this:

```
]30
]LIST
10 PRINT "THREE"
20 PRINT "TWO"
25 PRINT "ONE"
40 END
```

A range of line numbers may be removed all at once by using the delete command, called DEL, as follows:

```
]DEL 10,25
]LIST
40 END
```

The DEL command may be known by other names on other computers.
Earlier we recommended that the END statement be used as the last statement in a program even though it is optional. The reason is that as your program goes through frequent edits, lines may be inadvertently erased. If a complete LIST of your program fails to end with an END statement, then you will know that the program has been corrupted. Don't worry; such occurrences are rare. But the little effort it takes to type an END statement is worth it.

3.4 The NEW and CLEAR commands

Before you begin to type a new program into the computer, you should always type the command NEW in the immediate mode. The NEW command clears the memory of the computer of all previously stored deferred mode statements and also clears the contents of all variables. Numeric variables are initialized to zero, while string variables are initialized to the "null string" (which is a string of length zero). It is very important to remember to use the NEW command, or you may find unexpected lines when you LIST your program. IMPORTANT: It is NOT a good idea to use NEW as a deferred mode statement in a program, unless your intention is to have your program wipe itself out in mid execution!

If you only want to initialize all variables but keep your program intact, use CLEAR. The CLEAR instruction can be used in either the immediate or deferred modes.

EXERCISES 3.4

1. Write BASIC programs for the following sequences of BASIC instructions. Use the END statement. If you run them on a computer, be sure to type NEW before entering the program lines.

   (a) LET W = 126
       PRINT "A PERSON WEIGHING"
       PRINT W
       PRINT "POUNDS ON EARTH"
       PRINT "WOULD WEIGH"
       PRINT W/6
       PRINT "POUNDS ON THE MOON"

   (b) LET T1 = 80
       LET T2 = 85
       LET T3 = 93
       LET A = (T1 + T2 + T3)/3
       PRINT "MY TEST AVERAGE"
       PRINT A

2. Draw Box Diagrams for Problem 1.

3. Write a BASIC program for each Box Diagram below. Where possible, use only variables in the statements you write.

   (a)

	X	Q	L	CRT
	0	0	0	
10 LET X = 23	23	0	0	

(a)

	X	Q	L	CRT
20 LET Q = 2	23	2	0	
	23	2	21	
	25	2	21	
	25	2	21	(27)

(b)

	E1	R$	T	CRT
	0		0	
	−6		0	
	−6		1	
	−6	SMART	1	
	36	SMART	1	
	36	SMART	1	(SMART)

On the next few pages you will find several elementary applications of computer programming.

APPLICATION: BALANCING THE CHECKBOOK

The following BASIC PROGRAM will balance Ms. Smith's checkbook, assuming that her current balance is $458.65, her check entry amount is $45.76, and her new deposit is $125.50.

```
100 LET B = 458.65
110 LET D = 125.50
120 LET C = 45.76
130 LET S = B + D − C
140 PRINT S
150 END
```

```
]RUN
538.39
```

EXERCISES 3.4 contd.

4. Write a Box Diagram for the checkbook program above.

5. Assume we interchange the instructions at lines 100 and 130 as follows:

```
100 LET S = B + D − C
130 LET B = 458.65
```

Write a new Box Diagram. Does the program work correctly? Explain.

APPLICATION: SOLVING FOR AN ANGLE OF A TRIANGLE

In geometry, it is well known that the sum of the angles of a triangle is 180 degrees. If A, B, and C represent the angles of a triangle, we can say that $A + B + C = 180$. If two of the angles are known, the third angle A can be derived from the formula:

$A = 180 - B - C$

The following BASIC program will compute A, given the values of B and C:

```
100 LET B = 34
110 LET C = 110
120 LET A = 180 - B - C
130 PRINT A
140 END
```

```
]RUN
36
```

**EXERCISES
3.4   contd.**

6. Construct a Box Diagram for the program above.

7. Interchange the instructions in lines 100 and 120. Construct a new Box Diagram. Explain what effect the interchange had on the outcome.

8. All right triangles have one 90-degree angle. Assume the other two angles are called A and B. Write a BASIC program to compute angle B given that angle A equals 26.72 degrees. Assume that the triangle is a right triangle.

APPLICATION: INTEREST CHARGES

Mr. Getty purchased a new automobile for $6,000. He paid $1,000 down and financed the remainder with a loan at 1.5% per month. The following BASIC program will compute the total interest owed at the end of the first month:

```
100 LET P = 6000
110 LET D = 1000
120 LET R = .015
130 LET I = (P - D)*R
140 PRINT I
150 END
```

```
]RUN
75
```

**EXERCISES
3.4   contd.**

9. Fill out a Box Diagram for the program above.

10. Assume Mr. Getty pays $250 for the first month's payment. Modify the above program to also compute the amount he owes on the car after the first month.

APPLICATION: INTEREST EARNED

Mr. Floser invested $5,000 in a savings account at 1.5% per month. The following BASIC program will compute the interest earned after the first month and the total amount in the account:

```
 5 LET P=5000
10 LET R=.015
15 LET I=P*R
20 LET P=P+I
25 PRINT "INTEREST EARNED"
30 PRINT I
35 PRINT "AMOUNT IN ACCOUNT AFTER ONE MONTH"
40 PRINT P
45 END
```

```
]RUN
INTEREST EARNED
75
AMOUNT IN ACCOUNT AFTER ONE MONTH
5075
```

EXERCISES 3.4   contd.

11. Construct a Box Diagram for the program above.

12. Modify the program for a principal investment of $4,800 and interest at 2% per month.

13. Modify the program in problem 12 to compute and print the total interest earned and total principal for two months.

APPLICATION: STOCK MARKET ANALYSIS

Mr. Jones purchased 120 shares of IBM stock for $76.75 a share, and 76 shares of ITT for $23.50 a share. The following BASIC program will compute and print his total investment.

```
100 LET IBM=120
200 LET P1=76.75
300 LET ITT=76
500 LET P2=23.50
550 LET T=IBM*P1+ITT*P2
575 PRINT "MR. JONES' TOTAL INVESTMENT IS"
600 PRINT T
800 END
```

```
]RUN
MR. JONES' TOTAL INVESTMENT IS
10996
```

EXERCISES 3.4   contd.

14. Construct a Box Diagram for the program above.

15. Assume that Mr. Jones also purchased 250 shares of Ford Motors at $65.25 a share. Modify the above program to compute and print his total investment.

3.5 The REMark statement

The REM statement is one of several nonexecutable statements in BASIC. When the computer encounters the REM statement in a program, it will ignore it and continue on to the next statement in sequence. REM stands for REMark and is used to document a program for clarity. It is useful for placing comments in the program to describe such things as who wrote it and when, what the program is supposed to do, what a certain formula means, and what variables are being used. REM statements can be seen only when the program is LISTed.

Example

APPLICATION: CONVERTING YEARS TO MINUTES

```
10 REM PROGRAM TO CONVERT FIVE YEARS TO MINUTES
20 REM WRITTEN BY JANE Q. STUDENT
30 REM ON DEC. 31, 1982
40 REM
50 REM VARIABLE LIST
60 REM Y IS NUMBER OF YEARS
63 REM D IS NUMBER OF DAYS
65 REM H IS NUMBER OF HOURS
67 REM M IS NUMBER OF MINUTES
69 REM
70 LET Y=5
80 LET D=365*Y
90 LET H=24*D
100 REM HOURS HAVE BEEN FOUND, NOW GET MINUTES
120 LET M=60*H
130 PRINT "THE NUMBER OF MINUTES EQUALS"
140 PRINT M
150 END
```

EXERCISES 3.5

1. Complete a Box Diagram for the program above.

2. Write a program that will convert minutes back to years.

3.6 Multiple statements on a single line

Putting several instructions on one program line is possible in Applesoft, and many other versions of BASIC. In Applesoft, a colon (:) is used to separate the statements.

Example   Lines 70, 80, and 90 in the program above could be written as one line, like this:

70 LET Y = 5 : LET D = 365*Y : LET H = 24*D

The disadvantages of multiple statement lines generally outweigh the advantages. For one thing, inserting a new instruction in a program is difficult if it must go between two statements on a single line. Also, a REM statement cannot be put into a multiple statement line unless it goes at the end of the line. This is because colons which follow REM are considered part of the remark.

Example   The statement

100 REM ADD TWO NUMBERS : LET X = Y + Z

is strictly a REMark. There is no LET instruction, since everything following the REMark is ignored.
The statement

100 LET X = Y + Z : REM ADD TWO NUMBERS

is a LET statement followed by a REMark.
The advantages of using multiple statements will be seen in Chapters 6 and 8.
Except for special situations in which multiple statement lines are advantageous, we use single statement lines for the sake of clarity.

3.7 Structured programming, the A.C.O. module method

To be a successful BASIC programmer you must learn a method for organizing BASIC instructions. The A.C.O. MODULE METHOD fulfills this need for simple programs.
The A.C.O. method divides the BASIC program into three modules indicated by the letters A, C, and O:

I. ASSIGNMENT: The first module is called ASSIGNMENT. In this module, data are assigned to variables.

II. COMPUTE   : The second module is called COMPUTE. In this module, values are computed.

III. OUTPUT   : The third module is OUTPUT. In this module, data are displayed.

For simple programs, a good rule to follow is: WRITE THE ASSIGNMENT MODULE FIRST, THE COMPUTE MODULE SECOND, AND THE OUTPUT MODULE THIRD.
In later chapters we will broaden the module concept to handle more complex programming. Study the examples which follow.

Example   10 REM DEMO OF A.C.O. MODULE METHOD
20 REM
30 REM THIS PROGRAM FINDS THE HYPOTENUSE OF
40 REM A RIGHT TRIANGLE WHOSE LEGS ARE KNOWN
50 REM
60 REM ASSIGNMENT MODULE

```
65 REM
70 LET A=6
80 LET B=8
90 REM
100 REM COMPUTE MODULE
105 REM
110 REM THIS IS THE PYTHAGOREAN THEOREM
120 LET C=SQR(A^2+B^2)
130 REM
140 REM OUTPUT MODULE
150 REM
160 PRINT "THE HYPOTENUSE EQUALS"
170 PRINT C
180 END
```

Example The following program should be familiar. It is the INTEREST EARNED program organized using the A.C.O. method.

```
100 REM INTEREST EARNED BY MR. FLOSER
110 REM
120 REM ASSIGNMENT MODULE
130 LET P=5000
140 LET R=.015
150 REM
160 REM COMPUTE MODULE
170 LET I=P*R
180 LET P=P+I
190 REM
200 REM OUTPUT MODULE
203 REM
205 PRINT "INTEREST EARNED"
210 PRINT I
215 PRINT "AMOUNT IN ACCOUNT AFTER ONE MONTH"
220 PRINT P
240 END
```

It should be said that the A.C.O. method is a set of guidelines, not a hard and fast rule. BUT TO AS GREAT AN EXTENT AS IS POSSIBLE, USE THE A.C.O. MODULE METHOD. It will help you to organize your thoughts and to write logically sound programs.

EXERCISES 3.7

1. Rewrite the following two programs using the A.C.O. MODULE METHOD.

(a)
```
20 LET X = 24
30 LET Y= -4
40 PRINT X
50 LET Z=X+Y
60 PRINT Z
70 LET T=2*X-Y^3
80 PRINT T
90 END
```

(b)
```
10 LET Q$="MY"
15 PRINT Q$
20 LET R$="NAME"
30 PRINT R$
40 LET E1$="IS"
50 PRINT E1$
60 LET W$="MOZART"
80 PRINT W$
90 PRINT "!"
100 END
```

3.8 Projects

Write as BASIC programs the projects given in Chapter 1.

LAB 3-1 Immediate & deferred modes

Type in the command: NEW

The computer will execute instructions in two different modes, the immediate mode and the deferred mode.

Instructions that are executed in the immediate mode are called *commands* and instructions that are executed in the deferred mode are called *statements*. Statements have line numbers, commands do not. Whenever a statement is typed in, the computer will store the instruction in memory, and defer the execution of the statement until the command RUN is typed in. Whenever you type in a command, the computer will execute it immediately.

Certain instructions can only be used as commands while others can only be used as statements. Most instructions, however, can be used as both! For example, the LET and PRINT instructions can be used either as commands or statements.

Type in the statement: 10 LET X=5

The number 10 is called the line number of the statement.

Type in the command: PRINT X

What is the output of the computer? _____

Explain why the computer printed 0 instead of 5. _____

_____

_____

The reason why 0 was printed instead of 5 is because the computer has not executed the statement 10 LET X=5. The computer will not execute this statement until the command RUN is typed.

Type in the command: RUN

What value do you expect the variable X to hold now? _____

Type in the command: PRINT X

What is the output of the computer? _____

Explain why the output is 5. _____

_____

_____

After the command RUN is typed, the statement 10 LET X=5 is then executed, assigning the number 5 to the variable X. Thus, 5 was displayed when the command PRINT X was typed.

Whenever the command RUN is executed, the computer first initializes the storage memory for all variables. That is, all numeric variables will be set to zero and all string variables will be set to the null string (string of length zero).

Type in the command: LET Y=7

What value is stored in the variable Y? _____

Since this instruction is a command, the computer assigns the number 7 to Y.

Type in the command: RUN

What value is now stored in the variable Y? _____

Type in the command: PRINT Y

What is the output of the computer? _____

Explain why the computer printed 0 instead of 7?

_____

_____

_____

The computer initialized the memory when the command RUN was executed. Thus, Y was assigned the value 0.

LAB 3-2 LIST and DEL

Type in the command: NEW

Type in the statements: 10 LET X=5
                            20 PRINT X

Type in the command: HOME

As you just observed the HOME command cleared your screen. Don't panic! Your program is still in memory.

To make the computer display the statements that are stored in its memory, the LIST command is used.

Type in the command: LIST

What is the output of the computer? _____

_____

The LIST command will always display the statements stored in memory in numerical order of the line numbers.

Type in the statements: 30 PRINT Y
                                        15 LET Y = 8

Type in the command: LIST

What is the output of the computer? _____

_____

_____

_____

It doesn't matter in what order you type the statements of a program. The listing and execution of the program will always be in numerical order of the line numbers.

The LIST command can be used to display one or more line numbers.

Type in the command: LIST 15

What is the output of the computer? _____

The output is 15 LET Y = 8. To display a range of line numbers, the arguments of the LIST command are the beginning line number and ending line number separated by a comma.

Type in the command: LIST 10,20

What line numbers are displayed by the computer? _____

To change a statement in a program, type in the new statement with the same line number. For example, let's change the statement 15 LET Y = 8 to the statement 15 LET Y = 8*X.

Type in the statement: 15 LET Y = 8*X

Type in the command: LIST

What change do you see in the program? _____

_____

Editing may also require deleting a statement from the program. To delete one statement, type in the line number of the statement.

Type: 20 (*and press the* RETURN key)

Type in the command: LIST

What is the output of the computer? _____

What statement was deleted from the program? _____

    The statement 20 PRINT X was deleted from the program.

Type in the statements: 40 PRINT X
                                 50 LET A = 2
                                 60 PRINT X + A

Type in the command: LIST

What is the output of the computer?   10 _____

                                                    15 _____

                                                    30 _____

                                                    40 _____

                                                    50 _____

                                                    60 _____

    To delete a range of line numbers in a program, the command DEL is used.

Type in the command: DEL 15,40

Type in the command: LIST

    The DEL command requires two numbers separated by a comma. The numbers are the first and last line numbers of the range to be deleted.

What line numbers were deleted from the program? _____

    You should have written line numbers 15, 30, and 40. Note that these line numbers are between 15 and 40, inclusive.

LAB 3-3 Structuring programs using A.C.O.

Type in the command: NEW

    A set of statements typed in the deferred mode is called a *program*. Programs are executed by the computer one statement at a time. The computer executes these statements in sequential order of the line numbers.

    The logical order of the statements in a program is of most importance.

Type in the statements: 10 LET F = 9/5*C + 32
                                   20 LET C = 20
                                   30 PRINT F

Type in the command: RUN

What is the output of the computer? _____

> The intention of this program is to convert 20 degrees Celsius into Fahrenheit. Twenty degrees Celsius is equivalent to sixty-eight degrees Fahrenheit.

Explain why the computer printed 32 instead of 68.

_____

_____

> The computer will execute the program in numerical order of the line numbers. Line number 10 is executed first, assigning the computed value of 9/5*C+32 to F, when C contains the value 0. Thus, the computed value of 9/5*C+32 is 32. C is assigned the value 20 AFTER the assignment of F.

Type in the statements: 10 LET C=20
                             20 LET F=9/5*C+32

Type in the commands: LIST

How does this differ from the previous program?

_____

> Line numbers 10 and 20 are interchanged.

Type in the command: RUN

What is the output of the computer? _____

> The first statement executed in this program is 10 LET C=20. After 20 has been assigned to C, the execution of the statement 20 LET F =9/5*C+32 is performed.

> Most programs have three parts: 1. Assignment
>   2. Computation
>   3. Output

> Whenever a program is written, an outline of the program is done first. The outline helps the programmer write the program in a logical order. For example, the outline for a program that will evaluate and print all the possible sums of three given numbers may look like this:

> 1. Assign the first number to X.
> 2. Assign the second number to Y.
> 3. Assign the third number to Z.
> 4. Evaluate the sum of X and Y and store it in A.
> 5. Evaluate the sum of X and Z and store it in B.
> 6. Evaluate the sum of Y and Z and store it in C.
> 7. Evaluate the sum of X, Y and Z and store it in D.
> 8. Print A.

9. Print B.
10. Print C.
11. Print D.

Using the outline above, write the program that will print all the possible sums of the numbers 2, 5, and 8.

10 _____

20 _____

30 _____

40 _____

50 _____

60 _____

70 _____

80 _____

90 _____

100 _____

110 _____

120 _____

Except for the REM statements which we include as documentation, your program should look like the one below.

Type in the program:
```
5 REM ASSIGNMENT MODULE
6 REM
10 LET X = 2
20 LET Y = 5
30 LET Z = 8
34 REM
35 REM COMPUTATION MODULE
36 REM
40 LET A = X + Y
50 LET B = X + Z
60 LET C = Y + Z
70 LET D = X + Y + Z
74 REM
75 REM OUTPUT MODULE
76 REM
80 PRINT A
90 PRINT B
```

```
100 PRINT C
110 PRINT D
120 END
```

Type in the command: RUN

What is the output of the computer? _____

_____

_____

_____

Type in the command: NEW

The different modules can be combined together. For example, suppose we wrote the outline of the program in this way:

1. Assign the first number to X.
2. Assign the second number to Y.
3. Assign the third number to Z.
4. Evaluate the sum of X and Y and print it.
5. Evaluate the sum of X and Z and print it.
6. Evaluate the sum of Y and Z and print it.
7. Evaluate the sum of X, Y and Z and print it.

Using the outline, write the program that will display all the possible sums of the numbers 2, 5 and 8.

10 _____

20 _____

30 _____

40 _____

50 _____

60 _____

70 _____

80 _____

Except for the REM statements which we include as documentation, your program should look like the one below.

Type in the statements:
```
5 REM ASSIGNMENT MODULE
10 LET X = 2
20 LET Y = 5
30 LET Z = 8
35 REM COMPUTATION AND OUTPUT MODULE
```

```
40 PRINT X + Y
50 PRINT X + Z
60 PRINT Y + Z
70 PRINT X + Y + Z
80 END
```

Type in the command: LIST

Note that the computation and output modules are in one module.

Type in the command: RUN

What is the output of the computer? _____

_____

_____

Although this program was written differently, the output is the same. The A.C.O module method should be adhered to as much as possible. However, it is not a mandatory method for writing programs. We emphasize here that the logical order of the statements in a program is very crucial.

LAB 3-4 Disk commands

Before doing this lab, be sure you have initialized your floppy disk. Instructions on how to INIT diskettes are given in Appendix A.

Type in the command: NEW

Type in the program:
```
10 REM CONVERT CELSIUS TO FAHRENHEIT
20 LET C = 20
30 LET F = 9/5*C + 32
40 PRINT F
50 END
```

To store a program on the diskette for later use, the SAVE command is used. The argument of the SAVE command is the name of the program.

Type in the command: SAVE FAHRENHEIT

When the computer executes this command, a copy of the program in memory will be stored on the diskette. The program will be stored on the diskette under the name given in the SAVE command. Programs stored on disk are called files.

Type in the command: NEW

Type in the program:
```
10 REM CONVERT FAHRENHEIT TO CELSIUS
20 LET F = 50
30 LET C = 5/9*(F-32)
40 PRINT C
50 END
```

Type in the commands: SAVE CELSIUS
                           LIST

Note that the program was not erased from memory after the program was SAVEd. Remember, the computer makes a copy of the program in memory and stores it on the disk.

The CATALOG command will list all of the names of the files you have stored on your diskette.

Type in the command: CATALOG

You should see three program names that were saved: HELLO, FAHRENHEIT and CELSIUS. The HELLO program was created and saved when you initialized your disk.

To retrieve a program stored on your disk, the LOAD command is used. The argument of the LOAD command is the name of the program.

Type in the commands: LOAD FAHRENHEIT
                           LIST

Which program is now stored in the computer's memory? _____

_____

Note that CELSIUS was erased from the memory, and FAHRENHEIT is now stored in memory. The LOAD command will clear the memory, retrieve the program you wanted from the diskette, and store it in memory.

Type in the command: SAVE CELSIUS

Saving a program using the same name of a program already stored on disk will cause the computer to replace the program stored on the disk with the program in memory.

Type in the command: LOAD CELSIUS

Type in the command: LIST

Are FAHRENHEIT and CELSIUS the same program? _____

_____

Your answer should be YES.

Explain why this occurred. _____

_____

_____

To erase a program on the disk, the DELETE command is used. The argument of the DELETE command is the name of the program.

Type in the commands: DELETE CELSIUS
CATALOG

What program no longer exists on the disk?   _____

4

More On Printing

4.0 Introduction

In Chapter 1, the PRINT instruction was introduced in its simplest form. Here we discuss three additional features of the PRINT instruction which can be used to create more interesting screen displays. They are the comma, the semicolon, and TAB(X). For additional Applesoft instructions which affect the appearance of the screen, see the section in Chapter 12 called "Prettyprinting."

4.1 The comma

In Applesoft II BASIC, each line of the screen is divided into three invisible print zones, something like fixed tab sets on a typewriter. If a comma is used to separate the items in a PRINT statement, printing will begin in the next available print zone in the line. If there are no more print zones on the current line, printing will continue to the next line of the screen.

The print zones begin at the first, seventeenth, and thirty-third character positions in the line. Since the Apple displays text on a forty character screen, the print zones are not of equal length. The first two are sixteen characters long and the third is eight. Be aware that other versions of BASIC will format the print zones differently, although the function of the comma will remain the same.

Example   10 PRINT "12345678901234567890123456789012345678903"
20 PRINT "ONE","TWO","THREE"
30 END

```
]RUN
12345678901234567890123456789012345678903

ONE             TWO             THREE
```

The numbers are there to help you count character positions.
IMPORTANT: The blank line which occurred after the number guide
happened because the print line was filled to capacity. An automatic linefeed (new line) is caused when Applesoft prints to the fortieth character
position.

Example   10 PRINT "12345678901234567890123456789001234567890"
20 PRINT "HELLO, HOW ARE YOU?","FINE!"
30 END

```
]RUN
12345678901234567890123456788901234567890

HELLO, HOW ARE YOU?              FINE!
```

Notice that the first print item ran into the second print zone, so the
second print item started in the third zone.

Example   10 PRINT "12345678901234567890123456789001234567890"
20 PRINT "TESTING","ONE","TWO","THREE","FOUR"
30 END

```
]RUN
12345678901234567890123456788901234567890

TESTING          ONE              TWO
THREE            FOUR
```

There are more items than print zones, so printing goes automatically
to the next line.

Example   10 PRINT "12345678901234567890123456789001234567890"
20 PRINT ,,"TINTINABULATION"
30 END

```
]RUN

12345678901234567890123456789001234567890

                                   TINTINAB
ULATION
```

Two things should be noted in this example. First, the two commas
before the string force the printing to be done in the third print zone.
Second, since the string to be printed is too large to fit in the eight spaces
of the last print zone, it "wraps around" the screen. This feature is true
of the Applesoft, but may not happen in other versions of BASIC.

Example   10 PRINT "12345678901234567890123456789001234567890"
20 PRINT "TESTING",
30 PRINT "ONE","TWO"
40 END

```
]RUN
12345678901234567890123456789012345678900
TESTING          ONE          TWO
```

Notice the comma after the string TESTING. When a comma occurs at the end of a PRINT statement, items printed by a subsequent PRINT statement start in the next available print zone, just as if the two PRINT statements had been combined into one.

4.2 The semicolon

The effect of the semicolon is similar to the comma, except that wherever we have said "next available print zone," we should now say "next available character position." Another way of saying it is that when an item follows a semicolon in a PRINT statement, it is printed on the screen immediately following the last thing printed. The examples below should make this clear.

Example 10 PRINT "RUNNING";"OFF";"AT";"THE";"MOUTH"
20 PRINT 1;2;2;3;4
30 END

```
]RUN
RUNNINGOFFATTHEMOUTH
12234
```

Example 10 PRINT "RUNNING";"OFF";"AT";"THE";"MOUTH";
20 PRINT 1;2;2;3;4
30 END

```
]RUN
RUNNINGOFFATTHEMOUTH12234
```

This shows that if a semicolon is the last character on the PRINT line, then the next data printed will stay on the same line.

Example 10 PRINT "RUNNING ";"OFF ";"AT ";"THE ";"MOUTH"
20 END

```
]RUN
RUNNING OFF AT THE MOUTH
```

The run-on effect was prevented by including the space character as part of the strings printed.

Remember, the contents of variables may be displayed on the screen using the PRINT statement. In fact, variables and strings may be mixed in the same PRINT statement.

Example 10 LET X = 5
20 LET Y = 3
30 LET Z = X − Y

```
40 PRINT "THE ANSWER IS ";Z
50 END
```

```
]RUN
THE ANSWER IS 2
```

Since arithmetic can take place within a PRINT statement, the following sequence would have the same output:

```
10 LET X=5
20 LET Y=3
30 PRINT "THE ANSWER IS ";X−Y
40 END
```

```
]RUN
THE ANSWER IS 2
```

Example
```
10 LET N$="MR. LUCKY"
20 PRINT "YES YOU, ";N$;", MAY HAVE ALREADY WON!"
30 END
```

```
]RUN
YES YOU, MR. LUCKY, MAY HAVE ALREADY WON!
```

Actually, this last output exceeds 40 characters. On the Apple we would really see

```
YES YOU, MR. LUCKY, MAY HAVE ALREADY WON
!
```

EXERCISES 4.2

1. Show what the output will look like for the following:

   (a)
   ```
   10 LET X=25
   20 PRINT X,SQR(X),X^2
   30 PRINT X;SQR(X);X^2
   40 PRINT X;"   ";SQR(X);"    ";X^2
   50 END
   ```

   (b)
   ```
   10 LET N$="MR. TALKER"
   20 LET T$="555-8324"
   30 PRINT N$;"'S PHONE NUMBER IS ";T$
   40 END
   ```

   (c)
   ```
   10 LET W$="ANTIDISESTABLISHMENTARIANISM"
   20 PRINT  W$;"  HAS  ";LEN(W$) ;"  LETTERS."
   30 END
   ```

4.3 The tab function, TAB(X)

The TAB(X) function is unlike any of the functions we discussed in Chapter 2. Instead of returning a numeric or string value, it has a physical effect on the position that items are printed on a line. The TAB(X) function moves the cursor* to the Xth character position FROM THE LEFT MARGIN OF THE SCREEN. TAB(X) can only be used within a PRINT instruction.

Example   10 PRINT "12345678901234567890123456789012345678 90"
20 PRINT TAB(20);"MARCH 15, 1982"
30 PRINT
40 PRINT "DEAR MR. LUCKY,"
50 PRINT TAB(5); "THESE ARE YOUR PRIZES: ";TAB(30);"LUGGAGE"
60 PRINT TAB(30);"LAWNMOWER"
70 PRINT TAB(30);"FURNITURE"
80 PRINT
90 PRINT TAB(5);"AND A GRAND PRIZE OF";TAB(30);"$25,000"
95 END

```
JRUN
12345678901234567890123456789012345678 90

                     MARCH 15, 1982
DEAR MR. LUCKY,
     THESE ARE YOUR PRIZES:    LUGGAGE
                               LAWNMOWER
                               FURNITURE
          AND A GRAND PRIZE OF    $25,000
```

This example also brings up a point not mentioned earlier. A blank line can be generated by an "empty" PRINT statement. You should know, however, that the blank line below the number guide at the top is not due to an empty PRINT statement. As mentioned before, an automatic linefeed is generated when the fortieth character position of the line is occupied.

Avoid using commas in PRINT statements which use the TAB(X) function. A comma will force the printing to take place at the next print zone, regardless of where you have tabbed. The statement

PRINT TAB(5),"HI"

will print in the seventeenth character position, not the fifth. Always use semicolons, as in

PRINT TAB(5);"HI"

Another caution: Do not use TAB(0), unless you want to print in the 256th character position from the left edge of the screen! That's six lines down! The first character position on the line is TAB(1).

4.4 Projects

1. Write a program to print the following zodiac table.

SIGN	PERIOD				
CAPRICORN	DEC 22	TO	JAN 19		
AQUARIUS	JAN 20	TO	FEB 18		

---

*The cursor is the blinking rectangle which shows where the next character will be printed.

PISCES	FEB 19	TO	MAR 20
ARIES	MAR 21	TO	APR 19
TAURUS	APR 20	TO	MAY 20
GEMINI	MAY 21	TO	JUNE 20
CANCER	JUNE 21	TO	JULY 22
LEO	JULY 23	TO	AUG 22
VIRGO	AUG 23	TO	SEPT 22
LIBRA	SEPT 23	TO	OCT 22
SCORPIO	OCT 23	TO	NOV 21
SAGITTARIUS	NOV 22	TO	DEC 21

2. The following table shows distances between cities in miles:

CITIES	GOOSE BAY	RAIN HILL	BUTTON RIVER
GOOSE BAY	***	235	400
RAIN HILL	235	***	600
BUTTON RIVER	400	600	***

Write a BASIC program that will print the table.

3. Tables of mathematical functions are very important. Consider the following table:

X	X * X	SQR(X)
1	1	1
2	4	1.414
3	9	1.732
4	16	2
5	25	2.236
6		
7		
8		
9		
10		

Write a BASIC program that will complete this table. Round square roots to three decimal places.

4. Mrs. Lucey wishes to rent a car to drive from Los Angeles to San Francisco (400 miles). The local auto club provided her with the following information on auto rentals:

MAKE	MODEL	COST/ DAY	RATE/ MILE	TOTAL COST
FORD	ESCORT	$20	$0.23	
AUDI	5000	$32	$0.32	
FIAT	STRADA	$21	$0.20	
CHEVY	IMPALA	$45	$0.55	
DATSUN	210	$31	$0.22	

Write a program that will complete the last column and print the entire table.

5. Pascal's Triangle has many useful applications. The first nine rows of the Triangle look like this:

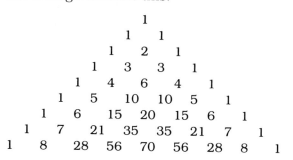

```
                    1
                 1     1
              1     2     1
           1     3     3     1
        1     4     6     4     1
     1     5    10    10     5     1
  1     6    15    20    15     6     1
1    7    21    35    35    21    7    1
1    8    28    56    70    56    28    8    1
```

Write a BASIC program that will generate and print Pascal's Triangle in the form shown above. Use LET statements to generate each number from the preceding lines. Notice that each number in the interior of the Triangle is the sum of the two numbers just above it.

LAB 4-1 The PRINT instruction using commas

Type in the command: NEW

The screen on the APPLE computer is 40 characters wide consisting of three print zones. The use of commas in a PRINT instruction will place data into these print zones. The first two print zones are sixteen (16) characters in length and the third is eight (8) characters in length.

The first print zone is from character position 1 through 16, inclusive. The second print zone is from character position 17 through 32, inclusive. And the third print zone is from character position 33 through 40, inclusive.

Type in the program: 10 HOME
20 PRINT "12345678901234567890123456789012345678 90"
30 PRINT "A","B","C"
40 END

Type in the command: RUN

In what character positions are the strings A, B, and C displayed on the CRT?

_____

The strings A, B, and C are displayed at the first character position of each print zone (character positions 1, 17, and 33).

Type in the statement: 30 PRINT "BASIC PROGRAMMING",123

Type in the command: LIST

How many characters are in the string BASIC PROGRAMMING? _____

Type in the command: RUN

In what character position does the 123 begin? _____

Since the string BASIC PROGRAMMING has 17 characters, two print zones are needed to display this string. Thus, 123 was printed in the next available print zone, the third print zone.

Type in the statement: 30 PRINT "BASIC PROGRAMMER",123

Type in the command: LIST

How many characters are in the string BASIC PROGRAMMER? _____

Type in the command: RUN

In what character position does the number 123 begin? _____

The string BASIC PROGRAMMER has sixteen characters and is printed in the first print zone. Yet the number 123 is printed in the third print zone! The Apple computer will skip the second print zone if the sixteenth (16th) character position of the first print zone is used. When the twenty-fourth (24th) character position is used (this is in the second print zone), the third print zone will be skipped.

Type in the statement: 30 PRINT 123,"PROGRAMS",456

Type in the command: LIST

In which print zone will the number 456 appear when the program is run?

_____

Type in the command: RUN

Since the letter S of the string PROGRAMS occupies the 24th character position, the third print zone is skipped. The number 456 is printed in the next available print zone, which is the first print zone of the next line.

Type in the statements: 20 PRINT "ONE",
                             30 PRINT "TWO",
                             40 PRINT "THREE"

Type in the command: LIST

What is the last character in line numbers 20 and 30? _____

Type in the command: RUN

The output of this program is on the same line, even though there are three different PRINT statements in the program.

Whenever a PRINT statement ends with a comma, the next printed data will be displayed in the next available print zone.

LAB 4-2 The PRINT instruction using semicolons

Type in the command: NEW

Whenever semicolons are used to separate data in a PRINT instruction, the data are printed next to each other without spaces.

Type in the command: PRINT "A";"B";"C"

What is the output of the computer? _____

Type in the program: 10 LET X$ = "ONE"
                         20 LET Y = 5
                         30 PRINT X$;23;"FOUR";Y
                         40 END

Type in the command: RUN

What is the output of the computer? _____

> The output ONE23FOUR5 consists of four different data printed together without spaces.

Type in the statements: 30 PRINT X$;
                          40 PRINT 23;
                          50 PRINT "FOUR";
                          60 PRINT Y
                          70 END

Type in the command: LIST

What is the last character in line numbers 30, 40, and 50?

_____

Type in the command: RUN

What is the output of the computer? _____

> Note that the output is the same as the previous program. Although there were four different PRINT statements executed, the output is on the same line. Whenever a PRINT statement ends with a semicolon, the next item printed will be adjacent to the last.

LAB 4-3 The TAB function

Type in the command: NEW

> While the comma forces printing in the next print zone and the semicolon displays data in the next available character position, the TAB function permits data to be displayed in any character position of the output line.

> The Apple computer sets the display screen to forty characters per output line. That is, only forty characters can be printed on one line. The argument of the TAB function must be a numeric expression which evaluates to a positive number less than 256. A semicolon should always be used after TAB function.

Type in the program: 10 HOME
                         20 PRINT "1234567890123456789012345678901234567890"

```
30 PRINT TAB(7);"A"
40 END
```

Type in the command: RUN

What is the argument of the TAB function? _____

In what character position on the display screen is the string A printed?
_____

> Both of your answers should be 7. The TAB function moves the cursor to the specified character position, and the data following the TAB function is printed there.

Type in the statement: 30 PRINT TAB(5);"A";TAB(26);"B"

Type in the command: LIST

How many TAB functions are there in line number 30? _____

Type in the command: RUN

Explain what the computer did when it executed line number 30. _____

_____

_____

_____

_____

> When the computer executed line number 30, the TAB(5) moved the cursor to the fifth character position of the output line. The computer then printed the string A at that character position. Next the TAB(26) moved the cursor to the 26th character position of the same output line and displayed the string B at that position.
>
> The TAB function will only move the cursor to the right, not to the left.

Type in the statement: 30 PRINT TAB(33);"A";TAB(12);"B"

Type in the command: LIST

What is the argument of the first TAB function? _____

What is the argument of the second TAB function? _____

Type in the command: RUN

What character position is the cursor moved to first? _____

> When TAB(33) is executed, the cursor was moved to the 33rd character position of the output line.

In what character position is the string B displayed? _____

When the computer tries to execute TAB(12), the cursor is at the 34th character position of the output line. Since the TAB function moves the cursor only to the right, the cursor cannot be moved to the 12th character position of the output line. Thus, the TAB(12) is not executed and the computer displayed the string B at the 34th character position.

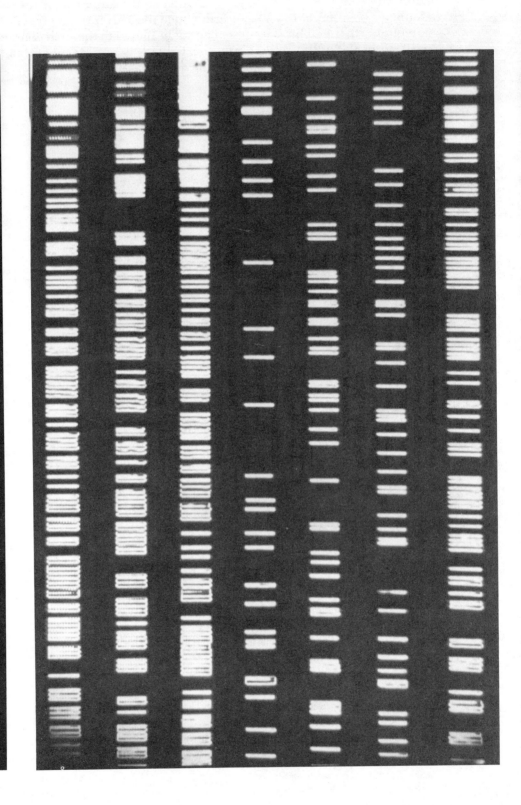

5

The READ/DATA and INPUT Statements

5.0 Introduction

In Chapter 1 we mentioned that the LET statement is only one of four kinds of assignment statements in the BASIC language. In this chapter, we introduce two more BASIC instructions for assigning data to variables: the READ/DATA and INPUT statements. The fourth assignment statement, GET, is discussed in Chapter 12.

5.1 The READ/DATA Statement

Although we seem to refer to the READ/DATA statement as a unit, they are really two separate statements which work together. The DATA statement allows us to list the data which will be assigned to variables at some point in the program. It is another example of a nonexecutable statement. The actual assigning of values from a data list is accomplished by the READ statement. The instruction READ is followed by a list of one or more variables, separated by commas, which are to receive the values listed in the DATA statement.

Example

```
10 DATA "COOL,JOE", 23, MALE
20 READ N$, A, S$
```

N$	A	S$
	0	
COOL,JOE	23	MALE

The idea is simple. The computer just matches the variables listed in line 20 with the data listed in line 10. As you can see, both numeric values and string values can be assigned using the READ and DATA statements. String values must be matched with string variables, and numeric values with numeric variables, or else a SYNTAX ERROR will occur and the program will halt. Quotation marks enclosing string data are optional, unless the string contains commas or colons or has leading spaces. For

83

the sake of clarity, we will make it a habit to enclose all string data in quotation marks.

A quotation mark may be used as a character within a string as long as it is not the first character. In a DATA statement a string containing quotes cannot be enclosed in quotation marks.

Example

A$

```
10 DATA AN "ACUTE" ANGLE
20 READ A$
```

    | AN "ACUTE" ANGLE |

Notice that there is no way that a LET statement could have made the same assignment. In the LET instruction, string data must be enclosed in quotation marks and therefore cannot contain them as characters.

READ statements should occur in your program where assignment of data is needed. But DATA statements can be anywhere. The computer will find them. To illustrate, the three programs in the next example all assign 4, 5, and 8 to A, B, and C, respectively. The DATA statements, however, appear in different places.

Example

```
10 DATA 4,5,8         10 READ A,B,C         10 READ A,B,C
20 READ A,B,C         20 PRINT A*B+C        20 PRINT A*B+C
30 PRINT A*B+C        30 DATA 4,5,8         30 END
40 END                40 END                40 DATA 4,5,8
```

```
]RUN                  ]RUN                  ]RUN
28                    28                    28
```

The placement of the DATA statement is up to the programmer. If there are several DATA statements in a program, it is generally a good idea to collect them together. They should be easy to find in case the program needs debugging.

The number of READ statements need not match the number of DATA statements in a program, as long as the variables and data items match up. The two programs which follow both assign 5, 6, and 7 to the variables A, B, and C, respectively.

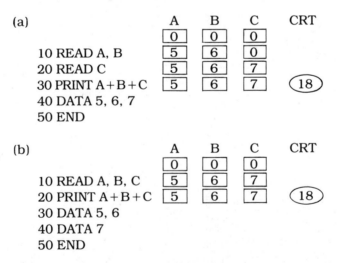

(a)

	A	B	C	CRT
	0	0	0	
10 READ A, B	5	6	0	
20 READ C	5	6	7	
30 PRINT A+B+C	5	6	7	18
40 DATA 5, 6, 7				
50 END				

(b)

	A	B	C	CRT
	0	0	0	
10 READ A, B, C	5	6	7	
20 PRINT A+B+C	5	6	7	18
30 DATA 5, 6				
40 DATA 7				
50 END				

Program (b) shows that if there are too few data items in a DATA statement, the computer will automatically find the next DATA statement in the program.

When there is not enough data to satisfy a READ statement, an OUT OF DATA error occurs and the program halts.

Example

```
10 READ A, B, C
20 DATA 5, 6
30 PRINT A+B+C
40 END
```

```
]RUN
?OUT OF DATA ERROR IN 10
]
```

EXERCISES 5.1

1. Complete a Box Diagram for each of these programs.

   (a)
   ```
   200 READ A,D,F1
   210 LET H=2*A−D/2*F1
   220 PRINT H
   230 DATA 5, 6, −2
   240 END
   ```

   (b)
   ```
   30 READ R$,T,E,F$
   35 PRINT R$,T,E;
   40 PRINT F$
   50 DATA "TEA"
   60 DATA 4,2
   70 DATA "?"
   80 END
   ```

   (c)
   ```
   10 DATA 2, 3, 4
   20 READ X, Y, Z
   30 LET Z=X+Y+Z
   40 PRINT Z
   50 END
   ```

2. Three of the six programs below will not run. Find them and explain the errors that have been made. For the programs that will run, what is the output?

   (a)
   ```
   10 DATA 23,"NOT","WELL",4
   20 READ X,C$,T,R
   25 PRINT X,C$,T,R
   30 END
   ```

   (b)
   ```
   10 READ X,Y,Z
   20 DATA 2,47
   25 PRINT X,Y,Z
   30 END
   ```

   (c)
   ```
   100 READ R$,T
   110 DATA "MOZART",4,"MATH"
   115 PRINT R$,T
   120 END
   ```

   (d)
   ```
   40 READ R,T,P
   45 PRINT R,T
   50 END
   ```

   (e)
   ```
   10 READ A,A,A
   20 DATA 5,6,7
   30 PRINT A,A,A
   40 END
   ```

   (f)
   ```
   10 DATA 3,5
   15 LET X=5
   20 LET Y=3
   40 READ X,Y
   50 PRINT X,Y
   60 END
   ```

3. The application program called INTEREST EARNED from Chapter 3 can be rewritten using READ/DATA as follows:

```
100 REM INTEREST EARNED
110 READ P,R
120 LET I=P*R
130 LET P=P+I
140 PRINT "INTEREST EARNED ";I
150 PRINT "AMOUNT IN ACCOUNT AFTER ONE MONTH ";P
```

160 DATA 5000,.015
170 END

Rewrite these Chapter 3 programs:

(a) BALANCING THE CHECKBOOK
(b) SOLVING FOR AN ANGLE OF A TRIANGLE
(c) INTEREST CHARGES
(d) STOCK MARKET ANALYSIS

Use READ/DATA to assign data to variables.

5.2 Iterative addition

Iterative addition means repeated addition using the same variables over and over again. The following examples demonstrate this process. IMPORTANT: The variable S in the programs below is called an *accumulator*. An accumulator is like the "memory plus" key on a calculator. It keeps a running total.

Example   This program adds the numbers 5, 35, and 60.

		S	X	CRT
100 REM DEMONSTRATION				
105 REM OF ITERATIVE ADDITION				
110 LET S = 0		0	0	
120 READ X		0	5	
130 LET S = S + X		5	5	
140 READ X		5	35	
150 LET S = S + X		40	35	
160 READ X		40	60	
170 LET S = S + X		100	60	
180 PRINT S		100	60	(100)
190 DATA 5,35,60				
200 END				

Certainly the same result could have been found with the shorter program:

10 READ X,Y,Z
20 LET S = X + Y + Z
30 PRINT S
40 DATA 5,35,60
50 END

But the iterative method has merits which won't be fully appreciated until the next chapter. Learn it now.

Example   Mrs. Homer has six children. The following program prints their names and ages and computes their average age. It uses iterative addition.

```
100 REM COMPUTES AVERAGE AGE
110 LET S = 0
120 READ N$,A
130 PRINT N$;" IS ";A" YEARS OLD."
140 LET S = S + A
150 READ N$,A
160 PRINT N$;" IS ";A;" YEARS OLD."
170 LET S = S + A
180 READ N$,A
190 PRINT N$;" IS ";A;" YEARS OLD."
200 LET S = S + A
210 READ N$,A
220 PRINT N$;" IS ";A;" YEARS OLD."
230 LET S = S + A
240 READ N$,A
250 PRINT N$;" IS ";A;" YEARS OLD."
260 LET S = S + A
270 READ N$,A
280 PRINT N$;" IS ";A;" YEARS OLD."
290 LET S = S + A
300 LET M = S/6
310 PRINT "THEIR AVERAGE AGE IS ";M
320 DATA "ERIC",6,"KRISTIN",8,"MELANIE",10
330 DATA "ROY",12,"KIM",13,"PAUL",18
340 END
```

EXERCISES 5.2

1. Modify the program above to compute the average age of Mrs. Homer's girls only. Do not change the DATA statements.

5.3 The RESTORE statement

Once any of the values in the DATA statement have been used up, they can be restored with the RESTORE statement.

Example   The following will be interrupted by an OUT OF DATA error since there is insufficient data for the variables:

```
100 READ A,B,C,D,E,F,G
110 DATA 2,1,5,6,24
120 END
```

However, by restoring the data before F and G are read, we solve the problem, as follows:

	A	B	C	D	E	F	G
	0	0	0	0	0	0	0
100 READ A,B,C,D,E	2	1	5	6	24	0	0
110 RESTORE	2	1	5	6	24	0	0
120 READ F,G	2	1	5	6	24	2	1

```
130 DATA 2,1,5,6,24
140 END
```

Observe that F and G take on the first two values in the data list, because ALL of the data is put back as a result of the RESTORE instruction. (Some versions of BASIC can restore data selectively.)

EXERCISES 5.3	

1. The following table shows test grades for four students in Mr. Smith's BASIC class.

	TEST 1	TEST 2	TEST 3
DENNIS	78	89	56
ALAN	56	66	89
TOM	81	55	99
ANDY	66	78	80

Using the DATA statement: DATA 78,89,56,56,66,89,81,55,99,66,78,80

Write ONE program that

(a) computes and prints the average test score for each of the students, and

(b) computes and prints the average score for each test.

Use the iterative addition technique, and restore the data between the two parts of the program.

5.4 The INPUT statement

With the INPUT statement, data can be assigned to variables directly from the keyboard by the user at the time the program is run. This is in contrast to the LET and READ/DATA statements which require assignments to be made by the programmer at the time the program is written. A programmer writes the program; a user runs it. Always assume that the user has no knowledge of programming and cannot modify the program to change the data in LET or DATA statements. The INPUT statement, therefore, is a way in which a user can supply data to the program. Programs which use INPUT statements are called *interactive*.

The simplest form of the INPUT instruction is:

INPUT X

The variable may be either numeric or string. When the computer encounters this instruction in a BASIC program, the CRT will display a question mark. The question mark is called a *prompt* because it is prompting the user for a response. All data supplied by the user in response to an INPUT statement will be shown in this book with an underline.

Example   Assume we wish to assign the numeric value 3.6 to X and the string "YOGURT" to P$ by using an INPUT statement. (NOTE: The CRT box shows only what appears after the RUN command is typed.)

	X	P$	CRT
	0		
10 INPUT X	3.6		?3.6
20 INPUT P$	3.6	YOGURT	?YOGURT

Don't forget that the underline means the user was responding to an INPUT prompt.

It is not necessary to put quotation marks around a string that is being entered in response to an INPUT statement, unless that string contains a comma or a colon.

Example

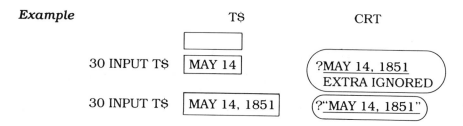

The EXTRA IGNORED message means that the data to the right of the comma was not assigned to T$.

Several variables may be assigned values with a single INPUT statement. This is done by separating the variables with commas after the INPUT instruction.

Example

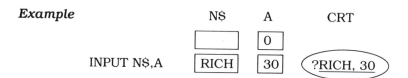

In response to the INPUT statement, the user types in the data he wishes to enter. The data may be typed all at once separated by commas, or else the RETURN key may be pressed after each item.

If the user is not familiar with the program that is running, or if there are several different INPUT statements in the program, a simple question mark prompt may not be sufficient. To remove the confusion, you (as the programmer) can insert a prompting message in quotation marks after an INPUT instruction. BASIC will print this message instead of the question mark. A semicolon MUST go between the prompt message and the list of variables. (Some versions of BASIC use a comma instead of a semicolon.)

Example
```
100 INPUT "ENTER YOUR NAME AND AGE>>" ;N$,A
105 PRINT
110 PRINT N$;", YOU HAVE SPENT NEARLY"
120 PRINT A/3;" YEARS OF YOUR LIFE ASLEEP!"
130 END
```

```
]RUN
ENTER YOUR NAME AND AGE>> RICH, 30
RICH, YOU HAVE SPENT NEARLY
10 YEARS OF YOUR LIFE ASLEEP!
```

Example
```
10 REM THIS PROGRAM PRINTS THE SUM
20 REM OF TWO ARBITRARY NUMBERS
30 INPUT "FIRST NUMBER: ";X
40 INPUT "NEXT PLEASE! ";Y
```

50 PRINT "THE SUM OF ";X;" AND ";Y;" IS ";X+Y
60 END

```
]RUN
FIRST NUMBER: 3
NEXT PLEASE! 5
THE SUM OF 3 AND 5 IS 8
```

APPLICATION: STOCK ANALYSIS

Mr. Jones purchased S1 shares of IBM for D1 dollars a share and S2 shares of SONY for D2 dollars a share. The following program will compute and print his total investment. Below the program we show a sample run for

S1 = 450
D1 = 75.50
S2 = 200
D2 = 25.25

100 REM STOCK ANALYSIS FOR ARBITRARY VALUES
110 REM
115 REM   ASSIGNMENT MODULE
117 REM
120 INPUT "HOW MANY SHARES OF IBM? "; S1
130 INPUT "HOW MUCH PER SHARE? "; D1
140 INPUT "HOW MANY SHARES OF SONY? "; S2
150 INPUT "HOW MUCH PER SHARE? "; D2
155 REM
160 REM   COMPUTE MODULE
165 REM
170 LET I=S1*D1+S2*D2
173 REM
175 REM   OUTPUT MODULE
178 REM
180 PRINT
185 PRINT "YOUR TOTAL INVESTMENT IS ";I;" DOLLARS."
190 END

```
]RUN
HOW MANY SHARES OF IBM? 450
HOW MUCH PER SHARE? 75.50
HOW MANY SHARES OF SONY? 200
HOW MUCH PER SHARE? 25.25
YOUR TOTAL INVESTMENT IS 39025 DOLLARS.
```

EXERCISES 5.4

1. Assume Mr. Jones also purchased S3 shares of ITT at D3 dollars a share. Modify the above program to compute and print the total he invested in each of the three stocks and the total amount invested.

2. Modify the program called INTEREST EARNED in Chapter 3 by replacing appropriate LET statements with INPUT statements.

5.5 Projects

1. APPLICATION: THE STANDARD DEVIATION
   The standard deviation is used by statisticians to measure the dispersion of data from the statistical average. The following table will show how the standard deviation is computed for the data listed under X.

X	X − AVE	(X − AVE)^2
3	0	0
7	4	16
−2	−5	25
8	5	25
3	0	0
0	−3	9
2	−1	1

SUM = 21
AVE = 21/7 = 3

SUM = 76
AVE = 76/7 = 10.857
STANDARD DEVIATION = SQR(10.857)
                   = 3.295

Rem. Ms Smith's Investments

Assume the DATA statement for X values: DATA 3,7,−2,8,3,0,2
   Write a program that will compute and print the AVERAGE and the STANDARD DEVIATION.

2. Ms. Smith purchased S1 shares of IBM at P1 dollars a share; S2 shares of SONY at P2 dollars a share; and S3 shares of ITT at P3 dollars a share.
   Several months later she received D1 dollars a share in dividends for IBM; D2 dollars a share in dividends for SONY; and D3 dollars a share in dividends for ITT.
   Later she sold the stocks for the following prices:

Q1 dollars a share for IBM,
Q2 dollars a share for SONY,
Q3 dollars a share for ITT.

Write a BASIC program to compute and print the TOTAL PURCHASE COST, THE TOTAL DIVIDENDS, THE TOTAL REVENUES RECEIVED FROM SALES, AND THE TOTAL NET PROFITS, where

TOTAL PURCHASE COST = SUM OF (NUMBER OF SHARES PURCHASED * PRICE PER SHARE)

TOTAL DIVIDENDS = SUM OF (NUMBER OF SHARES PURCHASED * DIVIDENDS PER SHARE)

TOTAL REVENUE RECEIVED FROM SALES = SUM OF (NUMBER OF SHARES PURCHASED * SALE PRICE PER SHARE)

TOTAL NET PROFITS = TOTAL REVENUE FROM SALES + TOTAL DIVIDENDS − TOTAL COSTS

one w/ input + one w/ Data Statements

In the assignment module section of the program, assign all values using INPUT statements only.

LAB 5-1 The READ and DATA statements

Type in the command: NEW

> The READ and DATA statements are used to assign data to variables within a program.
>
> The DATA statement is a non-executable statement containing data. The data listed in the DATA statement can be either numeric or string and must be separated by commas.
>
> The READ statement assigns data contained in a DATA statement. The arguments of the READ statement are variables and must be separated by commas.

Type in the program: 10 READ A$, X
　　　　　　　　　　　　　20 PRINT A$, X
　　　　　　　　　　　　　30 DATA "ONE", 2
　　　　　　　　　　　　　40 END

What are the variables of the READ statement? _____

What are the data of the DATA statement? _____

Type in the command: RUN

What is the output of the computer? _____

> When the computer executed line number 10, the first item in the DATA statement is assigned to the first variable of the READ statement. The second item in the DATA statement is assigned to the second variable of the READ statement.
>
> The type of variables listed in the READ statement must match the type of data in the DATA statement.

Type in the statement: 30 DATA 2,"ONE"

Type in the command: LIST

What is the second item in the DATA statement? _____

What is the second variable of the READ statement? _____

Type in the command: RUN

What is the response of the computer? _____

Type in the command: PRINT A$

What is the output of the computer? _____

> The ERROR was not caused by the assignment of 2 to A$. The computer interpreted the data 2 as a string and assigned it to A$. However, the second item in the DATA statement is the string ONE, and the attempt to assign it to the numeric variable X caused the ERROR.

Type in the statement: 30 DATA "HELLO"

Type in the command: LIST

How many variables are in the READ statement? _____

How many items are there in the DATA statement? _____

Type in the command: RUN

What is the response to the computer? _____

> The ERROR was caused by the lack of data in the DATA statement. There must be enough data in the DATA statement for each assignment done by the READ statement.

Type in the statement: 40 DATA 1,THERE,2
                          50 READ A$,X
                          60 PRINT A$,X
                          70 END

Type in the command: LIST

> The DATA statement can be anywhere in the program, since it is a non-executable statement.

Type in the command: RUN

What is the output of the computer? _____

_____

> When the READ statement assigns data to its variables, it starts with the data statement with the lowest line number. Thus, the string HELLO was first assigned. After all of the data is assigned in a particular DATA statement, the data in the next DATA statement in numerical order of the line numbers will be assigned.
>
> Note that the string THERE is not enclosed in quotes. Quotes are needed when the string contains a comma or a colon.

LAB 5-2 RESTORE

Type in the command: NEW

> The function of the RESTORE statement can be best shown by the following program.

Type in the program: 10 READ X
                        20 RESTORE
                        30 READ Y
                        40 RESTORE
                        50 READ Z
                        60 PRINT X, Y, Z
                        70 DATA 4, 5, 6
                        80 END

Type in the command: RUN

What values are assigned to X, Y, and Z? _____

> The number 4 is assigned to each of the variables. Whenever a value is assigned by the READ statement, the next value to be read is the next

item in the DATA statement. However, when the RESTORE statement is executed, the next value to be read will be the first item in the first DATA statement of the program.

Type in the command: NEW

Type in the program: 10 READ X
20 READ Y
30 RESTORE
40 PRINT X,Y
50 DATA 3
60 END

Type in the command: RUN

What is the response of the computer? _____

Explain why the error occurred. _____

_____

_____

There is no more data in line number 50 to be assigned to the variable Y in line number 20. The RESTORE statement at line number 30 occurs too late in the program to prevent the error.

Type in the statements: 20 RESTORE
30 READ Y

Type in the command: LIST

Type in the command: RUN

Note that the RESTORE statement is executed before the READ Y statement. This allows the first item in the data statement to be reread.

LAB 5-3 INPUT

Type in the command: NEW

The INPUT statement allows the user to assign data to variables from the keyboard.

Type in the program: 10 HOME
20 INPUT X
30 PRINT "THE VALUE OF X IS ";X
40 END

The argument of the INPUT statement can be one or more string variables or one or more numeric variables.

What is the argument of the INPUT statement in line number 20?

_____

The argument of the INPUT statement is the numeric variable X.

Type in the command: RUN

What is the output of the computer? _____

> You should see a question mark (?) displayed on the screen. This is the computer's way of asking for an input from the user. That is, it is prompting the user for a response.

Type in the number: 7

What is the output of the computer? _____

> The argument of the INPUT statement and the data typed in must match. That is, if the argument of the INPUT statement is a numeric variable, only numbers will be accepted.

Type in the command: RUN

Type in the string: HELLO

What is the response of the computer? _____

> The computer did not like what was entered. Thus, it displayed the prompt message ?REENTER and a question mark for another input.

Explain why the computer did not accept the string HELLO?

_____

_____

> The argument of the INPUT statement is a numeric variable. Thus, only numbers will be accepted.

Press the RESET key.

> Pressing the RESET key interrupts a program while it is running.

Type in the statements: 20 INPUT "ENTER YOUR NAME: ";X$
                          30 PRINT "YOUR NAME IS ";X$

Type in the command: LIST

> The expression "ENTER YOUR NAME: " before the variable X$ in the INPUT statement is called a prompt message. The prompt message must be a string enclosed in quotation marks. The variable and the prompt message of an INPUT statement must be separated by a semicolon.

Type in the command: RUN

What is the output of the computer? _____

> The output is the prompt message of the INPUT statement. Note that the question mark is not printed.

Type in the string: JOHN DOE

What is the output of the computer? _____

> Whenever a string variable is used in an INPUT statement, all strings will be accepted as input except strings containing commas (,) or colons (:).

Commas and colons can be entered if they are part of a string which is enclosed in quotation marks.

Type in the command: RUN

Type in the string: DOE, JOHN

What is the output of the computer? _____

_____

The computer's response, ?EXTRA IGNORED, was caused by the comma in the string DOE, JOHN.

Type in the command: RUN

Type in the string: "DOE, JOHN"

What is the output of the computer? _____

Explain why the computer accepted the string DOE, JOHN?

_____

_____

Remember, commas and colons can be entered if they are part of a string which is enclosed in quotation marks.

6

Decision and Branching Statements

6.1 The IF-THEN statement

How does the computer know to tell us when a flight is sold out or when we have overdrawn our checking account? How does the computerized cash register know what price to assign to a jar of pickles? The answer lies in the IF-THEN statement which gives the computer the ability to check a condition and take an action if the condition is true. The general form is

IF *condition* THEN *action*

where *condition* is an expression which is either TRUE or FALSE, and *action* is any BASIC instruction. The action is carried out ONLY if the condition is true. The following rules govern the IF-THEN statement:

(a) If the condition is FALSE, the action instruction is ignored and the program passes automatically to the next line number
(b) If the condition is TRUE, the action instruction is carried out. After the action is performed, control passes to the next BASIC instruction. The next BASIC instruction will either be on the same line number (for a multiple statement line) or the next line number (for a single statement line).

Examples of   IF N = 250 THEN PRINT "FLIGHT IS SOLD OUT"
IF-THEN   IF B − C<0 THEN PRINT "INSUFFICIENT FUNDS"
statements   IF I$ = "PICKLES" THEN LET P = .89

There are six different ways to compare data in a condition. The comparison symbols are called *relational operators*.

99

OPERATOR	MEANING
=	"is equal to"
<	"is less than"
>	"is greater than"
< =	"is less than or equal to"
> =	"is greater than or equal to"
<>	"is not equal to"

Example

	A	B	X	CRT
10 LET A = 2 : LET B = 4	2	4	0	
20 LET X = 10	2	4	10	
30 IF A = B − 2 THEN PRINT "EQUAL"	2	4	10	EQUAL
40 IF X< B + 8 THEN LET A = 1	1	4	10	
50 IF A<>2 THEN LET X = 5	1	4	5	
60 IF "HI" = "MY" THEN LET A = 2	1	4	5	
70 IF "HI"<>"MY" THEN LET A = 0	0	4	5	

The relation

B>18

tests a condition on a number and a numeric variable. But what would it mean to compare strings? What does

R$ > "GLASS"

really say? The answer is that a string is considered "greater" than another string if it comes later alphabetically. Imagine that you are looking up both strings in a dictionary. The one you find closer to the beginning is said to be "less than" the other. Suppose R$ contains the string GRAPES. Then the relation R$ > "GLASS" is TRUE.

A relation may test a condition on numeric values or on string values, but there can be no mixing of data types. It doesn't make sense to ask if the string SOUP is greater than the number 14.

Caution.   In Applesoft, no comparison in an IF-THEN statement may end with an "A", as in

IF B<A THEN LET C = 5

This is because "AT" is a reserved word. And the statement, when listed, would come out like this:

IF B< AT HEN LET C = 5

To avoid this problem, use parentheses:

IF (B<A) THEN LET C = 5

EXERCISES 6.1

1. State whether the conditions are true or false.

(a) A$>"HOUSE" where A$ is HOME
(b) Z$<A$ where Z$ is APE and A$ is APES

(c) C$> = D$ where C$ and D$ are both PURPLE
(d) F$<"M" where F$ is "MAXWELL"

2. Explain what is wrong with these IF-THEN statements:

(a) IF X$<>2 THEN LET F = 3
(b) IF B = "4" THEN PRINT R + 2*B
(c) IF PRINT R THEN LET X = 4
(d) IF B<>3 THEN X4$<>"HELLO"

3. Complete a Box Diagram for the following program:

100 LET X = 2
110 LET X1$ = "HELLO"
120 LET T = 4
130 LET Z$ = "SO LONG"
140 IF X + 1<>2 THEN LET T = 0
150 IF T = 0 THEN PRINT X
160 IF X1$<Z$ THEN LET Z$ = "TOMORROW"
170 IF T>X + 6 THEN LET T = 5
180 END

LOGICAL CONNECTIVES

Conditions can be connected together by the two *connectives*, AND and OR.

The following rules apply for connecting conditions:

(a) The expression
condition1 AND *condition2*
is TRUE only if *condition1* and *condition2* are both TRUE. Otherwise it is FALSE.
(b) The expression
condition1 OR *condition2*
is TRUE when at least one of the conditions is TRUE. Otherwise it is FALSE.

Examples of Logical Connectives   For the examples below assume X = 2, A = 3, B = 5, A$ = "NO".

	X	A	B	A$
	2	3	5	NO
IF X>2 AND A = 3 THEN LET B = 4	2	3	5	NO
IF A$ <>"YES" OR B>= 100 THEN LET X = 6	6	3	5	NO
IF B<= 5 AND A$ = "NO" THEN LET A$ = "YES"	6	3	5	YES
IF X = 1 OR (B<>3 and X = B + 1) THEN LET B = 8	6	3	8	YES

The examples bring out two more points. Both numeric and string relations may appear together in the same logical expression. Also, parentheses may be used to identify which part of the logical expression is to be evaluated first.

**EXERCISES
6.1, contd.**

4. Complete a Box Diagram for the following programs.

(a)

```
100 LET R = 2
110 LET V1 = 45
120 LET K$ = "HE"
130 IF K$>"SHE" OR V1 = 100 THEN LET R = R + 1
140 IF K$<"SHE" OR V1 = 100 THEN LET R = R - 2
150 IF K$<"SHE" AND V1<>100 THEN LET R = R - 2
160 END
```

(b)

```
10 LET G3$ = "CAT"
20 LET T$ = "DOG"
30 LET R = 3
40 IF G3$<>"KITTY" AND R<2 THEN LET Y = Y + R*2
50 IF G3$<>"KITTY" OR R<2 THEN LET Y = Y + R*2
60 IF (R = 5 AND T$ = "DOG") OR T$<>"POOCH" THEN LET
      T$ = "CHOW"
70 IF (R = 5 OR T$ = "PUPPY") AND T$<>"POOCH" THEN LET
      T$ = "BONE"
```

MULTIPLE STATEMENT LINES

In Applesoft many instructions may follow the THEN as long as they are separated by colons (:).

Example   Single statement lines

```
10 IF B - C<0 THEN PRINT "INSUFFICIENT FUNDS"
20 IF B - C<0 THEN LET B1 = ABS(B - C)
30 IF B - C<0 THEN PRINT "YOU ARE OVERDRAWN BY" ;B1;
      "DOLLARS"
```

Multiple statement lines

```
10 IF B - C<0 THEN PRINT "INSUFFICIENT FUNDS" : LET
      B1 = ABS(B - C) : PRINT "YOU ARE OVERDRAWN BY" ;B1;
      "DOLLARS"
```

Example   100 LET X = 2 : IF X>1 THEN PRINT "IT" : PRINT " WORKS!"

Since X is 2, it is certainly greater than 1. So the output is

IT WORKS!

Example

	X	Y	Z
100 LET X = 1 : IF X>1 THEN LET Y = 5: LET Z = 4	1	0	0
110 LET Y = 44	1	44	0

In this case the X is not greater than 1. So NONE of the statements following THEN are executed on line 100. Execution passes on to line 110.

Example

10 LET L\$ = "2" : IF 2 = VAL(L\$) THEN LET X = 1 :
    LET Z = 4 : LET Y = 9

X	Y	L\$	Z
1	9	2	4

20 LET L\$ = "THREE"

X	Y	L\$	Z
1	9	THREE	4

In this case VAL(L\$) is equal to 2. So the statements following THEN on line 10 are executed.

Colons may be used to join as many statements as will fit on one program line. A program line may be up to 239 characters long, which is nearly six lines on the Apple's forty character screen.

Caution

Given the statement

100 REM ADD TWO NUMBERS : LET X = Y + Z

The computer will not execute the LET statement to the right of the colon because it is considered part of the REMark.

**EXERCISES
6.1, contd.**

5. This program finds the larger of two numbers.

```
 5 REM FINDS THE LARGER OF TWO NUMBERS
10 INPUT X,Y
20 LET L = X
30 IF Y>L THEN LET L = Y
40 PRINT "THE LARGER ONE IS ";L
50 END
```

(a) Complete a Box Diagram when 35 and 72 are entered for X and Y.

(b) Modify the program so that the smaller of the two numbers is printed instead.

(c) Modify the program so that it prints a message if the two numbers are equal, or prints the larger one if they are not.

6. The following BASIC program finds the largest of three numbers.

```
100 REM FINDS THE LARGEST OF THREE NUMBERS
120 INPUT X,Y,Z
130 LET L = X
140 IF L<Y THEN LET L = Y
150 IF L<Z THEN LET L = Z
160 PRINT "THE LARGEST IS ";L
170 END
```

```
]RUN
?5,23,17
THE LARGEST IS 23
```

(a) Complete a Box Diagram when 5, 23, and 17 are entered.

(b) Explain the purpose of the variable L.

(c) Modify the program to find the smallest of four numbers.

7. The Nutty Nut Shop sells a variety of nuts: peanuts, walnuts and cashews. The prices for the three kinds of nuts are $1.85/lb for peanuts, $2.34/lb for walnuts, and $4.85/lb for cashews. The following BASIC program will compute the total retail cost to a customer who buys one kind of nut.

```
100 REM PROGRAM TO COMPUTE TOTAL RETAIL PRICE FOR
       NUTS.
110 INPUT "WHAT KIND OF NUTS DO YOU WANT? ";N$
120 IF N$ = "PEANUTS" OR N$ = "WALNUTS" OR N$ = "CASHEWS"
       THEN LET X = 1
130 IF X = 0 THEN PRINT "SORRY, WE DON'T HAVE ANY ";N$:
       GOTO 200
140 PRINT "HOW MANY POUNDS DO YOU WANT OF ";N$;
150 INPUT P
160 IF N$ = "PEANUTS" THEN LET Q = P*1.85
170 IF N$ = "WALNUTS" THEN LET Q = P*2.34
180 IF N$ = "CASHEWS" THEN LET Q = P*4.85
190 PRINT "THE PRICE YOU MUST PAY IS $";Q
200 END
```

```
]RUN

WHAT KIND OF NUTS DO YOU WANT? PEANUTS
HOW MANY POUNDS DO YOU WANT OF PEANUTS?3
THE PRICE YOU MUST PAY IS $5.55
```

(a) In line 120, X is called a "flag." Explain its function in this program.

(b) Modify the program so that if a customer wishes to purchase several kinds of nuts offered, the program will print the total cost.

(c) Rewrite the program to utilize the DATA statement:
DATA 1.85, 2.34, 4.85

(d) What is the purpose of the semicolon at the end of line 140?

(e) How can this program be rewritten to avoid the logical connectives in line 120?

6.2 The GOTO statement

In Chapter 3 you learned that the instructions in a BASIC program are normally carried out in increasing line order. It is possible, however, to change this normal sequence. Altering the normal flow of a program is called *branching.* Known as an *unconditional branch*, the GOTO statement causes an abrupt no-matter-what change in the flow of a program.

Example   10 REM THIS PROGRAM PRINTS SQUARE ROOTS
20 INPUT "ENTER ANY POSITIVE NUMBER ";X

```
30 PRINT SQR(X)
40 GOTO 20
50 END
```

```
]RUN
ENTER ANY POSITIVE NUMBER 2
1.41421356
ENTER ANY POSITIVE NUMBER 53
7.28010989
ENTER ANY POSITIVE NUMBER (press CTRL-C and RETURN)
]BREAK IN 20
```

Line 40 sends control back to line 20, so that lines 20, 30, and 40 are executed over and over again. Pressing CTRL-C and then RETURN breaks this endless loop. A message appears which tells us the line number of the statement being processed at the time of the interruption. (Pressing RESET would also break the endless loop, but no message would appear.)

The GOTO statement becomes very powerful when used as the action in an IF-THEN statement. The IF-THEN GOTO statement is known as a *conditional branch* instruction. It causes a branch only when the IF condition is true.

Example   Let's rewrite the program in the example above:

```
10 REM THIS PROGRAM PRINTS SQUARE ROOTS
20 INPUT "ENTER ANY POSITIVE NUMBER ";X
30 PRINT SQR(X)
40 INPUT "ARE YOU DONE? ";D$
50 IF D$<>"YES" THEN GOTO 20
55 PRINT "BYE!"
60 END
```

```
]RUN
ENTER ANY POSITIVE NUMBER 2
1.41421356
ARE YOU DONE? NO
ENTER ANY POSITIVE NUMBER 53
7.28010989
ARE YOU DONE? YES
BYE!
```

EXERCISES 6.2

1. If we replace line 50 above with

   50 IF D$ = "NO" THEN GOTO 20

   what difference would it make?

2. Why do you think it might be preferable to compare D$ to YES, as we did in the example, than to compare it to NO as in problem 1? (Think of it from a user's point of view.)

The following examples demonstrate a few of the many uses of the IF-THEN GOTO statement.

Example   The following program will sum the list of numbers 34, 66, 89, 53, −23, 134, 45:

```
100 REM SUMMING A LIST OF NUMBERS
110 DATA 34,66,89,53,-23,134,45,0
120 LET S=0
130 READ X
150 LET S=S+X: REM ITERATIVE ADDITION
160 IF X<>0 THEN GOTO 130
180 PRINT "THE SUM IS ";S
190 END
```

```
]RUN
THE SUM IS 398
```

Notice that the last value, 0, is used as a flag to denote the end of the data list. Line 160 checks for the flag.

Example   The following BASIC program will sum all the even numbers from 2 to 100:

```
100 REM ADD UP ALL OF THE EVEN NUMBERS FROM 2 TO 100
112 REM
113 REM      ASSIGNMENT MODULE
115 LET S=0
120 LET D=2
125 REM
128 REM      COMPUTE MODULE
130 LET S=S+D
140 IF D=100 THEN GOTO 160
145 LET D=D+2
150 GOTO 130
155 REM
158 REM      OUTPUT MODULE
160 PRINT "THE SUM IS ";S
170 END
```

```
]RUN
THE SUM IS 2550
```

Example   The following three line program also computes and prints the sum of the even numbers from 2 to 100.

```
10 LET I=0 : LET S=0
20 LET I=I+2 : IF I<=100 THEN LET S=S+I : GOTO 20
30 PRINT "THE SUM IS ";S :END
```

We prefer the structured and documented program of the previous example. Don't sacrifice clarity for brevity in your programs.

EXERCISES   3. Write a BASIC program to sum all of the odd numbers from 3 to 1001.
6.2, contd.
4. Find the sum of the first 50 terms of the series:

$$1 + (1/2)^2 + (1/3)^2 + (1/4)^2 + \ldots$$

Example   Mr. Smith uses his personal computer to keep track of important telephone numbers. Assume his list of telephone numbers is:

JOE'S BUTCHER SHOP	234-5678
BILLY SMITH	435-6789
MARY LU SANDERS	234-8888
MARSHA RYLE	345-5567
CALIFORNIA BANK	445-5678

The following program will permit Mr. Smith to retrieve a telephone number by entering only the name:

```
10 REM TELEPHONE DIRECTORY
20 DATA "JOE'S BUTCHER SHOP","234-5678"
25 DATA "BILLY SMITH", "435-6789"
30 DATA "MARY LU SANDERS","234-8888"
35 DATA "MARSHA RYLE", "345-5567"
40 DATA "CALIFORNIA BANK", "445-5678"
45 DATA "*","*"
50 INPUT "TYPE NAME PLEASE ";N$
60 READ X$,Y$
70 IF X$="*" THEN PRINT "NO SUCH NAME" : GOTO 110
90 IF X$<>N$ THEN GOTO 60
100 PRINT N$;"'S NUMBER IS ";Y$
110 END
```

```
]RUN

TYPE NAME PLEASE MARSHA RYLE
MARSHA RYLE'S NUMBER IS 345-5567
```

**EXERCISES
6.2, contd.**

5. The asterisk (*) is used as a flag to signal the end of the data list. Why are there two of them?

6. Write a BASIC program that is a reverse directory. The user may type in a telephone number, and the name will be printed. Use the same DATA statement.

7. Modify the program so that the list can also contain addresses.

Example   The following is a modification of the BALANCING THE CHECKBOOK program from Chapter 3. This version permits multiple entries of deposits and checks.

```
100 REM BALANCING THE CHECKBOOK
105 REM ASSIGNMENT MODULE
110 INPUT "ENTER THE CURRENT BALANCE: ";B
120 INPUT "DO YOU WISH TO MAKE A DEPOSIT? ";A$
125 LET D=0
130 IF A$="YES" THEN INPUT "TYPE DEPOSIT: ";D
140 INPUT "ENTER CHECK'S VALUE: ";C
145 REM COMPUTE MODULE
150 LET B=B+D-C
170 INPUT "DO YOU WISH TO MAKE ANOTHER ENTRY? ";A$
```

```
190 IF A$ = "YES" THEN GOTO 120
195 REM OUTPUT MODULE
200 PRINT "YOUR NEW BALANCE IS $";B
210 END
```

```
]RUN

ENTER THE CURRENT BALANCE: 59
DO YOU WISH TO MAKE A DEPOSIT? YES
TYPE DEPOSIT: 200
ENTER CHECK'S VALUE: 25.25
DO YOU WISH TO MAKE ANOTHER ENTRY? NO
YOUR NEW BALANCE IS $233.75
```

EXERCISES 6.2, contd.

8. Explain the need for line 125.

9. Modify the program so that all the checks can be entered at the same time. Use iterative addition.

6.3 Projects

1. Write a BASIC program that will find the largest number in an arbitrary list of numbers. Allow the numbers to be typed in by the user.

2. Write a BASIC program that will

   (1) Allow the user to enter three arbitrary words
   (2) Alphabetize the words in ascending order
   (3) Print the alphabetized list.

3. APPLICATION: CALCULATING INCOME TAX

   In the country of Appleland, the income tax tables are as follows:

   TABLE A
   MARITAL STATUS: SINGLE

ADJUSTED INCOME	TAX TO BE PAID
$0 − $5,000	5% of adjusted income
$5,001 − $10,000	$250 + 10% of amount over $5,000
$10,001 − $20,000	$1,250 + 20% of amount over $10,000
$20,001 − and over	$5,250 + 40% of amount over $20,000

   TABLE B
   MARITAL STATUS: MARRIED

ADJUSTED INCOME	TAX TO BE PAID
$0 − $5,000	2% of adjusted income
$5,001 − $10,000	$100 + 7% of amount over $5,000
$10,001 − $20,000	$800 + 15% of amount over $10,000
$20,001 − and over	$3,800 + 32% of amount over $20,000

   The Government allows $800 for each dependent.

   Write a BASIC program that will compute an individual's income tax under the following conditions:

I. ASSIGNMENT MODULE
   Use only INPUT statements to assign the following:
   (1) Marital status
   (2) Number of dependents
   (3) Income

II. COMPUTE MODULE
    Compute the adjusted income and the income tax.

III. OUTPUT MODULE
     Print the income tax.

Here is an explanation and example:

The formula for ADJUSTED INCOME is

ADJUSTED INCOME = INCOME − (# of dependents) ∗ $800.

Suppose Mrs. Carter had a total income for the year of $28,500 and claims three dependents. Her ADJUSTED INCOME will be

$28,500 − 3 ∗ 800 = $26,100.

She is married, so checking TABLE B, we find that her ADJUSTED INCOME falls in the "$20,001 − and over" category. Her tax will be $3800 + 32% of 6100, which is $5752.

4. APPLICATION: REAL ESTATE LISTINGS

The OK REALTY CO. has five new listings of homes:

ADDRESS	#BEDROOMS	#BATHS	PRICE
22 ELM ST.	5	3	$99,995
567 JOY ST.	3	2	$125,900
23 HART AVE.	6	2	$235,400
111 TERRY PL.	5	4	$125,000
5 MAY ST.	3	1	$67,500

Write the following programs:

(1) A price range can be entered and the program will find the houses falling in that range.

(2) A price range and number of bedrooms range can be entered and the program will find the houses satisfying both conditions.

Use DATA statements to store the information in the table, and use INPUT statements to enter the price and bedroom ranges.

LAB 6-1 The IF-THEN statement

Type in the command: NEW

The IF (comparison) THEN (instruction) is called the conditional or decision statement.

The instruction that follows THEN is only executed when the comparison that follows IF is true.

Type in the program: 10 LET X=5
20 IF X=5 THEN PRINT "X IS FIVE"
30 END

Type in the command: RUN

What is the output of the computer? _____

> When the computer executes line number 20, it first determines whether the comparison (X = 5) is true or false. Since the comparison is true, the computer executes the instruction (PRINT "X IS FIVE") following the THEN.

Type in the statements: 30 PRINT "NOT EQUAL TO FIVE"
                             40 END

Type in the command: LIST

Will the comparison be true in line number 20? _____

Type in the command: RUN

What is the output of the computer? _____

_____

> Since the comparison X = 5 is true in line number 20, the instruction PRINT "X IS FIVE" is executed. After executing this instruction the computer executes the next line number, line number 30.

Type in the statement: 20 IF X<>5 THEN PRINT X

Type in the command: LIST

Will the comparison be true in line number 20? _____

Type in the command: RUN

What is the output of the computer? _____

> When the computer executes line number 20, it determines whether the comparison (X<>5) is true or false. Since the comparison is false, the computer ignores the instruction following the THEN and executes the next line number.

> The logical connectives (AND, OR) can be used in the comparison.

Type in the statements: 20 IF X = 5 OR X = 7 THEN PRINT 20
                             30 IF X = 5 AND X = 7 THEN PRINT 30

Type in the command: LIST

> Line number 20 uses the connective OR in its comparison, and line number 30 uses the connective AND in its comparison.

Type in the command: RUN

What is the output of the computer? _____

> Whenever the comparison uses the connective OR only one of the sub-comparisons needs to be true for the whole comparison to be true. However, when the connective AND is used, both subcomparisons need to be true for the whole comparison to be true.

LAB 6-2 Branching

Type in the command: NEW

There are two types of branching: conditional and unconditional.

The GOTO statement is called the unconditional branch. When the computer executes this instruction, the program branches to the line number in the GOTO instruction.

Type in the program: 10 GOTO 30
20 PRINT "LINE NUMBER 20"
30 PRINT "LINE NUMBER 30"
40 END

Type in the command: RUN

What is the output of the computer? _____

Note that line number 20 was not executed. When the computer executed line number 10, the program transferred to line number 30.

The program below is an example of an infinite loop.

Type in the program: 10 LET X = 0
20 LET X = X + 1
30 PRINT X
40 GOTO 20
50 END

Type in the command: RUN

When you have seen enough numbers on the CRT, press the RESET key.

The conditional branch uses the IF-THEN statement with the GOTO instruction.

Type in the statement: 40 IF X< = 10 THEN GOTO 20

Type in the command: LIST

Line number 40 is a conditional branch. The branch will occur only when the condition, X< = 10 is true.

Type in the command: RUN

This time the program comes to an end. Explain why. _____

_____

_____

_____

Type in the command: PRINT X

What is the output of the computer? _____

The value of X is 11. When X was finally incremented to 11, the condition in line number 40 was false. Control therefore, is passed to line number 50 which ended the program.

Courtesy of Knotts Berry Farm Buena Park, CA

7

The FOR-NEXT Statement

7.0 Introduction

In Chapter 6 we saw how the IF-THEN and GOTO statements can be used to repeat a section of a program over and over. Branching for the purpose of repetition is called *looping*. The following BASIC program uses a loop to add the even numbers from 2 to 100:

```
100 REM ADD ALL EVEN NUMBERS FROM 2 TO 100
115 LET S = 0
120 LET K = 2
130 LET S = S + K
140 IF K = 100 THEN GOTO 160
150 LET K = K + 2
155 GOTO 130
160 PRINT S
170 END
```

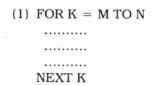

```
]RUN
2550
```

Looping has so many important applications in programming that a set of statements dedicated to looping have been included in the BASIC language. They are the FOR and the NEXT statements, and they greatly simplify the task of looping. Because the two statements must function together, we will refer to them as the FOR-NEXT statement.

7.1 Understanding the FOR-NEXT statement

There are two forms of the FOR-NEXT statement. They are

(1) FOR K = M TO N

....

....

....

NEXT K

113

(2) FOR K = M TO N STEP Q

     ....

     ....

     ....

     NEXT K

where .... are any BASIC statements, and M, N, and Q stand for numbers, numeric variables, or arithmetic expressions. K is called the index. Any numeric variable can be used as the index.

FORM 1

Form (1) of the FOR-NEXT statement operates under the following rules:

1. The FOR K = M TO N instruction sets K initially to the value M, and the BASIC instructions are carried out downward until the NEXT K statement is reached.
2. The NEXT K instruction increases the value of K by one, checks to see if K is LARGER than N, and if not, returns control to the instruction immediately following the FOR statement.
3. When the NEXT K statement increases K to a value larger than N, the program will go to the first instruction after the NEXT K statement.

Example   This program does an iterative addition three times on the variable S.

```
 5 LET S = 0
10 FOR K = 2 TO 4
20 LET S = S + K
30 NEXT K
40 PRINT S
50 END
```

```
]RUN
9
```

The FOR-NEXT statement repeats the loop three times. Below we show the program side by side with its Box Diagram.

	K	S	CRT
5 LET S = 0	0	0	
10 FOR K = 2 TO 4	2	0	
FIRST LOOP			
20 LET S = S + K	2	2	
30 NEXT K	3	2	
SECOND LOOP			
20 LET S = S + K	3	5	
30 NEXT K	4	5	
THIRD LOOP			
20 LET S = S + K	4	9	

		K	S	CRT
30 NEXT K		5	9	
40 PRINT S		5	9	⑨
50 END		5	9	

Example   100 FOR I = -1 TO 2
110 PRINT I + 2
120 NEXT I
130 IF I = 3 THEN PRINT "UNDERSTAND?"
140 END

```
]RUN

1
2
3
4
UNDERSTAND?
```

	I	CRT
100 FOR I = -1 TO 2	-1	
FIRST LOOP		
110 PRINT I + 2	-1	①
120 NEXT I	0	
SECOND LOOP		
110 PRINT I + 2	0	②
120 NEXT I	1	
THIRD LOOP		
110 PRINT I + 2	1	③
120 NEXT I	2	
FOURTH LOOP		
110 PRINT I + 2	2	④
120 NEXT I	3	
130 IF I = 3 THEN PRINT "UNDERSTAND?"	3	(UNDERSTAND?)
140 END	3	

EXERCISES 7.1

1. Complete a Box Diagram for the following program:

   100 DATA "CHINA","2", "EUROPE"
   110 FOR Q = 1 TO 3
   120 READ R$
   130 PRINT R$
   140 NEXT Q
   150 END

2. Complete a Box Diagram for the following:

   20 FOR I = 1 TO 10
   30 LET K = 2*I

```
40 IF K>4 THEN GOTO 60
50 NEXT I
60 PRINT "THAT'S ALL FOLKS"
70 END
```

3. Write a complete BASIC Program with a FOR-NEXT statement that goes with the following Box Diagram.

I	P	CRT
3	0	
3	1	
3	1	①
4	1	
4	3	
4	3	③
5	3	
5	5	
5	5	⑤
6	5	
6	7	
6	7	⑦
7	7	

FORM 2

Form (2) is known as the FOR-NEXT-STEP statement. It works in a similar manner, but has the ability to step the index by values other than one.

Form (2) of the FOR-NEXT-STEP operates under the following rules:

a) WHEN THE STEP Q IS A POSITIVE NUMBER

1. The FOR K=M TO N STEP Q instruction sets the index K initially to the value M, and the BASIC instructions are carried out downward until the NEXT K statement is reached.
2. The NEXT K instruction adds the value Q to K, checks to see if K is LARGER than N, and if not returns to the instruction immediately following the FOR statement.
3. Once the NEXT K statement increases K to a value LARGER than N, the program will go to the first instruction after the NEXT K statement.

b) WHEN THE STEP Q IS A NEGATIVE NUMBER

1. The FOR K=M TO N STEP Q instruction sets K initially to the value M, and the BASIC instructions are carried out downward until the NEXT K statement is reached.
2. The NEXT K instruction adds the value Q to K, checks to see if K is

SMALLER than N and if not returns control to the instruction immediately following the FOR statement.
3. Once the NEXT K statement decreases K to a value smaller than N,
the program will go to the first instruction after the NEXT K statement.

The following examples should help clarify the FOR-NEXT-STEP statement.

Example   This example demonstrates a step larger than one.

```
100 REM PRINTS THE ODD NUMBERS FROM 1 TO 9
105 REM Q IS POSITIVE 2
110 FOR I = 1 TO 10 STEP 2
120 PRINT I
130 NEXT I
140 END
```

```
JRUN
1
3
5
7
9
```

Here is the Box Diagram:

		I	CRT
	110 FOR I = 1 TO 10 STEP 2	1	
LOOP 1	120 PRINT I	1	(1)
	130 NEXT I	3	
LOOP 2	120 PRINT I	3	(3)
	130 NEXT I	5	
LOOP 3	120 PRINT I	5	(5)
	130 NEXT I	7	
LOOP 4	120 PRINT I	7	(7)
	130 NEXT I	9	
LOOP 5	120 PRINT I	9	(9)
	130 NEXT I	11	
	140 END	11	

Example   The following program demonstrates a negative step.

```
10 REM PRINTS THE NUMBERS 10,8,6
15 REM Q IS NEGATIVE 2
20 FOR J = 10 TO 5 STEP −2
```

```
30 PRINT J
40 NEXT J
50 END
```

```
]RUN
10
8
6
```

Here is the Box Diagram:

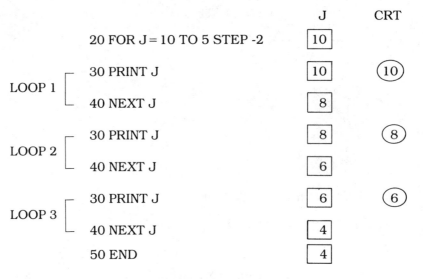

	J	CRT
20 FOR J = 10 TO 5 STEP -2	10	
LOOP 1 ⌐ 30 PRINT J	10	(10)
⌐ 40 NEXT J	8	
LOOP 2 ⌐ 30 PRINT J	8	(8)
⌐ 40 NEXT J	6	
LOOP 3 ⌐ 30 PRINT J	6	(6)
⌐ 40 NEXT J	4	
50 END	4	

Example   This program demonstrates a step that is a decimal fraction.

```
200 REM PRINTS THE NUMBERS .2, .3, .4, .5
210 FOR P = .2 TO .5 STEP .1
220 PRINT P
230 NEXT P
240 END
```

```
]RUN
.2
.3
.4
.5
```

	P	CRT
210 FOR P = .2 TO .5 STEP .1	.2	
LOOP 1 ⌐ 220 PRINT P	.2	(.2)
⌐ 230 NEXT P	.3	
LOOP 2 ⌐ 220 PRINT P	.3	(.3)
⌐ 230 NEXT P	.4	
LOOP 3 ⌐ 220 PRINT P	.4	(.4)
⌐ 230 NEXT P	.5	

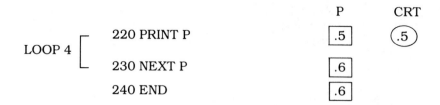

P   CRT

LOOP 4 ⌈ 220 PRINT P | .5 | (.5)

       ⌊ 230 NEXT P | .6 |

          240 END | .6 |

EXERCISES 7.1, contd.

4. What is the output for each of these programs?

(a) 10 FOR K = 1 TO 8
     20 LET T = .2*K + 1
     30 PRINT T
     35 NEXT K
     40 END

(b) 40 LET R = 3.5
     50 FOR U = R TO 0 STEP − .5
     60 PRINT U,U*U
     65 NEXT U
     70 END

(c) 100 LET E = 3
     110 FOR Q = E TO E + 5 STEP E
     120 PRINT Q
     130 NEXT Q
     140 END

(d) 100 FOR J = 8 TO 2
     110 PRINT J
     120 NEXT J
     130 END

     (careful on this one!)

The following programs demonstrate how easy iterative addition can be using a FOR-NEXT loop.

Example
```
100 REM ADDS ALL EVEN NUMBERS FROM 2 TO 100
110 LET S = 0
120 FOR K = 2 TO 100 STEP 2
130 LET S = S + K
140 NEXT K
150 PRINT "THE SUM IS ";S
160 END
```

```
]RUN
THE SUM IS 2550
```

Example
```
30 REM ADDS ALL NUMBERS IN THE DATA STATEMENT
40 DATA 34,56,35,45, − 8
50 DATA 2,34,445,67
60 LET S = 0
70 FOR I = 1 TO 9
80 READ X
90 LET S = S + X
100 NEXT I
110 PRINT "THE SUM IS ";S
120 END
```

```
]RUN
THE SUM IS 710
```

Example
```
100 REM ADD AN ARBITRARY NUMBER OF NUMBERS
110 INPUT "HOW MANY NUMBERS? ";Q
120 LET S = 0
130 FOR I = 1 TO Q
140 INPUT "TYPE A NUMBER: ";N
150 LET S = S + N
```

```
160 NEXT I
170 PRINT S
180 END
```

```
]RUN

HOW MANY NUMBERS? 5
TYPE A NUMBER: 10
TYPE A NUMBER: 2
TYPE A NUMBER: 1
TYPE A NUMBER: 66
TYPE A NUMBER: 4
83
```

7.2 Applications

The following programs are instructive applications of the FOR-NEXT statement.

APPLICATION

This program will print the name of the month if the number of the month is entered:

```
100 REM FINDS THE MONTH
110 INPUT "TYPE THE NUMBER OF THE MONTH DESIRED: ";N
120 IF N>12 OR N<1 THEN PRINT "SORRY, INVALID CHOICE.":
        GOTO 110
130 FOR I = 1 TO N
140 READ M$
150 NEXT I
160 PRINT "THAT MONTH IS ";M$
170 DATA "JANUARY","FEBRUARY","MARCH","APRIL"
180 DATA "MAY","JUNE","JULY","AUGUST","SEPTEMBER"
190 DATA "OCTOBER","NOVEMBER","DECEMBER"
200 END
```

```
]RUN

TYPE THE NUMBER OF THE MONTH DESIRED: 12
THAT MONTH IS DECEMBER
```

APPLICATION

Assume Mr. Smith invests $12,000 in a savings account for a period of ten years. Further assume that the interest is 9% compounded annually. The following program computes and prints the amount in his account at the end of each year.

```
10 REM COMPOUND INTEREST
20 LET P = 12000
30 FOR I = 1 TO 10
40 LET P = P + .09*P
45 PRINT "AMOUNT AFTER ";I;" YEARS IS ";P
50 NEXT I
60 END
```

```
]RUN

AMOUNT AFTER 1 YEARS IS 13080
AMOUNT AFTER 2 YEARS IS 14257.2
AMOUNT AFTER 3 YEARS IS 15540.348
AMOUNT AFTER 4 YEARS IS 16938.9793
AMOUNT AFTER 5 YEARS IS 18463.4875
AMOUNT AFTER 6 YEARS IS 20125.2013
AMOUNT AFTER 7 YEARS IS 21936.4695
AMOUNT AFTER 8 YEARS IS 23910.7517
AMOUNT AFTER 9 YEARS IS 26062.7194
AMOUNT AFTER 10 YEARS IS 28408.3641
```

EXERCISES 7.2

1. Write a BASIC program that will compute the total amount in a savings account after a period of N years paying an annual interest rate of R% assuming an initial investment of P dollars.

2. Modify the program in problem 1 to also compute and print the total amount of interest earned.

APPLICATION

It is known that the infinite sum

$$\frac{1}{2} + \frac{1}{6} + \frac{1}{12} + \dots + \frac{1}{K(K+1)} + \dots$$

is equal to 1. Although infinite summing is not possible on the computer, we can add as many terms as we desire, which we do in the following program:

```
25 REM SUMMING MANY TERMS
30 INPUT "HOW MANY TERMS DO YOU WANT? ";N
35 LET S=0
40 FOR K=1 TO N
50 LET S=S+1/(K*(K+1))
60 NEXT K
70 PRINT S
80 END
```

```
]RUN

HOW MANY TERMS DO YOU WANT? 500
.998003991
```

EXERCISES 7.2, contd.

3. Write a BASIC program to evaluate the infinite sum:

$$\frac{1}{6} + \frac{1}{24} + \dots + \frac{1}{K(K+1)(K+2)} + \dots$$

What is the sum of (a) 10 terms, (b) 100 terms, (c) 1000 terms? What value do you think the sum is approaching?

APPLICATION

In Chapter 1 we introduced factorial numbers. They are defined as follows:

$$1! = 1$$
$$2! = 2$$

3! = 3*2 = 6
4! = 4*3*2 = 24
5! = 5*4*3*2 = 120
6! = 6*5*4*3*2 = 720
and so on....

The following program computes factorials.

100 REM THIS PROGRAM COMPUTES N!
110 INPUT "ENTER N: ";N
120 LET S = 1
130 FOR I = N TO 2 STEP -1
140 LET S = S*I
150 NEXT I
160 PRINT S
170 END

```
]RUN
ENTER N: 10
3628800
```

APPLICATION

The following program computes the average of the numbers 45, 33, 67, 88, 22, 45 and prints those numbers that are greater than or equal to the average.

100 DATA 45,33,67,88,22,45
105 LET S = 0
110 FOR I = 1 TO 6
120 READ X
130 LET S = S + X
140 NEXT I
150 LET A = S/6
160 RESTORE
170 FOR I = 1 TO 6
180 READ X
190 IF (X> = A) THEN PRINT X
200 NEXT I
210 END

```
]RUN
67
88
```

EXERCISES 7.2, contd.

4. Write a BASIC program that computes the average of the numbers 567, 45, 668, 3322, −234, 44, 6789, −34, 67, 77 and prints the numbers that are smaller than or equal to the average.

5. Write a program that will generate and print 50 random whole numbers between 1 and 100 and their average.

APPLICATION

Mrs. Yankellow keeps a telephone directory on her personal computer. The directory list is:

MARY JONES	235-6666
LOUIS SMITH	245-4545
ACE HARDWARD	567-8989
MARY HART	234-5678
PHIL DOOR	556-6767

The following program will permit her to reference the list by name.

```
100 REM TELEPHONE LIST
110 DATA "MARY JONES", "235-6666"
120 DATA "LOUIS SMITH", "245-4545"
125 DATA "ACE HARDWARE", "567-8989"
130 DATA "MARY HART", "234-5678"
140 DATA "PHIL DOOR", "556-6767"
150 INPUT "WHAT IS THE NAME? ";N$
160 FOR I = 1 TO 5
170 READ X$,Y$
180 IF X$<>N$ THEN GOTO 200
190 PRINT "THE TELEPHONE NUMBER IS ";Y$ : GOTO 220
200 NEXT I
210 PRINT "SORRY, NAME UNAVAILABLE"
220 END
```

```
]RUN

WHAT IS THE NAME? MARY HART
THE TELEPHONE NUMBER IS 234-5678
```

EXERCISES 7.2, contd.

6. Modify the DIRECTORY program so it can produce a name given a telephone number.

7. The program is too specific. If more names and phone numbers are added to the DATA statements, it won't find them. Rewrite the program so that if the program is updated in the DATA statements only, it will work.

7.3 Nested FOR-NEXT statements

Since any set of BASIC statements can be included inside of a FOR-NEXT loop, one FOR-NEXT statement can be "nested" inside of another.

Example
```
100 FOR I = 1 TO 6
110 FOR J = 1 TO 5
115 PRINT I*J;" ";
120 NEXT J
130 PRINT
140 NEXT I
150 END
```

The printout on the CRT will appear as follows:

```
1  2  3  4  5
2  4  6  8  10
3  6  9  12  15
4  8  12  16  20
5  10  15  20  25
6  12  18  24  30
```

EXERCISES
7.3

1. What does line 130 do?

2. Write a program that will print the following table. Use nested FOR-NEXT statements.

$1+1=2$	$1+2=3$	$1+3=4$	$1+4=5$	$1+5=6$
$2+1=3$	$2+2=4$	$2+3=5$	$2+4=6$	$2+5=7$
$3+1=4$	$3+2=5$	$3+3=6$	$3+4=7$	$3+5=8$
$4+1=5$	$4+2=6$	$4+3=7$	$4+4=8$	$4+5=9$

7.4 Projects

1. THE FIBONACCI NUMBER SEQUENCE.

The Fibonacci numbers are the following:

1, 1, 2, 3, 5, 8, 13,...

To generate this list of numbers, follow these steps:

    a. Start with the numbers 1 and 1
    b. Add 1 + 1 to get 2
    c. Add 1 + 2 to get 3
    d. Add 2 + 3 to get 5
    e. The general rule is to add the last two numbers in the sequence to get the next number. Thus, in the above sequence, the next number after 13 is 21.

Write a BASIC program that will generate and print the first N numbers of the Fibonacci sequence, where N is chosen by the user.

2. APPROXIMATING π.

From Chapter 1 you may recall that π, the irrational number 3.1415926..., can be approximated by the infinite sum:

$$\pi = 4 - \tfrac{4}{3} + \tfrac{4}{5} - \tfrac{4}{7} + \tfrac{4}{9} - \ldots$$

Write a BASIC program to approximate π by adding as many terms as desired.

3. AUTOMOBILE FINANCING.

An automobile is financed for N dollars at a monthly interest charge of R% per month. Assume the monthly payment is P dollars. Write a BASIC program that will:

    a. Compute and print the total interest paid for K months, and
    b. Compute and print the balance owed after K months.

4. NUMERICAL CENTER PROBLEM.

A numerical center is a number which partitions a list of consecutive whole numbers (starting at 1) into two groups of numbers whose sums are equal. The first numerical center is 6. It separates the list

1, 2, 3, 4, 5, 6, 7, 8

into the two groups (1,2,3,4,5) and (7,8) whose sums are both equal to 15.

    The second numerical center is 35. It divides up the list from 1 to 49 into (1 to 34) and (36 to 49). The sum of the numbers in each group is 595.

Write a program to find all numerical centers between 1 and N, where N is chosen by the user.

5. THE GOLDEN RATIO

The Golden Ratio, a number that has fascinated many mathematicians since the ancient Greeks has as its value:

$$(1 + \sqrt{5})/2 = 1.618033989...$$

The Golden Ratio is a close relative of the Fibonacci Numbers (see above). The ratio of any two consecutive Fibonacci numbers is very nearly equal to the Golden Ratio. The approximation gets better and better as larger Fibonacci numbers are used. Write a BASIC program that tests this property.

6. PROBABILITY THEORY

The origins of Probability Theory comes from this true event:

> Chevalier de Méré wrote a letter to Pascal (1623–1662) where he sought an explanation to a gambling problem. Méré played a dice game with a single die where he would bet that in four throws of a die, a 6 would appear at least once. He won this game more often than he lost. He later changed the rules of the game and threw two dice instead, betting that at least one double-6 would occur in 24 throws of the two dice. To his surprise he lost more often than he won. (He felt the odds should be the same).

Write a BASIC program to simulate both dice games. You should get similar results.

LAB 7-1 The FOR-NEXT Statement

Type in the command: NEW

The FOR and NEXT statements are used to execute a sequence of statements a finite number of times. Suppose you wish to write a program that will display the string BASIC IS FUN twelve times. To accomplish this the statement PRINT "BASIC IS FUN" needs to be executed twelve different times.

Type in the program:
```
10 FOR K = 1 TO 12 STEP 1
20 PRINT "BASIC IS FUN"
30 NEXT K
40 END
```

Type in the command: RUN

How many times is the string BASIC IS FUN printed? _____

The statement 10 FOR K = 1 TO 12 STEP 1 does three things. First it initializes the index, K, to 1 (FOR K = 1). Second, it sets the limit value of 12 for the index K. And third, it defines an increment 1 which will be used later by the NEXT K statement.

The statement 30 NEXT K does several things. First, it increments the index by the step value. Second, it checks to see if the value of K is larger than 12. If not, the NEXT K instruction transfers control back to line number 20. Finally, when K exceeds 12, control is passed to the line number following the NEXT K statement.

The statements FOR and NEXT together with the statements between them are commonly called a loop.

Type in the program: 10 LET K = 97
20 FOR K = 2 TO 5 STEP 3
30 PRINT K
40 NEXT K
50 PRINT K
60 END

Type in the command: RUN

What is the output of the program? _____

_____

_____

Note that the first output is 2, not 97. This is because the FOR statement initializes the index K to 2. The second output is 5 because the index K, is incremented by 3. The last output, 8, was printed by line number 50, not line number 30. When the index K was incremented from 5 to 8, it became greater than the limit value of 5. The execution of the program then transferred to line number 50.

Type in the command: NEW

Type in the program: 10 FOR K = 1 TO 5
20 PRINT K
30 NEXT K
40 END

Type in the command: RUN

What is the output of the program? _____

_____

_____

What step value is the computer using? _____

When the STEP instruction is left out of the FOR statement, the increment is set to 1.

Type in the statement: 10 FOR K = 15 TO 7 STEP -2

Type in the command: LIST

Type in the command: RUN

What is the output of the program? _____

_____

_____

What is the increment value for the index? _____

You should have written -2. The index K is first set to 15 and is incremented by -2 until K passes the limiting value of 7.

What is the value of K after the loop is completed? _____

You should have written 5. Remember, the loop is not complete until after the index surpasses the limit value set by the FOR statement.

LAB 7-2 Nested loops

Type in the command: NEW

Whenever one FOR/NEXT statement is totally enclosed within another FOR/NEXT statement, the arrangement is called NESTING of loops. When nested loops are used in programs, two rules should be observed:

1. The inner loop must be totally enclosed within the outer loop.
2. Different index variables must be used for each FOR/NEXT statement.

Type in the program:
```
10 FOR I = 1 TO 3
20 PRINT "I = ";I
30 FOR K = 1 TO 2
40 PRINT " K IS ";K
50 NEXT K
60 PRINT "**********"
70 NEXT I
80 END
```

Type in the command: RUN

Note that the inner loop (line numbers 30, 40, and 50) is executed three different times: when I = 1, I = 2, and I = 3.

What line numbers belong to the outer loop? _____

You should have written line numbers 10, 20, 30, 40, 50, 60, and 70. Nested loops cannot overlap or cross each other.

Type in the statements:
```
50 NEXT I
70 NEXT K
```

Type in the command: LIST

What line numbers belong to the loop using index I? _____

You should have written line numbers 10, 20, 30, 40, and 50.

What line numbers belong to the loop using index K? _____

You should have written line numbers 30, 40, 50, 60, and 70.

Type in the command: RUN

What is the computer's response? _____

Explain why the error occurred. _____

_____

The loop using the index K overlaps the loop using the index I. Remember, the inner loop must be totally enclosed within the outer loop. Thus, the error was caused by the two loops being overlapped.

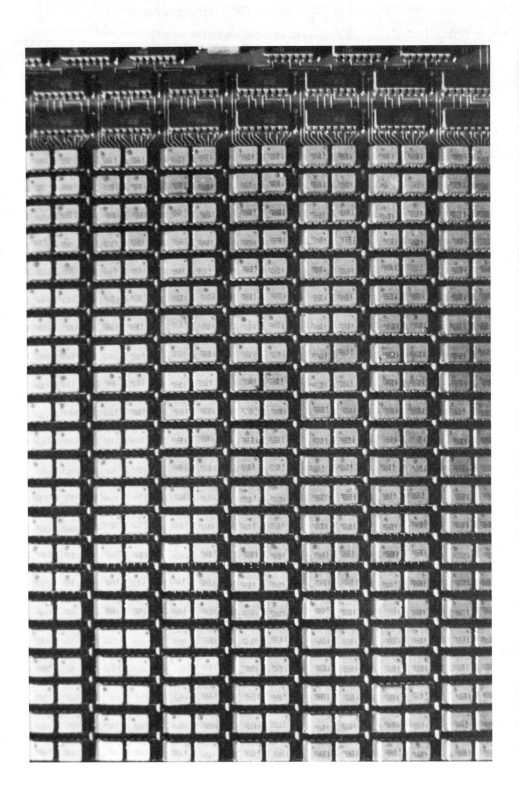

8

Arrays

8.0 Introduction

A moment's reflection may reveal to you what appears to be a large drawback to the way BASIC names numeric and string variables. Since Applesoft only recognizes the first two characters of a variable name, and the first one must be a letter, there are only 962 (= 26 * 37) unique variable names. (In fact, there are less due to reserved words.) This seems to suggest that during the course of running a program, less than 962 different values of numeric data and less than 962 different values of string data can be stored in the computer memory at any one time. This can be a huge handicap when you consider that certain applications may call for large amounts of data handling. Such might be the case for a program that computes the payroll for a large company, or a program that computes and stores the first 1000 prime numbers. So how do we overcome this obstacle? The answer lies in the concept of an array. Arrays come in two flavors, NUMERIC and STRING, and they come in a variety of sizes. First we will take up numeric arrays.

8.1 One-dimensional numeric arrays

A numeric array is a collection of numeric variables all of which have the same FIRST name, but are distinguished from one another by the use of SUBSCRIPTS. A subscript is a number in parentheses which follows the array's name.

Examples   A(0), A(1), A(2), A(3), ... , A(998), A(999), A(1000)
A6(0), A6(1), A6(2), ... , A6(8), A6(9), A6(10)

In this example, the array A can store 1001 different pieces of numeric data. We also say that there are 1001 cells in the array. The array A6, as given, can store eleven different pieces of numeric data.

RULES FOR NUMERIC ARRAYS

1. The array name is any valid numeric variable.
2. Each subscript must be a whole number (i.e., 0, 1, 2, ...) or any numeric variable or numeric expression which evaluates to a whole number. Subscripts which are not integers are truncated to integers.

Numeric values can be assigned to these arrays using the LET, READ and INPUT statements. The following is a simple example using the LET instruction.

Example

	A(3)	B(5)	J
	0	0	0
LET A(3) = 4	4	0	0
LET J = 3	4	0	3
LET A(J) = 5	5	0	3
LET B(J+2) = 6	5	6	3
LET B(A(J)) = 8	5	8	3

Example The following BASIC program will store and add the numbers 4, 9, and 8:

	C(1)	C(2)	C(3)	S	CRT
	0	0	0	0	
100 LET C(1) = 4	4	0	0	0	
110 LET C(2) = 9	4	9	0	0	
120 LET C(3) = 8	4	9	8	0	
130 LET S = C(1) + C(2) + C(3)	4	9	8	21	
140 PRINT S	4	9	8	21	21
150 END					

```
]RUN

21
```

Using READ/DATA the same program could have been written:

```
100 DATA 4,9,8
110 READ C(1),C(2),C(3)
120 LET S = C(1) + C(2) + C(3)
130 PRINT S
140 END
```

The same program can be written using a FOR-NEXT loop this way:

```
 90 REM ASSIGN DATA TO ARRAY
100 DATA 4,9,8
110 FOR I = 1 TO 3
120 READ C(I)
```

```
130 NEXT I
135 REM COMPUTE THE SUM
140 LET S = 0
145 FOR I = 1 TO 3
150 LET S = S + C(I)
160 NEXT I
165 REM PRINT THE SUM
170 PRINT S
180 END
```

```
]RUN

21
```

Example The above program can be generalized by assigning the data with an INPUT instruction.

```
100 REM ASSIGN DATA TO ARRAY
110 FOR I = 1 TO 3
120 INPUT "TYPE A NUMBER: ";C(I)
130 NEXT I
135 REM COMPUTE THE SUM
140 LET S = 0
150 FOR I = 1 TO 3
160 LET S = S + C(I)
170 NEXT I
180 REM PRINT THE SUM
190 PRINT "SUM is ";S
200 END
```

```
]RUN

TYPE A NUMBER: 23
TYPE A NUMBER: 5
TYPE A NUMBER: ¯22
SUM IS 6
```

EXERCISES 8.1

1. Complete a Box Diagram for the program in the last example.

2. Furnish correct LET statements for the following Box Diagram with the restriction that ONLY array variables can be used on the right side of the LET statements, after the first two statements.

	A(1)	A(2)	A(3)	A(4)
	0	0	0	0
LET A(2) = 4	0	4	0	0
LET A(4) = 6	0	4	0	6
	.5	4	0	6
	.5	1	0	6
	.5	1	0	8
	.5	1	9	8
	.5	0	9	8

3. Complete a Box Diagram for the following program.

	K	I	G(1)	G(2)	G(3)
10 DATA 3, 2	☐	☐	☐	☐	☐
15 READ I,K	☐	☐	☐	☐	☐
20 LET G(I) = 10	☐	☐	☐	☐	☐
25 LET G(K) = 4	☐	☐	☐	☐	☐
30 LET G(I-K) = 5*G(I)	☐	☐	☐	☐	☐
35 RESTORE	☐	☐	☐	☐	☐
40 READ G(K),K	☐	☐	☐	☐	☐
45 LET G(K-1) = G(G(K))	☐	☐	☐	☐	☐

4. Write a program which finds the average of ten numbers and prints the numbers in two groups: those less than or equal to the average, and those greater than the average. The ten numbers must be chosen by the user (INPUT) and stored in an array.

8.2 The DIMension statement

In order to store numbers into an array the computer must be told how many cells the array will have. This is done in a DIMension statement. If the array is called X, the form of the dimension statement is

DIM X(N)

where N is a whole number, or a variable or formula which evaluates to a whole number.

If several arrays need to be dimensioned, they may be included in the same DIM statement, such as

DIM G(100), Y(2*N + 1), Z(K)

If no more than the eleven cells numbered 0 through 10 are to be used, then the array does not have to be dimensioned.

Example   Here is a program that will store three exam grades for each of thirty students in a class.

```
100 DIM E1(30), E2(30), E3(30)
110 REM STORE GRADES
120 FOR I = 1 TO 30
130 PRINT "STUDENT NUMBER ";I
140 INPUT "WHAT ARE THE GRADES? ";E1(I),E2(I),E3(I)
145 PRINT
150 NEXT I
160 END
```

```
]RUN

STUDENT NUMBER 1
WHAT ARE THE GRADES? 56,78,49

STUDENT NUMBER 2
WHAT ARE THE GRADES? 78,85,93

STUDENT NUMBER 3
WHAT ARE THE GRADES? 95,98,88

(etc.)
```

EXERCISES 8.2

1. Add to the program so that it

   (a) Computes the average exam grade for each student and stores the averages in A(1), A(2), ..., A(30).

   (b) Prints the student number (i.e. 1, 2,..., 30) of each student whose average is greater than 80.

Example   The following steps will compute the standard deviation for a given set of array values:

   (a) Compute the average of the array values
   (b) Subtract this average from each of the array values
   (c) Square each of the values in (b)
   (d) Compute the average of the values in (c)
   (e) Take the square root of the average in (d).

The following program will find the standard deviation of twenty-five array values:

```
100 DIM A(25),B(25)
110 REM ENTER 25 NUMBERS INTO THE ARRAY A
120 FOR I = 1 TO 25
130 INPUT A(I)
140 NEXT I
150 REM PERFORM STEP (A)
155 LET S = 0
160 FOR I = 1 TO 25
170 LET S = S + A(I)
180 NEXT I
190 REM WE USE A FOR AVERAGE. THE SIMPLE VARIABLE A IS
200 REM DIFFERENT THAN THE ARRAY A.
210 LET A = S/25
220 REM PERFORM STEP (B)
230 FOR J = 1 TO 25
240 LET B(J) = A(J)-A
250 NEXT J
260 REM PERFORM STEP (C)
270 FOR J = 1 TO 25
280 LET B(J) = B(J)^2
290 NEXT J
300 REM PERFORM STEP (D)
```

```
310 LET S = 0
320 FOR I = 1 TO 25
330 LET S = S + B(I)
340 NEXT I
350 LET S = S/25
360 REM COMPLETE STEP (E)
370 LET S = SQR(S)
380 REM OUTPUT THE STANDARD DEVIATION
390 PRINT S
400 END
```

Example   The following BASIC program stores 200 random numbers into the array W, computes their average, prints all of the numbers which are larger than the average, and then tells us how many of them there were.

```
100 REM STORING AND AVERAGING 200 RANDOM NUMBERS
110 DIM W(200)
120 LET S = 0
130 LET C = 0
140 FOR K = 1 TO 200
150 LET W(K) = RND(1)
160 LET S = S + W(K)
170 NEXT K
180 LET A = S/200
190 PRINT "THE AVERAGE IS ";A
200 FOR K = 1 TO200
210 IF (W(K)>A) THEN PRINT W(K) : LET C = C + 1
220 NEXT K
230 PRINT C;" NUMBERS ARE LARGER THAN THE AVERAGE."
240 END
```

EXERCISES 8.2, contd.   2. What is the reason for writing (W(K) > A) instead of W(K) > A in line 210?

If the programmer wants to reserve an arbitrary number of cells in an array, then the DIM statement can be written in the form:

DIM A(N)

where N is any numeric variable or arithmetic expression. CAUTION: Once an array is dimensioned, it cannot be redimensioned unless the command CLEAR is given.

Example   The following program will store any number of random numbers:

```
100 INPUT "HOW MANY RANDOM NUMBERS TO STORE? ";N
110 DIM A(N)
120 FOR K = 1 TO N
130 LET A(K) = RND(1)
140 NEXT K
150 END
```

EXERCISES 8.2, contd.   3. Write a program that:

(a) stores N random integers between 1 and 100

(b) computes and prints their average

(c) prints all numbers larger than the average and

(d) prints all of the even numbers in the list.

Hint for (d): When an even number is divided by 2 it leaves no remainder. Use the INT function to help you check for this condition.

4. The STORING AND AVERAGING 200 RANDOM NUMBERS program needs generalizing. Rewrite it so that any number of random numbers can be stored and averaged.

5. Modify the standard deviation program so that any arbitrary number of values can be used.

8.3 Sorting

Sorting is the arranging of data into ascending or descending order. It plays an important role in computer applications, particularly in business.

Example
UNSORTED DATA: 45, 23, 78, 100, 2, 45, 2
SORTED IN ASCENDING ORDER: 2, 2, 23, 45, 45, 78, 100
SORTED IN DESCENDING ORDER: 100, 78, 45, 45, 23, 2, 2

There are many techniques for sorting. In this book we will discuss the BUBBLE SORT which is one of the most popular methods of sorting (even though it is also one of the slowest). To sort four numbers into ascending order using a bubble sort, the following procedure will be used:

1. Store the four numbers into the array A.
2. Compare the values in the first two cells. If A(1) is more than A(2) then switch the two values. Then compare A(2) and A(3), switching them if A(2) is more than A(3). Then compare A(3) and A(4), switching them if necessary. This is called a PASS.
3. Repeat Step 2 two more times.
4. Print the array.

Steps 2 and 3 can be better understood from the table below. Assume that the four numbers that we want to sort are 2, 8, 5, and −1. Our object is to arrange them from smallest to largest.

RELATION	T/F?	SWITCH?	A(1)	A(2)	A(3)	A(4)
			2	8	5	−1
PASS 1:						
A(1) > A(2)	FALSE	NO	2	8	5	−1
				switched		
A(2) > A(3)	TRUE	YES	2	5	8	−1

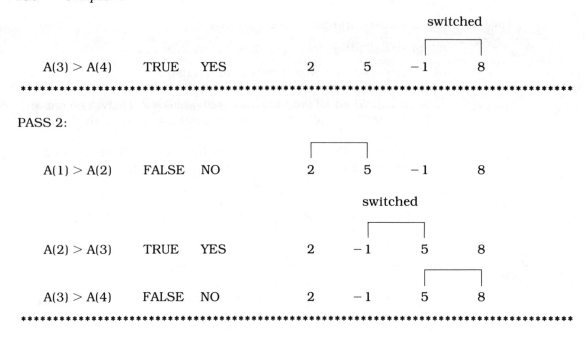

$$A(3) > A(4) \qquad \text{TRUE} \quad \text{YES} \qquad\qquad 2 \qquad 5 \qquad -1 \qquad 8$$

****

PASS 2:

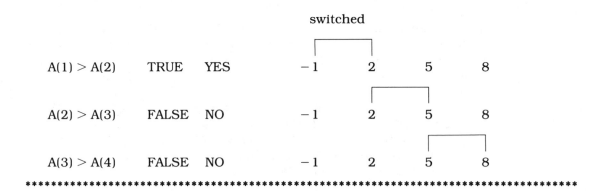

From this table the following BASIC program is written:

```
100 REM BUBBLE SORT, ASCENDING ORDER
110 DIM A(4)
120 DATA 2,8,5,-1
130 REM STORE NUMBERS IN ARRAY A
140 FOR I = 1 TO 4
150 READ A(I)
160 NEXT I
170 REM ********************
180 REM PASS ONE
190 FOR J = 1 TO 3
200 IF A(J) > A(J + 1) THEN LET L = A(J) : LET A(J) = A(J + 1) :
      LET A(J + 1) = L
210 NEXT J
220 REM ********************
230 REM PASS TWO
```

```
240 FOR J = 1 TO 3
250 IF A(J) > A(J + 1) THEN LET L = A(J) : LET A(J) = A(J + 1) :
      LET A(J + 1) = L
260 NEXT J
270 REM **********************
280 REM PASS THREE
290 FOR J = 1 TO 3
300 IF A(J) > A(J + 1) THEN LET L = A(J) : LET A(J) = A(J + 1) :
      LET A(J + 1) = L
310 NEXT J
320 REM PASSES ARE DONE, NOW PRINT ARRAY
330 FOR I = 1 TO 4
340 PRINT A(I);" ";
350 NEXT I
360 END
```

```
]RUN

-1  2  5  8
```

The alert reader will recognize that ALL THREE PASSES ARE IDENTI-CAL! This repetition can be eliminated in the program by inserting the FOR-NEXT loop which does the pass inside of another FOR-NEXT statement which loops three times. This is called NESTING OF FOR-NEXT LOOPS.

The following program demonstrates the nesting of loops.

```
100 REM BUBBLE SORT, ASCENDING ORDER
115 DIM A(4)
120 DATA 2,8,5,-1
130 FOR I = 1 TO 4
140 READ A(I)
150 NEXT I
155 REM THE "K" LOOP REPEATS THE PASS THREE TIMES
160 FOR K = 1 TO 3
170 FOR J = 1 TO 3
190 IF A(J) > A(J + 1) THEN LET L = A(J) : LET A(J) = A(J + 1) :
      LET A(J + 1) = L
230 NEXT J
240 NEXT K
250 REM SORTING IS DONE, NOW PRINT ARRAY
260 FOR I = 1 TO 4
270 PRINT A(I);" ";
280 NEXT I
290 END
```

```
]RUN

-1  2  5  8
```

EXERCISES 8.3

1. Three passes were required to sort four numbers. How many passes are necessary to sort six numbers? How many passes are necessary to sort N numbers?

2. Modify the bubble sort program so that it will sort the numbers

23, -56, 100, 45, 56, 34, 444, 67, 0, 45

into descending order.

3. If lines 220 to 310 were deleted from the first bubble sort program, what would the program accomplish?

4. Write a bubble sort so that the numbers to be sorted are arbitrary in number and entered by an INPUT statement.

5. The bubble sort method described above requires (N-1)*(N-1) comparisons of adjacent cells in an array containing N elements. (This is because there are N-1 passes with N-1 comparisons per pass.) Write a program to shorten the processing so that only N*(N-1)/2 comparisons would be required.

HINT: After the first pass is made the largest value is in A(N) (assuming you are sorting in ascending order). There is really no need in the other passes to keep comparing this largest value with the other values.

8.4 Applications

APPLICATION: DECIMAL TO BINARY NUMBER CONVERSION

The binary number system plays an important role in the internal operation of computers. Binary numbers are made up of the digits zero (0) and one (1).

Examples   11001 in binary equals 25 in decimal
111101 in binary equals 61 in decimal
1010101 in binary equals 85 in decimal

Decimal whole numbers can be converted into binary numbers by dividing repeatedly by 2 and storing the remainder. The following example demonstrates how this is done.

EXAMPLE OF CONVERTING DECIMAL NUMBERS INTO BINARY

Convert 25 to a binary number:

25 divided by 2 is	12 with a remainder of	1
12 divided by 2 is	6 with a remainder of	0
6 divided by 2 is	3 with a remainder of	0
3 divided by 2 is	1 with a remainder of	1
1 divided by 2 is	0 with a remainder of	1

The remainders are read from the bottom to the top to form the binary equivalent of 25. Thus, the decimal number 25 is equivalent to the binary number 11001.

The following program will convert decimal whole numbers to binary:

100 REM CONVERTS N FROM DECIMAL TO BINARY

```
115 DIM R(100)
120 REM ASSIGNMENT MODULE
125 LET I=0
130 INPUT "TYPE A DECIMAL NUMBER: ";N
140 LET I=I+ 1
145 REM COMPUTE MODULE. R(I) STORES THE I-TH REMAINDER
150 LET R(I)=N-2*INT(N/2)
160 LET N=INT(N/2)
170 IF N>0 THEN GOTO 140
180 REM OUTPUT MODULE
190 FOR K=I TO 1 STEP -1
200 PRINT R(K);
210 NEXT K
220 END
```

```
JRUN

TYPE A DECIMAL NUMBER: 100
1100100
```

EXERCISES 8.4

1. Complete a Box Diagram for the program above when the value for N is 6.

2. Modify the conversion program so that it will convert any whole number to the base 8.

3. Modify the conversion program so that it will convert any decimal whole number to the base 5 or base 7, depending on the user's choice.

APPLICATION: SEARCHING

A recent study has shown that people who sleep on the average more than seven hours a night live a shorter number of years. The following table contains sleeping and longevity statistics for eight deceased persons:

AVERAGE NO. OF HOURS SLEPT NIGHTLY	YEARS LIVED
6	67
6.5	72
5.75	80
9	55
8.5	62
5	81
6	70
9	50

In many programming applications, there is a need to pick out specific values from an array.

Example   The following BASIC program will find from the sleep-longevity table the average number of years lived by those who slept more than 6.5 hours a night.

```
100 DATA 6, 67, 6.5, 72, 5.75, 80, 9, 55
110 DATA 8.5, 62, 5, 81, 6, 70, 9, 50
120 DIM S(8),Y(8)
122 FOR K = 1 TO 8
124 READ S(K), Y(K)
126 NEXT K
128 LET T = 0
129 LET C = 0
130 REM THE FOR-NEXT LOOP WILL SEARCH THE ARRAY S
150 FOR I = 1 TO 8
160 IF S(I)< = 6.5 THEN GOTO 170
162 LET C = C + 1
165 LET T = T + Y(I)
168 PRINT S(I),Y(I)
170 NEXT I
175 PRINT "AVERAGE YEARS LIVED: ";T/C
180 END
```

```
JRUN

9                 55
8.5               62
9                 50
AVERAGE YEARS LIVED: 55.6666667
```

EXERCISES 8.4, contd.

4. Modify the above program so that it will search only for the array values of those individuals who slept more than 6.5 hours each night but didn't live beyond 70.

5. Write a program that will print only the array values for those who lived more than 65 years. Have the program average the sleeping time for the people who fall into that catagory.

6. Write a BASIC program that generates and stores 50 random whole numbers between 1 and 20 and counts and prints the number of 10's and 5's which are in the list.

APPLICATION: RANDOM SAMPLING

Example of Sampling with Replacement

The ability to perform sampling from a fixed set of data is important in many disciplines. The following program will randomly sample with replacement three values from the data list 34, 67, 345, 35, 678. Sampling with replacement means that each number may be picked more than once.

```
100 REM SAMPLE OF 3 RANDOM VALUES
115 DIM A(5)
120 DATA 34,67,345,35,678
130 FOR I = 1 TO 5
140 READ A(I)
150 NEXT I
155 FOR I = 1 TO 3
160 REM R IS A RANDOM SUBSCRIPT FOR THE ARRAY
```

```
180 LET R = INT(5*RND(1)) + 1
190 PRINT A(R)
200 NEXT I
210 END
```

```
]RUN

345
67
345
```

---

7. Write a program that will select 30 different random samples, each sample consisting of three numbers. Use the above data.

8. Write a program which picks 30 random numbers in the range from 1 to 365. If any number happens to be picked more than once, the program should print "SUCCESS." If all thirty numbers picked are different, the program should print "FAILURE."

9. If two or more people in a group of thirty share the same birthday (month and day), call this a "SUCCESS." Do you see that problem 9 is a simulation of this event? A famous result in probability theory, known as the "Birthday Problem," shows that the chances of two people out of a group thirty having the same birthday is nearly 70%. Test this claim by writing a program which counts the number of successes in 100 trials of the program in problem 9. There should be nearly seventy.

---

*Example of
Sampling
without
Replacement*

The following program will sample the values from the last program without replacement. This means that once a number is selected, it cannot be selected again.

```
100 REM SAMPLING 3 VALUES AT RANDOM WITHOUT REPLACEMENT
120 DIM A(5)
130 DATA 34, 67, 345, 35, 678
140 FOR I = 1 TO 5
150 READ A(I)
160 NEXT I
170 FOR I = 1 TO 3
180 LET L = INT(5*RND(1)) + 1
185 IF A(L) = -999 THEN GOTO 180
190 PRINT A(L)
195 REM -999 IS A FLAG
200 LET A(L) = -999
205 NEXT I
210 END
```

```
]RUN

34
35
345
```

EXERCISES
8.4, contd.

11. Write a program that will store the whole numbers from 1 to 80 in an array. Have the program pick a random sample of 20 of the numbers without repetition and print them. What "real world" situation does this model? Hint: think gambling.

8.5 Two-dimensional numeric arrays

Imagine a rectangle of boxes, say three rows by five columns. The three rows are numbered 0,1, and 2 and the five columns are numbered 0,1,2,3,and 4. Each box can be uniquely located by saying which row and which column it is in. This is exactly the idea behind a two-dimensional array, also called a *table*. The fifteen cells in the three by five array are actually individual variables, each capable of storing numeric data.

Suppose the array is named T. The statement

LET T(2,4)=9

assigns the number 9 to the box in row 2 and column 4. Keep in mind that the arrangement is always row first, column second. (Columns go up and down, like the columns in a Greek temple.) The statements

LET T(2,4)=9
LET T(2,1)=8
LET T(1,2)=7
LET T(0,0)=6

would produce the following Box Diagram:

		COLUMNS			
ARRAY T	0	1	2	3	4
0	6				
ROWS 1			7		
2		8			9

Notice that T(2,1) is not the same variable as T(1,2), and T(3,4) is meaningless in our example since we have only three rows, numbered 0,1, and 2.

If either subscript indicating rows or columns exceeds ten, then the array must be DIMensioned. An array U with four rows and thirteen columns would have to be set up at the outset of a program by writing

10 DIM U(3,12)

Remember that since there is a zeroth row and a zeroth column, the DIM statement above really creates an array with four rows and thirteen columns.

Example   The following program stores numbers into a two-dimensional array K. The zeroth row and column are not used in this example, which is fairly typical in applications.

ARRAY K

column

		1	2
	1	0	2
row			
	2	0	0

10 LET K(1,2) = 2

		1	2
	1	0	2
row			
	2	0	1

20 LET K(2,2) = 1

		1	2
	1	0	2
row			
	2	4	1

30 LET K(K(1,2),1) = 4

		1	2
	1	8	2
row			
	2	4	1

40 LET K(1,1) = K(1,2)*K(2,1)

**EXERCISES
8.5**

1. Fill in the array P for the following program.

```
10 DATA 45,56,2,5
20 FOR I = 1 TO 2
30 FOR J = 1 TO 2
40 READ P(I,J)
```

```
50 NEXT J : NEXT I
60 END
```

Example   Mr. Smith's electric bills from January to December were $31, $24, $23, $23, $21, $24, $26, $34, $33, $25, $28, and $30. His gas bills for the same months were $28, $25, $18, $15, $13, $14, $12, $10, $10, $17, $22, and $27. His phone bills for the year were $52, $61, $48, $99, $41, $38, $65, $40, $45, $57, $53, and $65. A two-dimensional array will store all of Mr. Smith's utility bills at one time. The columns represent the months, and the rows are the types of bills.

The following BASIC program will read and store Mr. Smith's bills.

```
10 DIM U(3,12)
20 FOR R = 1 TO 3
30 FOR C = 1 TO 12
40 READ U(R,C)
50 NEXT C
60 NEXT R
70 REM ELECTRIC BILLS DATA
80 DATA 31, 24, 23, 23, 21, 24, 26, 34, 33, 25, 28, 30
90 REM GAS BILLS DATA
100 DATA 28, 25, 18, 15, 13, 14, 12, 10, 10, 17, 22, 27
110 REM PHONE BILLS DATA
120 DATA 52, 61, 48, 99, 41, 38, 65, 40, 45, 57, 53, 65
```

Now consider the following application. Mr. Smith wants to be able to know his total utilities expense for any month of the year. He writes the rest of the program which we started above:

```
130 INPUT "WHICH MONTH (1 TO 12)? ";M
140 LET S = 0
150 FOR I = 1 TO 3
160 LET S = S + U(I,M)
170 NEXT I
180 PRINT "THE EXPENSE FOR THAT MONTH WAS $";S
190 INPUT "TRY IT AGAIN? ";A$
200 IF A$ = "YES" THEN GOTO 130
210 END
```

```
]RUN

WHICH MONTH (1 TO 12)? 10
THE EXPENSE FOR THAT MONTH WAS $99
TRY IT AGAIN? NO
```

EXERCISES   2. Add to Mr. Smith's program the ability to add up the total yearly expense
8.5   for any type of utility bill selected. (Hint: The row is fixed, but the months change from 1 to 12.)

3. Add a feature to the program so that Mr. Smith can ask the computer to print all the gas bills which exceed an amount he enters.

4. Modify your program in problem 3 so that Mr. Smith may also choose the utility he wants.

Example Mr. Dale wishes to store in the computer the M quiz grades of each of his N students in his statistics class.

```
 90 REM N IS THE NUMBER OF STUDENTS
 95 REM M IS THE NUMBER OF QUIZ GRADES PER STUDENT
100 INPUT "HOW MANY STUDENTS DO YOU HAVE? ";N
110 INPUT "HOW MANY QUIZZES FOR EACH STUDENT? ";M
120 DIM A(N,M)
130 FOR I = 1 TO N
140 PRINT "STUDENT NUMBER ";I
150 FOR J = 1 TO M
160 INPUT "TYPE A QUIZ GRADE: ";A(I,J)
170 NEXT J
180 NEXT I
190 END
```

```
JRUN

HOW MANY STUDENTS DO YOU HAVE? 3
HOW MANY QUIZZES FOR EACH STUDENT? 2
STUDENT NUMBER 1
TYPE A QUIZ GRADE: 70
TYPE A QUIZ GRADE: 75
STUDENT NUMBER 2
TYPE A QUIZ GRADE: 80
TYPE A QUIZ GRADE: 67
STUDENT NUMBER 3
TYPE A QUIZ GRADE: 89
TYPE A QUIZ GRADE: 98
```

EXERCISES 8.5, contd.

5. Mr. Dale needs to expand his program so that it can compute the average grade of each of his students and the class average for each exam. Expand the program for him.

Example Mr. Murtz, a famous real estate salesman, uses a computer to record his sales. The following program will find his total commissions and the total value of the houses he sold:

```
100 INPUT "TYPE THE NUMBER OF HOUSES SOLD: ";T
110 DIM N(T,2)
120 FOR I = 1 TO T
130 PRINT "FOR HOUSE NUMBER ";I
140 INPUT "WHAT WAS THE COMMISSION? "; N(I,1)
150 INPUT "WHAT WAS THE PRICE OF THE HOUSE? ";N(I,2)
160 NEXT I
170 REM SUM OF THE COMMISSIONS
175 LET S = 0
180 FOR I = 1 TO T
190 LET S = S + N(I,1)
```

```
200 NEXT I
210 PRINT "TOTAL COMMISSION IS $";S
220 LET S = 0
230 REM FIND THE TOTAL VALUE OF HOUSES
240 FOR I = 1 TO T
250 LET S = S + N(I,2)
260 NEXT I
270 PRINT "TOTAL VOLUME OF HOUSE SALES IS $";S
280 END
```

```
]RUN

TYPE THE NUMBER OF HOUSES SOLD: 2
FOR HOUSE NUMBER 1
WHAT WAS THE COMMISSION? 6000
WHAT WAS THE PRICE OF THE HOUSE? 100000
FOR HOUSE NUMBER 2
WHAT WAS THE COMMISSION? 12000
WHAT WAS THE PRICE OF THE HOUSE? 250000
TOTAL COMMISSION IS $18000
TOTAL VOLUME OF HOUSE SALES IS $350000
```

8.6 One- and two-dimensional string arrays

The popular versions of BASIC found on microcomputers nearly always have the ability to store string data in the cells of an array, known as a *string array*. String arrays have standard string variable names and follow the same rules regarding subscripts as numeric arrays. Each cell in a string array can hold a string of up to 255 characters in length, just as with standard string variables.

String arrays may be one- or two-dimensional. In fact, many versions of BASIC, including Applesoft, allow string and numeric arrays with dimensions greater than two.

Example   The following program assigns four strings to a one-dimensional string array.

	C$(1)	C$(2)	C$(3)	C$(4)
100 DATA "DALLAS", "CHICAGO"				
105 DATA "MIAMI", "BRONX"				
120 READ C$(1),C$(2),C$(3),C$(4)	DALLAS	CHICAGO	MIAMI	BRONX
130 LET C$(2) = C$(4)	DALLAS	BRONX	MIAMI	BRONX
140 IF C$(2)<>C$(1) THEN LET C$(2) = C$(1)	DALLAS	DALLAS	MIAMI	BRONX
150 END	DALLAS	DALLAS	MIAMI	BRONX

EXERCISES 8.6

1. Write a program that will sort the above array containing the four cities. Also have the program print the sorted array.

2. Write a general program that will sort an arbitrary one-dimensional string array.

Example   The following is an example of a two-dimensional string array containing people's names and ages.

100 DIM A$(2,2)

110 DATA "M. BERLE","72"

120 DATA "K. SMITH","68"

130 READ A$(1,1), A$(1,2)

column

	1	2
1	M. BERLE	72
2		

rows

140 READ A$(2,1), A$(2,2)

column

	1	2
1	M. BERLE	72
2	K. SMITH	68

rows

150 END

Example   The following list is the personal telephone directory of Ms. Manuel.

Roy's Garage	234-5456
Bill Blake	555-5655
Kym Osuna	234-5458
Jane Turner	874-5673
Ajax Bakery	871-2134
Dale's Deli	456-7676

What follows is a program which

(1) Stores the list in a string array K$,
(2) Finds a name requested and prints the name and telephone number.

```
100 DIM K$(6,2)
110 DATA "ROY'S GARAGE","234-5456","BILL BLAKE","555-5655"
120 DATA "KYM OSUNA","234-5458","JANE TURNER","874-5673"
130 DATA "AJAX BAKERY","871-2134","DALE'S DELI","456-7676"
150 REM NAMES GO INTO COLUMN 1 OF THE ARRAY
160 REM PHONE NUMBERS GO INTO COLUMN 2
170 FOR I = 1 TO 6
180 READ K$(I,1),K$(I,2)
190 NEXT I
200 INPUT "PLEASE TYPE IN THE COMPLETE NAME: ";N$
205 LET X = 0
210 FOR I = 1 TO 6
220 IF N$ = K$(I,1) THEN PRINT K$(I,1),K$(I,2) : LET X = 1
240 NEXT I
250 IF X = 0 THEN PRINT "SORRY, NAME NOT IN DIRECTORY."
270 END
```

```
]RUN

PLEASE TYPE IN THE COMPLETE NAME: BILL B
LAKE
BILL BLAKE        555-5655
```

EXERCISES 8.6, contd.

3. Modify the program above so that only a "search key" needs to be entered by the user. The search key is one or more letters from the beginning of the name. The computer must print the full name and the telephone number of anybody whose name matches the key. Hint: Only line 220 needs to be changed.

It is possible to sort strings in the same way numeric data is sorted.

Example   Dean Larton wishes to write a program that will sort some of the important academic courses offered in the Humanities Division at Jeffrey Street University.

INTENSIVE BASKET WEAVING
HISTORY OF ROCK AND ROLL
ASTROLOGY
HISTORY OF COMIC BOOKS
MINOR WRITERS AFTER SHAKESPEARE

The following program will sort and print the above list in alphabetical order.

```
100 REM ALPHABETIC SORT, ASCENDING
105 DATA 5
110 DATA "INTENSIVE BASKET WEAVING"
115 DATA "HISTORY OF ROCK AND ROLL"
120 DATA "ASTROLOGY","HISTORY OF COMIC BOOKS"
130 DATA "MINOR WRITERS AFTER SHAKESPEARE"
135 READ N
140 DIM R$(N)
150 FOR I = 1 TO N
160 READ R$(I)
170 NEXT I
```

```
180 FOR U = 1 TO N-1
190 FOR T = 1 TO N-1
200 IF R$(T)>R$(T+1) THEN LET L$=R$(T) : LET R$(T)=R$(T+1) :
        LET R$(T+1)=L$
210 NEXT T
220 NEXT U
230 FOR I = 1 TO N
240 PRINT R$(I)
250 NEXT I
260 END
```

```
]RUN

ASTROLOGY
HISTORY OF COMIC BOOKS
HISTORY OF ROCK AND ROLL
INTENSIVE BASKET WEAVING
MINOR WRITERS AFTER SHAKESPEARE
```

APPLICATION IN RANDOM SAMPLING

The Newport Magic Club has five members volunteering to serve on the Cleaning Committee. Since there are only three openings, the following BASIC program will select three members at random:

```
100 REM RANDOM SELECTION OF THREE MEMBERS FROM
110 REM A GROUP OF FIVE, WITHOUT REPETITION.
120 DATA "JOHN","BILL","MARY","HARRY","PHIL"
150 DIM P$(5)
160 FOR J = 1 TO 5
170 READ P$(J)
180 NEXT J
185 FOR I = 1 TO 3
190 LET L = INT(5*RND(1))+1
210 IF P$(L) = "ALREADY CHOSEN" THEN GOTO 190
220 PRINT P$(L)
230 LET P$(L) = "ALREADY CHOSEN"
240 NEXT I
250 END
```

```
]RUN

HARRY
PHIL
MARY
```

EXERCISES 8.6, contd.

4. Mr. Mas coaches a soccer team with fourteen players. He needs eleven players in the starting lineup. Write a program which chooses his starting lineup at random. Invent your own player names.

APPLICATION

The Lease A Lemon Co. wishes to enter into the computer the following information about each of its customers:

(1) The name of the customer

150   Chapter 8

(2) The address of the customer
(3) The phone number of the customer
(4) The serial number of the automobile
(5) The deposit of the customer.

The following assignment module will accomplish this task.

```
100 INPUT "ENTER THE NUMBER OF CUSTOMERS: ";K
110 DIM R$(K,5)
120 FOR I = 1 TO K
130 INPUT "ENTER THE NAME OF CUSTOMER: "; R$(I,1)
140 INPUT "ENTER THE ADDRESS OF THE CUSTOMER: ";R$(I,2)
150 INPUT "ENTER THE PHONE NUMBER OF THE CUSTOMER: "
        ;R$(I,3)
160 INPUT "ENTER THE SERIAL NUMBER OF THE AUTOMOBILE: "
        ;R$(I,4)
170 INPUT "ENTER THE DEPOSIT OF THE CUSTOMER: ";R$(I,5)
175 PRINT
180 NEXT I
```

```
]RUN

ENTER THE NUMBER OF CUSTOMERS: 2
ENTER THE NAME OF CUSTOMER: BOB JONES
ENTER THE ADDRESS OF THE CUSTOMER: 110 ELM
ENTER THE PHONE NUMBER OF THE CUSTOMER: 760-1111
ENTER THE SERIAL NUMBER OF THE AUTOMOBILE: 23456
ENTER THE DEPOSIT OF THE CUSTOMER: 500
ENTER THE NAME OF CUSTOMER: BILL SMITH
ENTER THE ADDRESS OF THE CUSTOMER: 333 HART ST
ENTER THE PHONE NUMBER OF THE CUSTOMER: 345-4566
ENTER THE SERIAL NUMBER OF THE AUTOMOBILE: 3444
ENTER THE DEPOSIT OF THE CUSTOMER: 345
```

This program can be expanded to search for a customer by name so that the record of any customer can be printed.

```
200 INPUT "ENTER NAME DESIRED: ";N$
205 LET G = 0
210 FOR I = 1 TO K
220 IF N$ = R$(I,1) THEN LET G = I
230 NEXT I
240 IF G = 0 THEN PRINT "SORRY, NAME NOT HERE." : GOTO 260
250 PRINT R$(G,1), R$(G,2), R$(G,3), R$(G,4), R$(G,5)
260 END
```

```
(continued from above)

ENTER NAME DESIRED: BILL SMITH
BILL SMITH        333 HART ST
345-4566          3444                    345
```

EXERCISES 8.6, contd.

5. Expand the above program to compute the total deposit taken from the customers.

6. Modify the above program so that one can request the names of customers who gave deposits between $100 and $200.

7. Modify the above program so that by entering a serial number the record of the customer can be printed.

8.7 Projects

1. A Magic Square is a square array of numbers such that all rows, columns, and diagonals have the same sum.

Examples

8	1	6
3	5	7
4	9	2

1	15	14	4
12	6	7	9
8	10	11	5
13	3	2	16

Write a BASIC program to check a square array to see if it is a Magic Square. The numbers in the square should be in DATA statements in the program.

2. Hexadecimal numbers have many important applications in Computer Science. Just as binary numbers are comprised of the two digits 0 and 1, hexadecimal numbers are made up of the 16 digits and letters 0, 1, 2, 3, 4, 5, 6, 7, 8, 9, A, B, C, D, E, and F. The letters A through F stand for the decimal numbers 10 through 15. The hexadecimal place-values from right to left are 1, 16, 256 ($=16*16$), 4096 ($=16*16*16$), etc.

Examples   1F (hex) = 31 (decimal)

A10 (hex) = 2576 (decimal)

(a) Write a program that will convert an arbitrary hexadecimal number into its decimal equivalent.

(b) Write a program that will convert an arbitrary decimal whole number into its hexadecimal equivalent. (See the decimal number to binary conversion program in Section 8.4.)

3. Consider the following DATA statements:

DATA "ACE","TWO","THREE","FOUR"
DATA "FIVE","SIX","SEVEN"
DATA "EIGHT","NINE","TEN"
DATA "JACK","QUEEN","KING"
DATA "DIAMONDS","SPADES"
DATA "HEARTS","CLUBS"

Using the above DATA statements, write a program that will:

(a) Store the fifty-two cards of an ordinary deck into a fifty-two row by two column two-dimensional array A. The first column of A contains the face-value, and the second contains the suit.

(b) Print four five-card hands, where all twenty cards are chosen at random without replacement.

4. The table below is the total dollar sales for four salespeople selling two models of automobiles.

SALESMAN	MODEL A	MODEL B	ROW TOTALS
JILL	$345,567	$567,543	
BILL	$897,444	$908,661	
PHIL	$123,199	$234,567	
LIL	$345,111	$222,333	
TOTALS			

Write a BASIC program that will print this table along with the sums of each of the columns and rows, labelled appropriately.

5. SIGNS OF THE ZODIAC

Given a month and day of birth, write a program that will determine the corresponding sign of the zodiac. The following information gives the birth date and the sign of the zodiac.

SIGN	PERIOD
CAPRICORN	DEC 22-JAN 19
AQUARIUS	JAN 20-FEB 18
PISCES	FEB 19-MAR 20
ARIES	MAR 21-APR 19
TAURUS	APR 20-MAY 20
GEMINI	MAY 21-JUNE 20
CANCER	JUNE 21-JULY 22
LEO	JULY 23-AUG 22
VIRGO	AUG 23-SEPT 22
LIBRA	SEPT 23-OCT 22
SCORPIO	OCT 23-NOV 21
SAGITTARIUS	NOV 22-DEC 21

This program should determine the sign of the zodiac when the user enters the month and day.

LAB 8-1 One-dimensional arrays

Type in the command: NEW

A subscripted variable consists of a variable name followed by a subscript enclosed in parentheses. For example: A(1) is a subscripted variable but A1 is not. A set of subscripted variables with the same variable name is called an ARRAY.

The ease in assigning and processing large amounts of data is the major reason for using arrays.

Type in the program: 10 FOR K = 0 TO 10
                          20 READ Z$(K)

```
30 LET X(K) = K + 1
40 NEXT K
50 PRINT "K","Z$(K)","X(K)"
60 FOR K = 0 TO 10
70 PRINT K,Z$(K),X(K)
80 NEXT K
90 END
100 DATA A,B,C,D,E,F,G,H,I,J,K
```

Type in the command: RUN

Note that the subscript K is a variable. When K = 0, Z$(K) is Z$(0) and X(K) is X(0). When K = 1, Z$(K) is Z$(1) and X(K) is X(1).

By studying the output of the program, Z$(0) contains the string A and X(0) contains the number 1.

What are the contents of Z$(K) and X(K) when K = 4? _____

The string E is stored in Z$(4) and the number 5 is stored in X(4).

Applesoft BASIC automatically allows up to 11 memory locations (0 through 10) for each one-dimensional array.

Type in the statements: 10 FOR K = 0 TO 15
                            60 FOR K = 0 TO 15
                            110 DATA L,M,N,O,P

Type in the command: LIST

Since K will be assigned integers 0 through 15, sixteen storage locations are needed in memory for both arrays, Z$(K) and X(K).

Type in the command: RUN

What is the computer's response? _____

The error was caused by the lack of memory locations for the array. That is, the computer has not reserved memory locations for Z$(11) through Z$(15) and X(11) through X(15). Remember, Applesoft BASIC automatically reserves only 11 memory locations for each one-dimensional array (subscripts 0 through 10).

When more memory locations are needed for the array, the DIM statement is used.

Type in the statement: 5 DIM Z$(15),X(15)

Type in the command: LIST

Note that the DIM statement is the first statement of the program. All DIM statements should be placed at the beginning of a program before any statements using arrays. This will insure that all arrays used in the program are properly dimensioned.

Type in the command: RUN

Explain what the computer does when it executes line number 5?

_____

_____

_____

When the computer executes line number 5, it reserves sixteen storage locations in memory for the arrays with variable names Z$(0) through Z$(15) and X(0) through X(15).

The subscript of the subscripted variable must be a nonegative number.

Type in the command: NEW

Type in the statement: 10 LET A(-2)$=5$
                            20 PRINT A(-2)
                            30 END

Type in the command: RUN

What is the computers response? _____

Explain why the error occurred? _____

_____

Remember, subscripts must be greater than or equal to 0.

If the subscript is not a whole number, BASIC will truncate the number to an integer.

Type in the command: NEW

Type in the statements: 10 LET A(1.8)$=5$
                             20 PRINT A(1)

Type in the commands: LIST
                           RUN

What is the output of the computer? _____

Explain why the output is 5? _____

_____

_____

The number 1.8 is truncated to the integer 1 in line number 10. Thus, the subscripted variable A(1) is assigned the value 5.

LAB 8-2 Two-dimensional arrays

Type in the command: NEW

A rectangular table of values consisting of rows and columns is called a two-dimensional array. The DIM statement is used to create a two-dimensional array of subscripted numeric or string variables.

Type in the statement: 10 DIM X$(2,3)

The two arguments inside the parentheses must be separated by a comma. They can be nonnegative numbers, or numeric variables, or arithmetic expressions generating nonnegative numbers.

The first argument, 2, is the highest subscripted value of the rows. The second argument, 3, is the highest subscripted value of the columns for the two-dimensional array. The lowest subscripted value for both row and column is 0.

Thus, the execution of the statement 10 DIM X$(2,3) creates a two-dimensional array with three rows (0, 1 and 2) and four columns (0, 1, 2, and 3). Twelve storage locations are reserved in memory with variable names as shown in the table below.

	Column 0	Column 1	Column 2	Column 3
Row 0	X$(0,0)	X$(0,1)	X$(0,2)	X$(0,3)
Row 1	X$(1,0)	X$(1,1)	X$(1,2)	X$(1,3)
Row 2	X$(2,0)	X$(2,1)	X$(2,2)	X$(2,3)

Type in the statement: 10 DIM X$(1,2)

When the computer executes this statement, how many storage locations will the computer reserve? _____

The computer will reserve six storage locations.

What are the variable names of the array? _____

_____

The variable names of the array are X$(0,0), X$(0,1), X$(0,2), X$(1,0), X$(1,1), and X$(1,2).

Type in the statement: 20 LET X$(2,2) = "HELLO"
                            30 END

Type in the commands: LIST
                          RUN

What is the computer's response? _____

Explain why the error occurred? _____

_____

The computer did not reserve a storage location for the variable name X$(2,2). The cell numbered (2,2) is out of the range for the dimensioned array.

Type in the command: NEW

Type in the program: 10 DIM A(1,2)
                         20 FOR J = 0 TO 2
                         30 READ A(0,J)
                         40 NEXT J
                         50 FOR J = 0 TO 2
                         60 READ A(1,J)
                         70 NEXT J
                         80 PRINT "A(0,0) = ";A(0,0)
                         90 PRINT "A(0,1) = ";A(0,1)
                         100 PRINT "A(0,2) = ";A(0,2)
                         110 PRINT "A(1,0) = ";A(1,0)

```
120 PRINT "A(1,1) = ";A(1,1)
130 PRINT "A(1,2) = ";A(1,2)
140 DATA 10,20,30,40,50,60
150 END
```

Type in the commands: LIST
                                 RUN

Normally, nested loops are used to assign data to a two-dimensional array and to print data from a two-dimensional array. What follows is an improvement over the program above.

Type in the command: NEW

Type in the program:
```
10 DIM A(1,2)
20 FOR I = 0 TO 1
30 FOR J = 0 TO 2
40 READ A(I,J)
50 NEXT J
60 NEXT I
70 FOR I = 0 TO 1
80 FOR J = 0 TO 2
90 PRINT "A(";I",";J") = ";A(I,J)
100 NEXT J
110 NEXT I
120 DATA 10,20,30,40,50,60
130 END
```

Type in the commands: LIST
                                 RUN

9

More on Strings

9.0 Introduction

Now we will zero in on some important applications which involve the handling of string data. The ability to join two or more strings together to form a single string is central to everything we will do in this chapter. The process is known as *concatenation*, which we turn to right now.

9.1 Concatenation

Concatenation is an operation on string data much like addition is an operation on numeric data. To concatenate two strings is to join them together to form one string. The symbol for the operation is a plus sign (+). It is placed between the two strings that are to be joined.

Example

	A$	B$	C$
10 LET A$ = "STRING"	STRING		
20 LET B$ = "CHEESE"	STRING	CHEESE	
30 LET C$ = A$ + B$	STRING	CHEESE	STRINGCHEESE

40 END

It is at line 30 that concatenation takes place. The string variables A$ and B$ are in the order they are to be joined, and they are separated by a plus sign, which is the concatenation operator. C$ is assigned the result of the operation.

Example The following program uses concatenation to generate the names of the fifty-two cards in a deck:

```
100 DATA "ACE","TWO","THREE"
110 DATA "FOUR","FIVE","SIX"
```

```
120 DATA "SEVEN","EIGHT","NINE"
130 DATA "TEN","JACK","QUEEN"
140 DATA "KING"
160 DATA "HEARTS","DIAMONDS"
170 DATA "CLUBS","SPADES"
180 DIM A$(13),B$(4),C$(52)
190 FOR I = 1 TO 13
200 READ A$(I)
210 NEXT I
220 FOR I = 1 TO 4
230 READ B$(I)
240 NEXT I
245 LET K = 0
250 FOR I = 1 TO 13
260 FOR J = 1 TO 4
265 LET K = K + 1
270 LET C$(K) = A$(I) + " OF " + B$(J)
280 NEXT J
290 NEXT I
300 FOR K = 1 TO 52
310 PRINT C$(K)
320 NEXT K
330 END
```

```
]RUN

ACE OF HEARTS
ACE OF DIAMONDS
ACE OF CLUBS
ACE OF SPADES
TWO OF HEARTS
TWO OF DIAMONDS
TWO OF CLUBS
TWO OF SPADES
        .
        .
        .
KING OF HEARTS
KING OF DIAMONDS
KING OF CLUBS
KING OF SPADES
```

**EXERCISES
9.1**

1. If line 270 were written LET C$(K) = A$(I) + B$(J) instead of the way it is in the program, what difference would it make?

2. Mr. and Mrs. Damoiselle have just had their first baby and it's a girl! Together they have decided that her first name should be Madeline, Kristin, Kymberly, or Charlotte. They have also narrowed the middle name down to May, Danielle, Erin, or Michelle. Help them decide on their daughter's full name by writing a program that will figure out all sixteen combinations of first, middle, and last names and print them. Use concatenation to create each full name.

3. Write a program to change any English word into Pig Latin. The rule is: remove the first letter, place it at the end of the word, and then add AY. For example, BASIC becomes ASICBAY. Assume that all words are translated the same way.

4. Write a program that will let the user enter a person's first and last name. Then it will print the name in reverse order. For example, JOHN DOE should come out DOE JOHN.

9.2 Printing numbers in dollars-and-cents format

Getting the computer to print numbers in dollars-and-cents format is quite a trick! Numbers like 3.5 and 23 need to be "padded" to 3.50 and 23.00. Other numbers such as 2.587 need to be rounded to 2.59. Here is an outline of what our program has to do:

1. Move the decimal point of the number two places to the right and round to the nearest whole number. For example, 2.587 becomes 259.
2. Change the result in Step 1 into a string and concatenate "00" to the front of it. Continuing the example above, 259 becomes 00259.
3. Assign the two rightmost digits to R$. For example, put 59 (from 00259) into R$.
4. Assign the remaining digits to L$. In our example, put 002 into L$.
5. Remove the leading zeros in L$ by changing L$ into a number (using the VAL function) and then back into a string (with STR$). For our example, the VAL of L$ is 2, which is changed back into a string and assigned to L$.
6. Concatenate L$ to R$ with a "." in between, and we're done! The result is 2.59.

Here is the program liberally documented with REMarks:

```
10 INPUT "WHAT IS THE NUMBER? ";N
30 REM
40 REM STEP 1 - MOVE DECIMAL POINT TWO PLACES AND ROUND
50 LET N1 = INT(100*N + .5)
60 REM
70 REM STEP 2 - CHANGE N1 TO A STRING AND ATTACH "00"
80 LET N1$="00"+STR$(N1)
85 REM
90 REM STEP 3 - EXTRACT THE TWO RIGHTMOST DIGITS
100 LET R$=RIGHT$(N1$,2)
105 REM
110 REM STEP 4 - EXTRACT THE REMAINING DIGITS
120 LET L$=LEFT$(N1$,LEN(N1$)-2)
125 REM
130 REM STEP 5 - REMOVE THE LEADING ZEROS IN L$
140 LET L$=STR$(VAL(L$))
145 REM
150 REM STEP 6 - PUT ALL OF THE PIECES TOGETHER
160 LET N$=L$+"."+R$
165 REM
170 PRINT "HERE IS YOUR NUMBER IN DOLLARS & CENTS: $";N$
180 END
```

```
]RUN

WHAT IS THE NUMBER? 2.587
HERE IS YOUR NUMBER IN DOLLARS & CENTS:
$2.59
```

**EXERCISE
9.2**

1. Combine Steps 1 and 2 into a single LET statement. Then combine Steps 3, 4, 5, and 6 into a single LET statement. The advantage of only two LET statements instead of six is that there is only one intermediate variable (namely N1$), instead of three.

9.3 Fields and records

In many applications, specific character positions within a string may have special meaning. A meaningful collection of characters is called a field. A collection of fields is called a record.

Here are three typical records from a telephone directory:

```
SMITH      PAT        555-2414
JOHNSON    RICHARD    592-3425
SHAKESPEARWILLIAM     342-1449
```

```
12345678911111111122222222        (number guide)
        012345678901234567
```

There are three fields in each record. They are the last name, first name, and telephone number. Notice that the same fields always begin in the same character position from record to record. It is good programming practice to require that records which contain the same kinds of information have fixed field lengths. From the number guide underneath the records you can see that the field lengths and positions in the record are as follows:

FIELD NAME	LENGTH	POSITION
Last Name	10	1 - 10
First Name	9	11 - 19
Telephone	8	20 - 27

It is obvious that not all last names will be ten letters long. Some will be less; some will be more. However, the fixed field concept requires that ALL ten characters of the last name field be filled. For short names, the remaining characters in the field are filled with spaces. For names longer than ten characters the name is truncated. (See William Shakespeare above.)

The following program accepts a last name, a first name, and a telephone number and prints a record with the fields described above:

```
10 REM CREATE A RECORD WITH THREE FIELDS
20 REM THE FOLLOWING B$ IS ASSIGNED 10 SPACES
30 LET B$ = "          "
40 REM
50 REM ASSIGN FIELDS
60 INPUT "TYPE LAST NAME: ";L$
70 INPUT "TYPE FIRST NAME: ";F$
80 INPUT "TYPE TELEPHONE NUMBER: ";T$
90 REM
100 REM PAD FIELDS TO CORRECT LENGTH
110 LET L$ = L$ + B$
120 LET L$ = LEFT$(L$,10)
130 LET F$ = F$ + B$
140 LET F$ = LEFT$(F$,9)
150 LET T$ = T$ + B$
```

```
160 LET T$ = LEFT$(T$,8)
170 REM
180 REM CONCATENATE ALL FIELDS TO CREATE A RECORD
190 LET R$ = L$ + F$ + T$
200 PRINT R$
210 END
```

```
]RUN

TYPE LAST NAME: SMITH
TYPE FIRST NAME: PAT
TYPE TELEPHONE NUMBER: 555-2414
SMITH     PAT      555-2414
```

The way in which each field is padded to the correct field length is really pretty clever. A string of spaces at least as long as the longest field is concatenated to each item entered. Then using the LEFT$ function, we cut the resulting string down to size.

The main reason for insisting on fixed field lengths is to be able to take an arbitrary record and know exactly where to look for whatever information is needed. The example below uses the fixed field idea to sort a telephone directory into ascending order on the telephone number.

Example The following program accepts the names and telephone numbers of N people and then sorts the list by telephone number.

```
10 REM          ASSIGNMENT MODULE
20 INPUT "HOW MANY PEOPLE? ";N
30 DIM R$(N)
40 LET B$ = "          "
50 FOR I = 1 TO N
60 PRINT
70 INPUT "TYPE LAST NAME: ";L$
80 INPUT "TYPE FIRST NAME: ";F$
90 INPUT "TYPE TELEPHONE NUMBER: ";T$
100 LET L$ = LEFT$(L$ + B$,10)
110 LET F$ = LEFT$(F$ + B$,9)
120 LET T$ = LEFT$(T$ + B$,8)
130 LET R$(I) = L$ + F$ + T$
140 NEXT I
150 REM COMPUTE MODULE, SORT ON TELEPHONE NUMBERS
160 FOR J = 1 TO N-1
170 FOR K = 1 TO N-1
180 REM TELEPHONE FIELD STARTS AT POSITION 20
190 IF MID$(R$(K),20,8)>MID$(R$(K + 1),20,8) THEN
        LET X$ = R$(K) : LET R$(K) = R$(K + 1) : LET R$(K + 1) = X$
200 NEXT K
210 NEXT J
220 REM          OUTPUT MODULE
230 PRINT
240 FOR I = 1 TO N
250 PRINT R$(I)
260 NEXT I
270 END
```

```
]RUN

HOW MANY PEOPLE? 3

TYPE LAST NAME: SMITH
TYPE FIRST NAME: PAT
TYPE TELEPHONE NUMBER: 555-2414

TYPE LAST NAME: JOHNSON
TYPE FIRST NAME: RICHARD
TYPE TELEPHONE NUMBER: 592-3425

TYPE LAST NAME: SHAKESPEARE
TYPE FIRST NAME: WILLIAM
TYPE TELEPHONE NUMBER: 342-1449

SHAKESPEARWILLIAM   342-1449
SMITH       PAT     555-2414
JOHNSON     RICHARD 592-3425
```

In the above program, N records are stored in the array R$. Such a collection of records dedicated to a specific list of data is called a *file*. Files are discussed in Chapter 11.

EXERCISES 9.3

1. Although all fields are stored as strings, some fields may represent numeric information such as age, weight, salary, grade point average, and so on. These fields should be RIGHT JUSTIFIED. That means that the information should be at the far right of the field with padded spaces at the left. This is done so that sorting on a numeric field will produce correct results. (If left justified, the string 25 would be considered larger than the string 195 because 2 comes later "alphabetically" than 1.) Rewrite the program above so that each record contains a fourth field, the person's monthly salary. Right-justify the salary in a field of length 5 and sort the entries by salary. (When entering a monthly salary, do not type in cents.)

2. Write a program that

   (1) Accepts as input an arbitrary number of integers (i.e., no decimal points)

   (2) Prints a sorted list, one number per line, without leading zeros, and right justified.

Example Input: 0342, 00013, 24, 92142, 1
Output: 1
             13
             24
            342
          92142

3. Write a program that

   (1) Accepts as input an arbitrary number of words

   (2) Prints the words alphabetized, one per line, so that the word list is left justified.

Example Input: ROCKET, GUARD, HAMLET, MISSISSIPPI
Output: GUARD

HAMLET
MISSISSIPPI
ROCKET

4. For problem 3, write a program so that the list will be printed right justified.

9.4 Projects

1. THE MINI WORD PROCESSOR—I.

Write a BASIC program that will perform the following functions:

(a) A sentence is typed by the user and then displayed.

(b) The user may replace any word in the sentence with another word, and the modified sentence is displayed.

2. THE MINI WORD PROCESSOR—II.

Write a BASIC program that will do the following:

(a) A sentence is typed by the user and then displayed.

(b) The user may insert a word between any two words in the sentence, and the modified sentence is displayed.

3. THE MINI WORD PROCESSOR—III. Word processing programs typically have the ability to take a standard form letter and "personalize" it. They do this by searching the letter for every occurrence of a special symbol, such as *NAME*, and replacing the symbol with an actual name. Write a program which will do the same thing.

4. Mrs. Otto wants to rent a car to drive from Los Angeles to San Francisco (400 miles). Due to the gas crunch she doesn't want to fill her tank on the way. In addition the total travel cost should not exceed $200. Help her to write a program to pick the car or cars from the following list which meet her requirements. Assume gas costs $1.50 a gallon.

AUTO	MODEL	M.P.G.	TANK CAPACITY	CHARGE/DAY	RATE/MILE
HOT ROD	FAST	18	16	$20	$.25
GASSER	SLOW	23	10	24	.27
STARS	SPEEDY	29	20	29	.30
FIRE	CLASSY	25	21	30	.22
TEVY	SHARP	17	15	22	.32
CABY	TOPS	27	17	23	.18

5. For the table above, write a program that produces and prints two sorted tables, where the sorts are on the m.p.g. field and the charge/day field.

LAB 9-1 Concatenation

Type in the command: NEW

To concatenate means to link strings together in a series. When strings need to be connected together in a program, CONCATENATION is used.

Type in the program: 10 LET A$ = "DOWN"
                               20 LET B$ = "TOWN"
                               30 LET C$ = A$ + B$
                               40 PRINT C$
                               50 END

Type in the command: RUN

What is the output of the program? _____

The concatenation occurred when the computer executed line number 30. The string in A$ is linked with the string in B$ using the operator +. The concatenated string is then stored in C$. Note the order in which the two string are linked. The ordering of the variables in a concatenation statement is important.

Type in the statements: 50 LET D$ = B$ + A$
                              60 PRINT D$
                              70 END

Type in the commands: LIST
                              RUN

What is the output of the program? _____

_____

Explain why C$ and D$ are different.

_____

_____

_____

Both strings stored in C$ and D$ were formed by concatenation of A$ and B$. However, the order of the variables in line number 30 is different than in line number 50.

Type in the statements: 30 LET C$ = "LOW" + A$
                              50 LET D$ = B$ + "FOLKS"

Type in the commands: LIST
                              RUN

What is the output of the program? _____

_____

You may concatenate as many string variables, strings, or functions that generate strings as you wish up to a limit of 255 characters in the concatenated string.

Type in the command: NEW

Type in the program: 10 DATA ONE,TWO,THREE,FOUR,FIVE
                               20 FOR I = 1 TO 5
                               30 READ N$

```
40 LET A$(I) = "THE SYMBOL FOR " + N$ + " IS " + STR$(I)
50 NEXT I
60 FOR K = 1 TO 5
70 PRINT A$(K)
80 NEXT K
90 END
```

Type in the command: RUN

Explain the concatenation in line number 40:

_____

_____

LAB 9-2 Padding and justifying

Type in the command: NEW

All records of a file should be constructed identically. That is, field lengths and positions should be the same from record to record. Since data stored in the same field of different records will have different lengths, PADDING is necessary to fill the unused character positions of the field. The following program shows what happens when fields are not padded.

Type in the program:
```
10 HOME
20 FOR K = 1 TO 3
30 INPUT "TYPE IN NAME: ";N$
40 INPUT "TYPE IN PHONE NUMBER: ";T$
50 LET A$(K) = N$ + " " + T$
60 PRINT
70 NEXT K
80 FOR K = 1 TO 3
90 PRINT A$(K)
100 NEXT K
110 END
```

Type in the command: RUN

Type in the following data: JOE COOL
(213) 555-1000
SUZY Q
731-2222
BEATRICE BENEVIDES
(805) 661-9999

How many fields does each record have? _____

Each record has two fields. The first field contains the name and the second field contains the phone number. But the fields are not consistent in length or position. In any record there is no way of knowing where the name field ends or the telephone field begins.

If the programmer is to be able to retrieve data from the fields of a record, he or she must know where the field is located within the record. This is possible only if the length of a field does not change from record to record. When designing a record, the programmer first determines the number of fields and the maximum number of characters each field must have.

For the program above, how many fields are needed and how many characters will be needed for each field?

_____

_____

Two fields are needed. However, the number of characters needed for each field may vary. For example, BEATRICE BENEVIDES has eighteen characters, but who is to say this will be the greatest number of characters needed for a name. The design of the record must be such that it will satisfy most cases. Let's design the record such that the first field will contain twenty characters and the second field fifteen characters. "Unused" character positions in any field will be filled with spaces. This is called PADDING.

How many characters will each record have? _____

Each record will contain thirty-five characters.

The process of padding begins by assigning to a string variable a number of spaces equal to the number of character positions in the longest field. In our case, the longest field has twenty characters.

Type in the statement: 5 LET B$ = "   " : REM (20 SPACES)

Type in the command: LIST

A field is said to be LEFT-JUSTIFIED if the first character of the data is in the left-most character position of the field. A field is said to be RIGHT-JUSTIFIED if the last character of the data is in the right-most character position of the field.

Continuing our example, we will design the record so that the name is left-justified in the first field and the phone number is right-justified in the second field.

Type in the statements: 45 LET F1$ = N$ + B$
50 LET F2$ = B$ + T$

Type in the command: LIST

Concatenating spaces after the data left-justifies a string variable. Concatenating spaces before the data right justifies a string variable.

Which line number left-justifies a string variable and which line number right-justifies a string variable in this program?

_____

Line number 45 concatenates twenty spaces after the data stored in N$. This left-justifies the string variable F1$. In line number 50, twenty spaces are concatenated before the data stored in T$. Therefore, this line number right-justifies the the string variable F2$.

Type in the statement: 55 LET A$(K) = LEFT$(F1$,20) + RIGHT$(F2$,15)

Type in the command: LIST

Which field is left-justified and which field is right-justified in this program?

_____

_____

The first field (containing the name) will be left-justified. The second field (containing the phone number) will be right-justified.

Type in the command: RUN

Type in the same data as before.

What is the most important reason for padding field?

_____

_____

_____

Padding forces fields containing similar kinds of information to have the same number of characters from record to record. Thus, locating data within a record is easier, since all records are structured in the same way.

10

Structured Programming

10.0 Introduction

The ability to program requires more than a knowledge of the syntax of a programming language; it demands of the programmer the ability to write *algorithms*, or short procedures which solve easily stated problems. The algorithms are then logically linked together to form *modules*. Modules are "miniprograms" which solve the specific tasks required of a more general problem. The full solution to a problem is made up of a collection of modules, and we call it a *program*. In this chapter we shall discuss algorithms, modules, and programs.

10.1 Algorithms

An algorithm is a rule or procedure which is used to solve a specific problem. For example, a well-known algorithm in arithmetic is long division. By always following the rules of long division we are assured of a correct answer, whether or not we understand why the rules work. Here we shall be concerned with several algorithms that can be useful in your BASIC programs. Many of these algorithms have already been discussed in previous chapters and should be familiar to you.

Notice that none of the algorithms below have line numbers. You are expected to put the algorithms at appropriate places in your programs and assign line numbers at that time.

ALGORITHM I: ENTERING AN ARBITRARY NUMBER OF VALUES
INTO A ONE-DIMENSIONAL ARRAY

```
INPUT "PLEASE ENTER THE NUMBER OF NUMBERS ";P
DIM N(P)
FOR I = 1 TO P
INPUT "ENTER A NUMBER: ";N(I)
NEXT I
```

Example   Mrs. Smith wishes to enter her students' final examination scores into the computer. The following algorithm will accomplish this task:

```
10 INPUT "HOW MANY GRADES DO YOU WISH TO ENTER? ";P
20 DIM N(P)
30 FOR I = 1 TO P
40 INPUT "ENTER AN EXAM GRADE: ";N(I)
50 NEXT I
```

Example   Mr. Yankellow wishes to enter into the computer the titles of the books in his library. The following algorithm will accomplish this task:

```
100 INPUT "HOW MANY TITLES TO BE ENTERED? ";N
110 DIM B$(N)
120 FOR I = 1 TO N
130 INPUT "TYPE A TITLE OF A BOOK: ";B$(I)
140 NEXT I
```

ALGORITHM II: SUMMING AN ARBITRARY NUMBER OF NUMBERS IN AN ARRAY

```
REM P IS THE NUMBER OF NUMBERS
REM S IS THE VARIABLE CONTAINING THE SUM
REM N( ) IS THE ARRAY
LET S = 0
FOR I = 1 TO P
LET S = S + N(I)
NEXT I
```

Example   Marcia sold several cars last month at the Lucky Auto Company. The following program will sum up her total commissions:

```
100 INPUT "TYPE THE NUMBER OF CARS SOLD ";P
110 DIM N(P)
120 FOR I = 1 TO P
125 PRINT "ENTER COMMISSION ON AUTO SALE #";I
130 INPUT N(I)
140 NEXT I
150 REM ALGORITHM II
160 LET S = 0
170 FOR I = 1 TO P
180 LET S = S + N(I)
190 NEXT I
200 PRINT "MARCIA'S TOTAL COMMISSION IS ";S
210 END
```

ALGORITHM III: ENTERING NUMBERS INTO A TWO-DIMENSIONAL ARRAY

```
REM A( , ) IS THE TWO-DIMENSIONAL ARRAY
REM N IS THE NUMBER OF ROWS
REM M IS THE NUMBER OF COLUMNS
INPUT "TYPE NUMBER OF ROWS ";N
INPUT "TYPE NUMBER OF COLUMNS ";M
DIM A(N,M)
```

```
FOR I = 1 TO N
FOR J = 1 TO M
INPUT A(I,J)
NEXT J
NEXT I
```

Example   Mrs. Larson wishes to store in the computer the M quiz grades of each of her N students in Statistics.

```
100 INPUT "HOW MANY STUDENTS DO YOU HAVE? ";N
105 INPUT "HOW MANY QUIZZES FOR EACH STUDENT? ";M
110 DIM A(N,M)
120 FOR I = 1 TO N
130 PRINT "FOR STUDENT #";I
140 FOR J = 1 TO M
150 PRINT "ENTER GRADE FOR QUIZ #";J
155 INPUT A(I,J)
160 NEXT J
170 NEXT I
```

EXERCISES 10.1

1. Write an algorithm that will enter strings into a two-dimensional array.

ALGORITHM IV: SUMMING THE NUMBERS IN EACH OF THE ROWS OF A TWO-DIMENSIONAL ARRAY

```
REM A( , ) IS THE ARRAY
REM N IS THE NUMBER OF ROWS
REM M IS THE NUMBER OF COLUMNS
REM S( ) IS THE ARRAY CONTAINING THE SUMS OF EACH ROW
FOR I = 1 TO N
LET S(I) = 0
FOR J = 1 TO M
LET S(I) = S(I) + A(I,J)
NEXT J
NEXT I
```

Example   Mrs. Larson wishes to sum the grades for each of her students. We shall assume the following lines are a continuation of the example above.

```
175 DIM S(N)
180 FOR I = 1 TO N
190 LET S(I) = 0
195 FOR J = 1 TO M
200 LET S(I) = S(I) + A(I,J)
210 NEXT J
220 PRINT "THE SUM OF THE GRADES FOR STUDENT #";I; " IS ";S(I)
230 NEXT I
```

EXERCISES 10.1, contd.

2. Write an algorithm that will sum the numbers in each column.

ALGORITHM V: ENTERING AN ARBITRARY NUMBER OF RECORDS
WHERE THE FIELDS ARE LEFT-JUSTIFIED

```
REM A1 IS THE LENGTH OF FIELD F1$,
REM A2 IS THE LENGTH OF FIELD F2$, etc...
REM B$ IS A STRING OF SPACES AS LONG AS LONGEST FIELD
LET B$ = "              "
INPUT "HOW MANY RECORDS? ";Q
DIM R$(Q)
FOR I = 1 TO Q
INPUT "ENTER FIELD 1: ";F1$
INPUT "ENTER FIELD 2: ";F2$
     :
   etc.
     :
LET F1$ = LEFT$(F1$ + B$, A1)
LET F2$ = LEFT$(F2$ + B$, A2)
     :
   etc.
     :
LET R$(I) = F1$ + F2$ + ...etc...
NEXT I
```

Example   The Yellow Stone Taxi Company wants to enter into the computer the following information for each taxi in service:

(1) The name of the driver
(2) The serial number of the taxi
(3) The age of the taxi
(4) The total distance traveled each day
(5) The amount of revenue taken in for each taxi.

The following program uses ALGORITHM V to accomplish this task:

```
100 INPUT "HOW MANY TAXIS ARE IN SERVICE? ";Q
110 DIM R$(Q)
120 FOR I = 1 TO Q
130 LET B$ = "                        "
140 INPUT "TYPE THE NAME OF THE DRIVER: ";F1$
150 INPUT "TYPE THE SERIAL NUMBER OF THE TAXI: ";F2$
160 INPUT "TYPE THE AGE OF THE TAXI: ";F3$
170 INPUT "TYPE TOTAL DISTANCE TRAVELED EACH DAY: ";F4$
180 INPUT "TYPE AMOUNT OF REVENUE TAKEN IN: ";F5$
190 LET F1$ = LEFT$(F1$ + B$,25)
200 LET F2$ = LEFT$(F2$ + B$,10)
210 LET F3$ = LEFT$(F3$ + B$,2)
220 LET F4$ = LEFT$(F4$ + B$,4)
230 LET F5$ = LEFT$(F5$ + B$,4)
240 LET R$(I) = F1$ + F2$ + F3$ + F4$ + F5$
250 NEXT I
```

EXERCISES   3. Starting after line 250, add to the program above so that it will find
10.1, contd.   the total distance traveled and the total revenue earned by all taxis.
                     Don't change anything before line 250.

4. The Snappy Shoe Co. wants to maintain their customer mailing list in the computer. For each customer, they want to store the following information:

   (1) Last Name
   (2) First Name
   (3) Street address
   (4) City
   (5) Zip code
   (6) Telephone number.

   Write a BASIC program that will do the job. Select field sizes as desired.

5. Modify Algorithm V so that the fields are right-justified.

ALGORITHM VI: BUBBLE SORTING IN ASCENDING ORDER

```
REM N IS THE NUMBER OF ITEMS TO BE SORTED
FOR K = 1 TO N-1
FOR J = 1 TO N-K
IF A(J) > A(J + 1) THEN LET L = A(J) : LET A(J)
       = A(J + 1) : LET A(J + 1) = L
NEXT J
NEXT K
```

**ALGORITHM VI-A: ALTERNATIVE VERSION OF THE BUBBLE
SORT IN ASCENDING ORDER**

```
FOR K = 1 TO N-1
FOR J = 1 TO N-K
IF A(J) <= A(J + 1) THEN GOTO line1
LET L = A(J)
LET A(J) = A(J + 1)
LET A(J + 1) = L
line1 NEXT J
NEXT K
```

**EXERCISES
10.1, contd.**

6. Write a bubble sort algorithm that will sort in descending order.

The field that a group of records is sorted along is called the key field.

**ALGORITHM VII: SORTING RECORDS IN ASCENDING ORDER
ALONG ANY KEY FIELD**

```
REM F IS THE LENGTH OF THE KEY FIELD
REM A IS THE POSITION OF THE BEGINNING OF KEY FIELD
FOR K = 1 TO N-1
FOR J = 1 TO N-K
IF MID$(R$(J),A,F) > MID$(R$(J + 1),A,F) THEN
    LET L$ = R$(J) : LET R$(J) = R$(J + 1) :
    LET R$(J + 1) = L$
NEXT J
NEXT K
```

Example   The following modification of the Yellow Stone Taxi program will permit the user to select the field on which to sort:

```
260 PRINT "1. NAME OF THE DRIVER"
270 PRINT "2. SERIAL NUMBER OF THE TAXI"
280 PRINT "3. AGE OF THE TAXI"
290 PRINT "4. TOTAL DISTANCE TRAVELED"
300 PRINT "5. REVENUE RECEIVED"
310 INPUT "SELECT BY NUMBER THE FIELD ON WHICH
        YOU WISH TO SORT ";P
320 IF P = 1 THEN LET A = 1 : LET F = 25
330 IF P = 2 THEN LET A = 26 : LET F = 10
340 IF P = 3 THEN LET A = 36 : LET F = 2
350 IF P = 4 THEN LET A = 38 : LET F = 4
360 IF P = 5 THEN LET A = 42 : LET F = 4
370 FOR K = 1 TO Q-1
380 FOR J = 1 TO Q-K
390 IF MID$(R$(J),A,F) > MID$(R$(J+1),A,F) THEN
        LET L$ = R$(J) : LET R$(J) = R$(J+1) :
        LET R$(J+1) = L$
400 NEXT J
410 NEXT K
```

If the key field is at the extreme left or extreme right of the record, the LEFT$ or RIGHT$ functions may be more convenient to use instead of the MID$ function.

Example   The following is a modification of the Yellow Stone Taxi program so that the array will be sorted along the revenue field:

```
260 REM SORTING ALONG THE RIGHTMOST FIELD
270 FOR K = 1 TO Q - 1
280 FOR J = 1 TO Q - K
290 IF RIGHT$(R$(J),4) > RIGHT$(R$(J+1),4) THEN
        LET L$ = R$(J) : LET R$(J) = R$(J+1) :
        LET R$(J+1) = L$
300 NEXT J
310 NEXT K
```

**EXERCISES
10.1, contd.**

7. Make a similar modification to the Yellow Stone Cab Company program so that the array is sorted along the name field. Use the LEFT$ function.

8. Add to the Snappy Shoe program (Exercise 10.1.4) so that the program will sort on any field selected by the user.

**ALGORITHM VIII: SEARCHING A TWO-DIMENSIONAL STRING
ARRAY ALONG ANY COLUMN**

```
REM R$(N,M) IS THE STRING ARRAY
REM S$ IS THE STRING SEARCHED FOR IN COLUMN C
LET L = 0
FOR I = 1 TO N
IF S$ = R$(I,C) THEN LET L = I : LET I = N
```

NEXT I
IF L = 0 THEN (instruction if string is not found)

Example   Professor Kawai has recorded four quiz grades for each of her N students. Each row of the two-dimensional string array G$ contains a student's last and first names (separated by a space) followed by the four quiz grades. The following program assigns the data to the array, asks the user for a student's name, searches the left-hand column of the array for the student's name, and computes and prints the student's average quiz grade.

```
100 INPUT "HOW MANY STUDENTS? ";N
110 DIM G$(N,5)
120 REM ASSIGN DATA TO ARRAY
130 FOR I = 1 TO N
140 PRINT : PRINT "STUDENT ";I
150 INPUT "ENTER NAME (LAST FIRST) ";G$(I,1)
160 FOR J = 2 TO 5
170 PRINT "ENTER QUIZ ";J-1;
180 INPUT " GRADE: ";G$(I,J)
190 NEXT J
200 NEXT I
210 REM ALGORITHM VIII
220 REM RETRIEVE DATA FROM ARRAY BY SEARCHING FOR NAME
230 PRINT
240 INPUT "TYPE STUDENT'S LAST NAME: ";L$
250 INPUT "TYPE STUDENT'S FIRST NAME: ";F$
260 LET S$ = L$ + " " + F$
270 LET L = 0
280 FOR I = 1 TO N
290 IF S$ = G$(I,1) THEN LET L = I : LET I = N
300 NEXT I
310 IF L = 0 THEN PRINT "NO SUCH NAME EXISTS" : GOTO 390
320 REM END OF ALGORITHM VIII
330 REM NOW AVERAGE THE GRADES
340 LET S = 0
350 FOR K = 2 TO 5
360 LET S = S + VAL(G$(L,K))
370 NEXT K
380 PRINT "THE AVERAGE GRADE FOR ";S$;" IS ";S/4
390 END
```

```
]RUN

HOW MANY STUDENTS? 2

STUDENT 1
ENTER NAME (LAST FIRST): MANUEL CONNIE
ENTER QUIZ 1 GRADE: 98
ENTER QUIZ 2 GRADE: 92
ENTER QUIZ 3 GRADE: 88
ENTER QUIZ 4 GRADE: 96

STUDENT 2
ENTER NAME (LAST FIRST): SARVAS ALAN
ENTER QUIZ 1 GRADE: 49
ENTER QUIZ 2 GRADE: 58
ENTER QUIZ 3 GRADE: 62
ENTER QUIZ 4 GRADE: 55
```

```
TYPE STUDENT'S LAST NAME: SARVAS
TYPE STUDENT'S FIRST NAME: ALAN
THE AVERAGE GRADE FOR SARVAS ALAN IS 56
```

EXERCISES 10.1, contd.

9. Write an algorithm that will search a two-dimensional string array along any row.

The next example incorporates ALGORITHM VIII and the algorithm you wrote for Exercise 10.1.9.

Example   Consider this table which shows the mileage between cities:

*	ROCKVILLE	HARTLAND	SOUTHVILLE
ROCKVILLE	0	679	458
HARTLAND	679	0	800
SOUTHVILLE	458	800	0

The following program will find the distance between any two cities in the table:

```
100 DATA "*","ROCKVILLE","HARTLAND","SOUTHVILLE"
110 DATA "ROCKVILLE","0","679","458"
120 DATA "HARTLAND","679","0","800"
130 DATA "SOUTHVILLE","458","800","0"
140 DIM R$(4,4)
150 FOR I = 1 TO 4
160 FOR J = 1 TO 4
170 READ R$(I,J)
175 NEXT J
178 NEXT I
180 INPUT "ENTER TOWN YOU ARE LEAVING: ";X$
190 INPUT "ENTER TOWN YOU ARE GOING TO: ";Y$
195 REM ALGORITHM VIII
198 LET L1 = 0
200 FOR I = 1 TO 4
210 IF X$ = R$(I,1) THEN LET L1 = I : LET I = 4
230 NEXT I
240 IF L1 = 0 THEN GOTO 300
245 REM ALGORITHM FROM EXERCISE 10.1.9
250 LET L2 = 0
260 FOR I = 1 TO 4
270 IF Y$ = R$(1,I) THEN LET L2 = I : LET I = 4
290 NEXT I
300 IF L2 = 0 THEN PRINT "SORRY, CITY DOES NOT EXIST" :
      GOTO 330
310 PRINT "THE DISTANCE IS ";R$(L1,L2)
330 END
```

```
JRUN

ENTER TOWN YOU ARE LEAVING: SOUTHVILLE
ENTER TOWN YOU ARE GOING TO: HARTLAND
THE DISTANCE IS 800
```

ALGORITHM IX: SEARCHING RECORDS ALONG ANY FIELD

```
REM R$( ) IS THE ARRAY CONTAINING THE RECORDS
REM A IS THE BEG. CHAR. POSITION OF THE FIELD SEARCHED
REM F IS THE LENGTH OF THE FIELD SEARCHED
REM N IS NUMBER OF RECORDS IN ARRAY
LET L = 0
FOR I = 1 TO N
IF S$ = MID$(R$(I),A,F) THEN LET L = I : LET I = N
NEXT I
IF L = 0 THEN (instruction if string is not found)
```

Example   The Rock And Roll Conservatory of Music needs a program that will

1. Create a student file (array) containing each student's name, student number, and phone number
2. Print a student's name and phone number when the student number is entered.

Here it is:

```
100 INPUT "ENTER NUMBER OF STUDENTS ";N
110 DIM R$(N)
120 LET B$ = "                    "
130 FOR I = 1 TO N
140 PRINT
150 PRINT "FOR STUDENT ";I
160 INPUT "ENTER STUDENT'S LAST NAME: ";L$
170 INPUT "ENTER STUDENT'S FIRST NAME: ";F$
180 INPUT "ENTER STUDENT NUMBER: ";M$
190 INPUT "ENTER STUDENT TELEPHONE NUMBER: ";T$
200 LET L$ = LEFT$(L$+B$,15)
210 LET F$ = LEFT$(F$+B$,10)
220 LET M$ = LEFT$(M$+B$,5)
230 LET T$ = LEFT$(T$+B$,8)
240 LET R$(I) = L$ + F$ + M$ + T$
250 NEXT I
260 PRINT
270 INPUT "ENTER STUDENT NUMBER DESIRED: ";S$
280 LET S$ = LEFT$(S$+B$,5)
290 REM BEGINNING OF ALGORITHM IX
300 LET L = 0
310 FOR I = 1 TO N
320 IF S$ = MID$(R$(I),26,5) THEN LET L = I : LET I = N
330 NEXT I
340 IF L = 0 THEN PRINT "NO SUCH STUDENT NUMBER" : GOTO 370
350 PRINT "NAME AND PHONE # ARE "
360 PRINT LEFT$(R$(L),15);" ";MID$(R$(L),16,10);
        TAB(30);MID$(R$(L),31,8)
370 END
```

```
]RUN

ENTER NUMBER OF STUDENTS: 2

FOR STUDENT 1
ENTER STUDENT'S LAST NAME: DICKINSON
```

```
ENTER STUDENT'S FIRST NAME: MIKE
ENTER STUDENT NUMBER: 12345
ENTER STUDENT'S TELEPHONE NUMBER: 555-3209


FOR STUDENT 2
ENTER STUDENT'S LAST NAME: OLMSTED
ENTER STUDENT'S FIRST NAME: SCOTT
ENTER STUDENT NUMBER: 32552
ENTER STUDENT'S TELEPHONE NUMBER: 555-2255


ENTER STUDENT NUMBER DESIRED: 12345
NAME AND PHONE # ARE
DICKINSON          MIKE              555-3209
```

**EXERCISES
10.1, contd.**

10. Modify the above program so that it will print a student's record by searching the telephone field.

10.2 Modules and programs

Writing a program is much like writing an essay or a book. The first thing to do is to write down in outline form what the program is to do. Order the items in your outline so that they fall into a logical progression. It shouldn't take you long to find some natural divisions in the outline which group certain related tasks together. We call each division a MODULE. The modules themselves are collections of one or more algorithms.

A good program is a consequence of a good MODULE OUTLINE, which is an ordered list of all of the modules which comprise the program. In the examples which follow, we will show you the module outline and then the actual modules written in Applesoft BASIC.

Example   Good Health Hospital needs a program that will keep records of its patients. Their requirements break down into three modules.

MODULE OUTLINE

I. ENTER THE INFORMATION ABOUT INCOMING PATIENTS.
II. SORT THE ARRAY ON THE PATIENTS' LAST NAMES.
III. PRINT A LIST OF PATIENT NAMES.
IV. SEARCH FOR PATIENT INFORMATION BY LAST NAME.

The program follows. Notice that three of the four modules are algorithms found in Section 10.1.

```
100 REM MODULE I (ALGORITHM V)
110 INPUT "HOW MANY PATIENTS ARE YOU ENTERING? ";N
120 DIM R$(N)
130 LET B$ = "                     "
140 FOR I = 1 TO N
150 PRINT
160 PRINT "FOR PATIENT ";I
170 INPUT "ENTER PATIENT'S LAST NAME: ";L$
180 INPUT "ENTER FIRST NAME: ";F$
190 INPUT "ENTER ADDRESS: ";A$
200 INPUT "ENTER HOME PHONE NUMBER: ";P$
210 INPUT "ENTER HOSPITAL ROOM ASSIGNED: ";K$
220 LET L$ = LEFT$(L$+B$,15)
```

MODULE I

```
230 LET F$ = LEFT$(F$ + B$,10)
240 LET A$ = LEFT$(A$ + B$,30)
250 LET P$ = LEFT$(P$ + B$,7)
260 LET K$ = LEFT$(K$ + B$,3)
270 LET R$(I) = L$ + F$ + A$ + P$ + K$
280 NEXT I
290 REM
300 REM MODULE II (ALGORITHM VII)
310 FOR K = 1 TO N-1
320 FOR J = 1 TO N-K
330 IF LEFT$(R$(J),15) > LEFT$(R$(J + 1),15) THEN
        LET L$ = R$(J): LET R$(J) = R$(J + 1):LET R$(J + 1) = L$
340 NEXT J
350 NEXT K
360 REM
370 REM MODULE III
380 PRINT "HERE IS A LIST OF PATIENT NAMES"
390 FOR I = 1 TO N
400 PRINT LEFT$(R$(I),15);", ";MID$(R$(I),16,10)
410 NEXT I
420 REM
430 REM MODULE IV (ALGORITHM IX)
440 PRINT
450 INPUT "ENTER LAST NAME OF PATIENT SOUGHT: ";N$
460 LET N$ = LEFT$(N$ + B$,15)
470 LET L = 0
480 FOR I = 1 TO N
490 IF N$ = LEFT$(R$(I),15) THEN LET L = I : LET I = N
500 NEXT I
510 IF L = 0 THEN PRINT "SORRY, PATIENT NOT LISTED" :
        GOTO 530
520 PRINT R$(L)
530 END
```

Example   The Shady Lane Retirement Community needs a BASIC program which computes and prints the average age of all residents, prints the names and ages of all residents sorted by last name, and prints an asterisk next to those ages which exceed the average.

MODULE OUTLINE

    I. READ THE DATA.
   II. COMPUTE AND PRINT THE AVERAGE AGE.
  III. MARK ALL RESIDENTS WHOSE AGE EXCEEDS THE AVERAGE.
   IV. SORT THE DATA ON THE LAST NAMES.
    V. PRINT THE SORTED TABLE.

We now write each module separately.

MODULE I

```
10 REM MODULE I - READ THE DATA
15 REM N IS THE NUMBER OF RESIDENTS
18 READ N
```

```
20 DIM T$(N)
30 LET B$ = "                    "
40 FOR I = 1 TO N
43 REM READ LAST NAME, FIRST NAME, AGE
45 READ L$,F$,A$
50 LET L$ = LEFT$(L$ + B$,15)
55 LET F$ = LEFT$(F$ + B$,10)
60 LET A$ = RIGHT$(B$ + A$,3)
70 LET T$(I) = L$ + F$ + A$
80 NEXT I
85 REM NUMBER OF RESIDENTS IN LINE 90
90 DATA 53
95 REM RESIDENTS NAMES AND AGES FOLLOW
100 DATA "SHENT","ANN","92","DEARLY","L.",72
105 DATA "OALD","CHIAM",104,"VAN WINKLE","RIP",119
110 (more data...)
120 REM END OF MODULE I
```

EXPLANATION OF MODULE I

Each cell in the string array T$ contains one record of information. The record has three fixed fields: the last name (fifteen characters), the first name (ten characters), and the age (three characters). The age has been right-justified in its field as all numeric data should be.

EXERCISES 10.2	1. Identify the algorithm from Section 10.1 which is similiar to this Module I, except that data is entered from the keyboard.

MODULE II

```
130 REM MODULE II - COMPUTE AND PRINT THE AVERAGE AGE
135 LET S = 0
140 FOR I = 1 TO N
160 LET S = S + VAL(RIGHT$(T$(I),3))
170 NEXT I
180 LET A = S/N
190 PRINT "THE AVERAGE AGE OF ALL RESIDENTS IS ";A
200 REM END OF MODULE II
```

EXPLANATION OF MODULE II

Here we sum all ages and divide by N, the number of residents. The VAL function in line 160 changes the age from a string into a number so that it may be added to S. See Chapter 2 for more information about the VAL function.

EXERCISES 10.2, contd.	2. Identify the algorithm from Section 10.1 which is used in Module II.

MODULE III

```
210 REM MODULE III - MARK ALL RESIDENTS WHOSE AGE EXCEEDS
220 REM THE AVERAGE WITH AN ASTERISK
```

```
230 FOR I = 1 TO N
240 IF (VAL(RIGHT$(T$(I),3)) > A) THEN LET T$(I) = T$(I) + " *"
250 NEXT I
260 REM END OF MODULE III
```

EXPLANATION OF MODULE III

In itself, this module is a search algorithm. The loop looks again at the ages, this time comparing them to the average age A. To "mark" an age which exceeds the average, we just concatenate an asterisk to the record.

MODULE IV

```
270 REM MODULE IV - SORT THE DATA ON THE LAST NAME
280 FOR I = 1 TO N-1
290 FOR J = 1 TO N-I
310 IF LEFT$(T$(J),15)<=LEFT$(T$(J+1),15) THEN GOTO 350
320 LET X$ = T$(J)
330 LET T$(J) = T$(J+1)
340 LET T$(J+1) = X$
350 NEXT J
360 NEXT I
370 REM END OF MODULE IV
```

EXPLANATION OF MODULE IV

This is the alternate version of the bubble sort (ALGORITHM VI-A) which we saw in Section 10.1. We are using the alternate version just for the sake of variety.

MODULE V

```
380 REM MODULE V - PRINT SORTED TABLE
390 REM PRINT A HEADER FOR THE REPORT
400 PRINT "LAST NAME";TAB(15);"FIRST NAME";TAB(35);"AGE"
410 FOR I = 1 TO N
420 PRINT LEFT$(T$(I),15);TAB(17);MID$(T$(I),16,10);
        TAB(35);MID$(T$(I),26)
430 NEXT I
440 REM END OF MODULE V
450 REM AND END OF PROGRAM!
460 END
```

EXPLANATION OF MODULE V

In printing the age field, we chose to use the MID$ function instead of the RIGHT$ function. This is because some of the records were made longer than others when the asterisk was concatenated. We can retrieve everything from the twenty-sixth character position to the end of the string by using MID$(T$(I),26).

**EXERCISES
10.2, contd.**

3. Write a program for Shady Lane that will print two lists of all residents, one sorted on the age field and another sorted on the first name field.

4. Write a program for Shady Lane to print a report that is sorted on the age field. Within the same report, alphabetize by last name all people who have the same age. Hint: From each record, extract the age and last name fields. Concatenate them together with the age first. Sort on this new "hybrid" field.

5. Mrs. Smith has a rather extensive personal library. Write a program for her which follows this module outline.

   I. Create a record for each book consisting of these fields:

      (a) Author's last name
      (b) Author's first name
      (c) Title of book
      (d) Publishing company
      (e) Price paid.

   II. Print two reports, one sorted by last name and the other by title.

   III. Print all records of books whose prices are less than X amount, where X is assigned with an INPUT statement.

Example   The Daytime Soap Opera Times magazine accepts classified advertising at the rate of $55.00 per line, where a line constitutes 35 characters and spaces. A portion of a line is charged the same as a full line. A BASIC program is to be written that will compute the total charges for a given classified advertisement.

For example, if the ad contains 87 characters and spaces, the number of lines would be computed as follows:

87 divided by 35 is 2 with a remainder of 17

Since the partial line is charged at the full rate, the number of lines used would be three. The charge is $55 times 3, or $165.

The following outline will be used to write the BASIC program.

MODULE OUTLINE

   I. ENTER THE ADVERTISEMENT.
   II. FIND THE NUMBER OF CHARACTERS AND SPACES IN THE AD.
   III. FIND THE NUMBER OF LINES AND THE TOTAL COST.
   IV. PRINT THE AD, THE NUMBER OF LINES, AND THE TOTAL COST.

The program follows.

```
10 REM DAYTIME SOAP OPERA TIMES ADVERTISEMENT COSTS
15 REM
20 REM VARIABLE TABLE
30 REM X$ IS THE ADVERTISEMENT
40 REM L IS THE NUMBER OF CHARACTERS IN AD
50 REM N IS THE NUMBER OF COMPLETE LINES IN AD
60 REM S IS THE NUMBER OF LINES THAT COST IS BASED ON
70 REM C IS THE TOTAL COST OF THE ADVERTISEMENT
80 REM
100 REM MODULE I - ENTER ADVERTISMENT
```

```
110 PRINT "ENTER THE AD. NO COMMAS OR COLONS!"
120 INPUT X$
125 REM END OF MODULE I
128 REM
130 REM MODULE II - COUNT THE NUMBER OF CHARACTERS AND
140 REM SPACES IN THE AD
150 LET L = LEN(X$)
155 REM END OF MODULE II
158 REM
160 REM MODULE III - FIND THE NUMBER OF LINES
165 REM AND TOTAL COST
170 LET N = INT(L/35)
180 IF L = 35*N THEN LET S = N
185 IF L>35*N THEN LET S = N + 1
190 LET C = 55*S
195 REM END OF MODULE III
198 REM
200 REM MODULE IV - PRINT AD, NUMBER OF LINES, AND COST
210 PRINT
220 PRINT "THE NUMBER OF LINES IS ";S
230 PRINT "THE PRICE OF THE ADVERTISEMENT IS  $";C
240 PRINT "THE AD READS: " : PRINT
250 FOR I = 1 TO S
260 PRINT MID$(X$,35*I-34,35)
270 NEXT I
280 REM END OF MODULE IV
290 END
```

```
]RUN

ENTER THE AD.  NO COMMAS OR COLONS!
?PERSONAL COMPUTER FOR SALE -- $2000 OR
BEST OFFER.  INCLUDES DISK DRIVE AND MON
ITOR.  CALL 555-2388 AFTER 6 PM.

THE NUMBER OF LINES IS 4
THE PRICE OF THE ADVERTISEMENT IS $220
THE AD READS:

PERSONAL COMPUTER FOR SALE -- $2000
 OR BEST OFFER.  INCLUDES DISK DRIV
E AND MONITOR.  CALL 555-2388 AFTER
 6 PM.
```

**EXERCISES
10.2, contd.**

6. Modify the program so that if the length of the last line is less than one-half of a full line, then only $28.00 is charged for the last line; otherwise the total price of $55.00 is charged.

7. Assume that the magazine has a pricing policy that if the number of lines exceeds four, then the cost per line exceeding four is $45.00. Modify the OUTLINE above and the BASIC program to compute the total cost.

Let us assume that the magazine changes its pricing policy for classified advertising by only charging for characters that are not spaces in the copy of the ad. This change in pricing would require us to change Module II. The module would be changed to read

II. COUNT THE NUMBER OF NONSPACE CHARACTERS IN THE AD
Unfortunately, the function LEN(X$) counts spaces as well. Hence, we will have to modify Module II in such a way that we count the number of nonspace characters. The following modification will do the job:

```
130 REM MODULE II - COUNT THE # OF NON-SPACE CHARACTERS
132 LET L=0
135 FOR I = 1 TO LEN(X$)
140 IF MID$(X$,I,1)<>" " THEN LET L=L+1
145 NEXT I
150 END OF MODULE II
```

NOTE THAT NO OTHER CHANGES HAVE TO BE MADE IN THE PROGRAM! This demonstrates the power of modular programming.

10.3 The GOSUB and RETURN statements and subroutines

Now and then it is necessary in a program to use the same procedure more than once. Notice that in the next example, Modules II, III, and IV are essentially the same.

Example   Mr. Clark, a salesman for a local computer firm, frequently travels between three cities. On his last trip he went from Hartland to Rockville, Rockville to Southville, and Southville to Hartland. Here is a module outline which will find the total distance traveled.

MODULE OUTLINE

I. STORE THE DISTANCES BETWEEN THE CITIES IN A TWO-DIMENSIONAL ARRAY.
II. FIND THE DISTANCE BETWEEN HARTLAND AND ROCKVILLE.
III. FIND THE DISTANCE BETWEEN ROCKVILLE AND SOUTHVILLE.
IV. FIND THE DISTANCE BETWEEN SOUTHVILLE AND HARTLAND.
V. SUM THE DISTANCES AND PRINT THE ANSWER.

As you study the program which was written from this module outline, notice the similarity of Modules II, III, and IV.

```
     ┌─ 100 REM MODULE I - STORE DATA
M    │  110 DATA "*","ROCKVILLE","HARTLAND","SOUTHVILLE"
O    │  120 DATA "ROCKVILLE","0","679","458"
D    │  130 DATA "HARTLAND","679","0","800"
U    │  140 DATA "SOUTHVILLE","458","800","0"
L    │  150 DIM R$(4,4)
E    │  160 FOR I = 1 TO 4
     │  170 FOR J = 1 TO 4
     │  180 READ R$(I,J)
     │  190 NEXT J
I    └─ 200 NEXT I
        210 REM
     ┌─ 220 REM MODULE II - HARTLAND TO ROCKVILLE
```

```
      230 LET X$ = "HARTLAND"
      240 LET Y$ = "ROCKVILLE"
      250 FOR I = 1 TO 4
 II   260 IF X$ = R$(I,1) THEN LET L1 = I
      270 NEXT I
      280 FOR I = 1 TO 4
      290 IF Y$ = R$(1,I) THEN LET L2 = I
      300 NEXT I
    └ 310 LET D1 = VAL(R$(L1,L2))
      320 REM
    ┌ 330 REM MODULE III - ROCKVILLE TO SOUTHVILLE
      340 LET X$ = "ROCKVILLE"
      350 LET Y$ = "SOUTHVILLE"
      360 FOR I = 1 TO 4
 III  370 IF X$ = R$(I,1) THEN LET L1 = I
      380 NEXT I
      390 FOR I = 1 TO 4
      400 IF Y$ = R$(1,I) THEN LET L2 = I
      410 NEXT I
    └ 420 LET D2 = VAL(R$(L1,L2))
      430 REM
    ┌ 440 REM MODULE IV - SOUTHVILLE TO HARTLAND
      450 LET X$ = "SOUTHVILLE"
      460 LET Y$ = "HARTLAND"
      470 FOR I = 1 TO 4
      480 IF X$ = R$(I,1) THEN LET L1 = I
 IV   490 NEXT I
      500 FOR I = 1 TO 4
      510 IF Y$ = R$(1,I) THEN LET L2 = I
      520 NEXT I
    └ 530 LET D3 = VAL(R$(L1,L2))
      540 REM
 V    550 PRINT "TOTAL DISTANCE TRAVELED WAS ";D1+D2+D3
      560 END
```

The algorithm at lines 250 through 300 appears again at lines 360 through 410 and then again at lines 470 through 520. We could have written the algorithm just once and reused it by branching back and forth. But soon the program would be a tangled mess of GOTO statements.

The GOSUB and RETURN statements solve this problem.

The GOSUB statement is somewhat similiar to the GOTO statement in that they both cause an unconditional branch to a given line number. For instance, the statement

100 GOSUB 340

will cause a branch to line 340 in the program. The big difference between GOSUB and GOTO is that GOSUB is always used in connection with a RETURN statement. When RETURN is encountered, the computer branches back to the original GOSUB statement and processing continues with the next statement. The program has made a kind of "round trip." The set of instructions (or module) which contains the RETURN statement is called a SUBROUTINE. This diagram should help clarify:

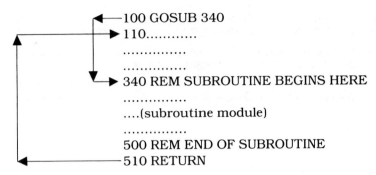

When line 100 is executed, the program branches to the subroutine at line 340. The arrows show that the RETURN statement sends control back to line 110, the line following the GOSUB statement. (If line 100 had had multiple statements separated by colons, the RETURN would have sent control back to the STATEMENT on line 100 just following GOSUB 340.)

We now rewrite the traveling salesman program above, using a subroutine to compute the distance between any two cities.

```
100 REM MODULE I - STORE DATA
110 DATA "*","ROCKVILLE","HARTLAND","SOUTHVILLE"
120 DATA "ROCKVILLE","0","679","458"
130 DATA "HARTLAND","679","0","800"
140 DATA "SOUTHVILLE","458","800","0"
150 DIM R$(4,4)
160 FOR I = 1 TO 4
170 FOR J = 1 TO 4
180 READ R$(I,J)
190 NEXT J
200 NEXT I
210 REM
220 REM MODULE II - HARTLAND TO ROCKVILLE
230 LET X$ = "HARTLAND"
240 LET Y$ = "ROCKVILLE"
250 GOSUB 500
260 LET D1 = D
270 REM
280 REM MODULE III - ROCKVILLE TO SOUTHVILLE
290 LET X$ = "ROCKVILLE"
300 LET Y$ = "SOUTHVILLE"
310 GOSUB 500
320 LET D2 = D
330 REM
340 REM MODULE IV - SOUTHVILLE TO HARTLAND
350 LET X$ = "SOUTHVILLE"
360 LET Y$ = "HARTLAND"
370 GOSUB 500
380 LET D3 = D
390 REM
400 PRINT "THE TOTAL DISTANCE TRAVELED WAS ";D1+D2+D3
410 GOTO 590
```

MODULE I

II

III

IV

V

```
S   ┌─ 500 REM SUBROUTINE MODULE
U   │  510 FOR I = 1 TO 4
B   │  520 IF X$ = R$(1,I) THEN LET L1 = I
R   │  530 NEXT I
O   │  540 FOR I = 1 TO 4
U   │  550 IF Y$ = R$(I,1) THEN LET L2 = I
T   │  560 NEXT I
I   │  570 LET D = VAL(R$(L1,L2))
N   └─ 580 RETURN
E      585 REM
       590 END
```

```
]RUN

TOTAL DISTANCE TRAVELED WAS 1937
```

Caution:

The ONLY way into a subroutine should be by a branch from a GOSUB statement. Line 410 in the program above is used to avoid "falling" into the subroutine. Without line 410 a "RETURN WITHOUT GOSUB" error would occur when line 580 is reached, and the program would bomb (computerese for "stopping with an error").

Example   A program is needed for the Shady Lane Retirement Community that will produce two reports: one is a list of the residents sorted by last name, and the other is a list sorted by age. We will follow this module outline:

MODULE OUTLINE

    I. ENTER RESIDENTS' NAMES AND AGES INTO AN ARRAY.
   II. SORT THE ARRAY ON THE LAST NAME FIELD.
 III. PRINT A REPORT.
 IV. SORT THE ARRAY ON THE AGE FIELD.
  V. PRINT A REPORT.

The tasks of sorting and printing a report will be written as subroutines.

```
100 REM MODULE I - ASSIGN NAMES AND AGES
110 INPUT "HOW MANY RESIDENTS? ";N
120 DIM R$(N)
130 LET B$ = "                "
140 FOR I = 1 TO N
145 PRINT
150 PRINT "FOR RESIDENT #";I
160 INPUT "ENTER LAST NAME: ";L$
170 INPUT "ENTER FIRST NAME: ";F$
180 INPUT "ENTER AGE: ";A$
190 LET R$(I) = LEFT$(L$+B$,15) + LEFT$(F$+B$,10) +
        RIGHT$(B$+A$,3)
200 NEXT I
210 REM
220 REM MODULE II - SORT BY LAST NAME
230 LET K = 1
```

```
240 LET Q = 15
250 GOSUB 1000
255 REM
260 REM MODULE III - PRINT REPORT
265 PRINT : PRINT "SORTED BY LAST NAME"
270 GOSUB 2000
280 REM
290 REM MODULE IV - SORT BY AGE
300 LET K = 26
310 LET Q = 3
320 GOSUB 1000
330 REM
340 REM MODULE V - PRINT REPORT
345 PRINT : PRINT "SORTED BY AGE"
350 GOSUB 2000
360 REM
370 GOTO 9999
380 REM
1000 REM SUBROUTINE TO SORT ON ANY FIELD
1010 FOR I = 1 TO N-1
1020 FOR J = 1 TO N-I
1030 IF MID$(R$(J),K,Q) > MID$(R$(J + 1),K,Q) THEN
        LET L$ = R$(J) : LET R$(J) = R$(J + 1) : LET R$(J + 1) = L$
1040 NEXT J
1050 NEXT I
1060 RETURN
1070 REM
2000 REM SUBROUTINE TO PRINT REPORT
2005 PRINT
2010 PRINT "LAST NAME"; TAB(16); "FIRST NAME";
            TAB(30);"AGE"
2020 FOR I = 1 TO N
2030 PRINT LEFT$(R$(I),15); MID$(R$(I),16,10);
            TAB(30);RIGHT$(R$(I),3)
2040 NEXT I
2050 RETURN
2060 REM
9999 END
```

```
]RUN
HOW MANY RESIDENTS? 3

FOR RESIDENT #1
ENTER LAST NAME: SHENT
ENTER FIRST NAME: ANN
ENTER AGE: 92

FOR RESIDENT #2
ENTER LAST NAME: DEARLY
ENTER FIRST NAME: L.
ENTER AGE: 72

FOR RESIDENT #3
ENTER LAST NAME: OALD
ENTER FIRST NAME: CHIAM
ENTER AGE: 104
```

```
SORTED BY LAST NAME

LAST NAME      FIRST NAME       AGE
DEARLY         L.                72
OALD           CHIAM            104
SHENT          ANN               92

SORTED BY AGE

LAST NAME      FIRST NAME       AGE
DEARLY         L.                72
SHENT          ANN               92
OALD           CHIAM            104
```

EXERCISE   1. Modify the program so that sorting is done on the full name, last and
10.3   first combined.

10.4 ON-GOTO, ON-GOSUB, and the menu

When the IF-THEN statement is combined with a branching statement, as in IF-THEN GOTO or IF-THEN GOSUB, we create a statement known as a "conditional" branch. Conditional branching is also done by the ON-GOTO and ON-GOSUB statements.

This sequence of IF-THEN GOTO statements sends control to various places in the program depending on the value of K:

100 IF K = 1 THEN GOTO 250
110 IF K = 2 THEN GOTO 500
120 IF K = 3 THEN GOTO 355
130 IF K = 4 THEN GOTO 999

The purpose of the ON-GOTO statement is to condense the above statements into one, as follows:

100 ON K GOTO 250, 500, 355, 999

The value of K determines where the program is to GOTO. If K is one, then control passes to the line 250, which is listed first. If K is two, then control passes to line 500, which is the second line number listed, and so on. We say that K acts as an index to the line numbers in the list. If K is less than one or greater than the number of line numbers listed, then control passes to the statement which follows the ON-GOTO statement.

The ON-GOSUB statement behaves similarly, except that control passes to a subroutine. The RETURN statement in the subroutine will send the program back to the line just following the ON-GOSUB statement.

The real value of the ON-GOSUB statement is in the use of "menus." We say that a program is "menu-driven" if the various functions that the program performs may be selected by the user from a list of options. The list is called the menu. The next example shows a menu-driven program.

Example   Green Bay College needs a program that is described by the following module outline:

      I. STORE IN AN ARRAY THE STUDENT NUMBER, LAST NAME, FIRST NAME, AND AGE OF EACH STUDENT.

II. SEARCH THE FILE BY STUDENT NUMBER.
III. SEARCH THE FILE BY LAST NAME.

M
E   10 REM LINES 20 TO 80 COMPRISE THE MENU
N   20 PRINT "1. STORE STUDENT INFORMATION"
U   30 PRINT "2. SEARCH BY STUDENT NUMBER"
      40 PRINT "3. SEARCH BY LAST NAME"
      50 PRINT "4. QUIT"
      60 INPUT "ENTER NUMBER DESIRED: ";K
      70 ON K GOSUB 90,190,260,330
      80 GOTO 10
      85 REM
      90 REM MODULE I - STORE STUDENT DATA
      100 INPUT "HOW MANY STUDENTS ARE YOU ENTERING? ";N
M   110 DIM S$(N,4)
O   120 FOR I = 1 TO N
D   130 INPUT "STUDENT NUMBER ";S$(I,1)
U   140 INPUT "STUDENT LAST NAME ";S$(I,2)
L   150 INPUT "STUDENT FIRST NAME ";S$(I,3)
E   160 INPUT "STUDENT AGE ";S$(I,4)
      170 NEXT I
I   180 RETURN
      185 REM
      190 REM MODULE II SEARCH BY STUDENT NUMBER
      200 INPUT "ENTER A STUDENT NUMBER: ";Q$
      205 LET L = 0
      210 FOR I = 1 TO N
II   220 IF Q$ = S$(I,1) THEN LET L = I
      230 NEXT I
      235 IF L <> 0 THEN PRINT S$(L,1), S$(L,2), S$(L,3),
          S$(L,4)
      240 RETURN
      250 REM
      260 REM MODULE III - SEARCH BY LAST NAME
      270 INPUT "ENTER STUDENT'S LAST NAME: ";Q$
      275 LET L = 0
III   280 FOR I = 1 TO N
      290 IF Q$ = S$(I,2) THEN LET L = I
      300 NEXT I
      310 IF L <> 0 THEN PRINT S$(L,1), S$(L,2), S$(L,3),
          S$(L ,4)
      320 RETURN
      330 END

Notice that each RETURN statement sends control back to line 80, which
then branches to line 10, the beginning of the menu.

**EXERCISES
10.4**

1. Note that Modules II and III are essentially the same and both can be
    replaced with a subroutine. Revise the above program so that one
    module subroutine will handle both of the searches.

2. This program has a serious defect in that if several students have the
    same last name, only the first one found will be printed. Modify the
    program so that if several students' last names match the search key,
    then all of their records will be printed.

10.5 Top-down programming

Modular programming is a simple yet powerful way of adding structure to your BASIC programs. But even programs built on modules can be messy if care is not taken to order them in a logical fashion. We advocate an arrangement in which control flows smoothly from the top module down. This is a style known as Top-Down Programming. The following is a summary of a few basic tenets of Top-Down Programming:

1. Move from the first module or the menu straight down.
2. Skipping one or more modules on the way down is acceptable.
3. The flow of the program should be downward. As much as possible, avoid moving up to a module (with the exception of the menu).
4. Each module should have only one entry and one exit point. The entry point should be the first line of the module, and the exit should be the last. This will force the flow to be from top to bottom.
5. Use of the GOTO statement should be kept to a minimum. Excessive branching in any program is frowned upon. Some programming languages are designed to have no need of a GOTO statement, but BASIC is not so lucky. While it may not be possible to write a "GOTO-less" program in BASIC, we encourage you to keep the following in mind:

   GENERALLY SPEAKING, GOTO STATEMENTS MAKE A PROGRAM HARDER TO READ, HARDER TO UNDERSTAND, AND HARDER TO DEBUG. THEY SHOULD BE USED AS A LAST RESORT, WHEN NO OTHER BASIC STATEMENTS WILL DO.

Excessive use of the GOTO statement will create a condition known in the industry as "spaghetti code" or pure pasta!

10.6 Documentation

There are two very compelling reasons for documenting programs. First, although you may know every infinite detail about your program today, it's a sure bet that your memory will be a little less sharp a year from now. For your own use, EVEN IF YOUR MEMORY RIVALS BORNSTEIN, document your programs! Secondly, other programmers may have reason to look at your programs. This is definitely true in businesses, where application programs may need updating, but the programmer has long since left the company. But again, even if you think no one will ever look...document that program!

Okay, now that we've driven the point home, the question still remains, "How much should you say"? It is never necessary to comment on the obvious. But, of course, what is obvious is very subjective. As a rule, we find two areas of documentation very helpful. The first is a variable table which lists all the variables in your program and provides a brief description of their purpose. Secondly, we suggest that REMarks should be used to denote the beginning of a program module, and to provide a brief description of what task it performs.

Example of Documentation

```
100 REM PROGRAM TO COMPUTE PROFIT
110 REM C = COMMISSION ON SALES
120 REM S = GROSS SALES
```

```
130 REM P = NET PROFIT
140 REM MODULE I - ASSIGN DATA
      ..........................
      ..........................
200 REM MODULE II - COMPUTE PROFIT
      ..........................
      ..........................
500 REM MODULE III - COMMISSION ON SALES
      ..........................
      ..........................
800 REM MODULE IV - GROSS SALES
      ..........................
      ..........................
1000 REM MODULE V - NET PROFIT
      ..........................
      ..........................
1300 END
```

10.7 Projects

1. Ms. Smith, a teacher of biology, needs to figure out the grades for each of the students in her class. Her grades are based on the following point system:

85 - 100	A
70 - 84	B
55 - 69	C
40 - 54	D
0 - 39	F

Ms. Smith uses the following procedure to compute the final grades:

1. Sum the individual quizzes
2. Add this sum to two times the score on the final
3. Divide the sum in (2) by the number of exams plus one.

Write a menu-driven program that:

1. Stores each of the students' quizzes and final exams
2. Computes the total scores and final grades
3. Does an alphabetic sort on the last names
4. Does a sort on the final letter grade
5. Prints all students whose grades are a specific letter
6. Prints all students whose grades are higher or lower than a specified grade

2. The telephone company needs a program that performs the following tasks:

1. Stores the name, address, and telephone number of each resident.
2. Sorts records by:
    (a) telephone number

(b) last name
(c) zip code
and prints the sorted records.
3. Given any portion of the last name the program selects all residents who match, and prints their records.

3. Write a program for the Golden House Realty Co. that will do the following:

1. Stores information on the location, number of bedrooms, square footage, and price of the houses that it is selling
2. Sorts on any chosen field
3. Prints the sorted table.

LAB 10-1 GOSUB/RETURN

Type in the command: NEW

The GOSUB and RETURN statements are used to form a subroutine.

Type in the program: 10 GOSUB 40
20 PRINT "LINE NUMBER 20"
30 GOTO 60
40 PRINT "LINE NUMBER 40"
50 RETURN
60 END

Line numbers 40 and 50 form a subroutine. The first line number of the subroutine is the line number given in the GOSUB statement. The last line number in the subroutine is the RETURN statement.

Type in the command: RUN

What is the output of the program? _____

_____

The statement 10 GOSUB 40 causes a branch to line number 40. The statement 50 RETURN causes a branch back to line number 20.

List the line numbers in the order in which they are executed.

_____

The order in which the statements are executed is : 10, 40, 50, 20, 30, and 60. Line number 10 is executed first. Then the program branches to line number 40. The execution of line number 50 sends control back to line number 20.

The RETURN statement causes a branch to the statement following the last GOSUB executed.

When a GOSUB statement is executed, BASIC puts the line number of the GOSUB statement in a special list, called a stack. A RETURN statement causes a branch to the last line number listed in the stack, and that line number is erased from the list. Every executed RETURN statement erases a line number from the stack. Thus, a GOSUB statement must be executed prior to the execution of a RETURN statement.

Type in the statement: 30 PRINT "LINE NUMBER 30"

Type in the commands: LIST
                           RUN

Why did the computer print an error?

_____

_____

_____

When the computer executed 50 RETURN for the second time, the stack was empty. To avoid accidently "falling" into a subroutine and thus causing an error, separate your subroutines from the main program. Do this by ending the main program with a branch to the end (as in 30 GOTO 60), or simply use an END statement (as in 30 END).

Explain why subroutines are needed in a program.

_____

_____

_____

_____

Sometimes a particular set of statements must be executed a number of different times within a program. Subroutines let you organize a program such that only one set of statements needs to be written.

LAB 10-2 The ON-GOTO and ON-GOSUB statements

Type in the command: NEW

The ON-GOTO and ON-GOSUB are multi-branch conditional transfer statements.

The argument following the ON can be an arithmetic expression or a numeric variable. The line numbers listed following the GOTO or GOSUB must be separated by a comma. For example:

ON X GOTO 110,230,80

ON K + 7 GOSUB 430,220,550

Type in the program: 10 INPUT "TYPE IN NUMBER: ";K
                          20 ON K GOTO 40,60,80
                          30 END
                          40 PRINT "LINE NUMBER 40"
                          50 GOTO 10
                          60 PRINT "LINE NUMBER 60"
                          70 GOTO 10
                          80 PRINT "LINE NUMBER 80"
                          90 GOTO 10

Type in the command: RUN

Type in the number: 1

What is the output of the program? _____

>After K was assigned the value 1, execution of line number 20 transferred the control to line number 40.

Type in the number: 2

What is the output of the program? _____

>After K was assigned the value 2, the control was transferred to line number 60.

Type in the number: 3

What is the output of the program? _____

To which line number did the program branch when line 20 was executed? _____

>The answer is line number 80.

What is the relationship between the value assigned to K and the line numbers listed after the GOTO?

_____

_____

_____

>If K is assigned 1, transfer is to the first line number listed. If K is assigned 2, transfer is to the second listed number, and so forth. The variable K is an "index" to the list of line numbers.

Type in the number: 1.7

What is the output of the program? _____

>Note that the output is LINE NUMBER 40. This is because the value of K is truncated to the integer of the number, in this case the integer 1.

What would the output be if the number 3.5 were typed in? _____

Type in the number: 3.5

What is the output of the program? _____

Explain why LINE NUMBER 80 was printed? _____

_____

_____

>The number 3.5 is truncated to the integer 3. Thus, the program transferred to the third line number following the GOTO.

>Whenever the argument following the ON is equal to zero or is larger than the number of line numbers listed after the GOTO or GOSUB, the program

transfers to the next statement following the ON-GOTO or ON-GOSUB statement.

Type in the number: 6

Explain why the program ended. _____

_____

_____

The program ended at line number 30. Since there are only three line numbers listed after the GOTO, and K was assigned 6, control passed to the next line number.

Type in the command: RUN

Type in the number: −2

What is the computer's response? _____

The index variable following the ON must be positive.

Type in the command: NEW

Type in the program:
```
10 HOME
20 PRINT "0. SUM OF 1-100"
30 PRINT "1. SUM OF EVEN NUMBERS 2-100"
40 PRINT "2. SUM OF ODD NUMBERS 1-99"
50 PRINT "3. QUIT"
60 PRINT
70 INPUT "TYPE IN MENU NUMBER: ";X
80 ON X + 1 GOSUB 110,140,170,200
90 INPUT "PRESS RETURN KEY TO CONTINUE: ";X$
100 GOTO 10
110 REM SUBROUTINE SUM 1-100
120 PRINT "SUM 1-100 IS ";5050
130 RETURN
140 REM SUBROUTINE SUM OF EVEN NUMBERS
150 PRINT "SUM OF EVEN NUMBERS 2-100 IS ";2550
160 RETURN
170 REM SUBROUTINE SUM OF ODD NUMBERS
180 PRINT "SUM OF ODD NUMBERS 1-99 IS ";2500
190 RETURN
200 END
```

Type in the command: RUN

Select one of the menu numbers and type it in. Explain why line number 90 is important?

_____

_____

The best way to explain the importance of line number 90 is to remove it from the program and RUN the program again.

Explain why in line number 80, the argument following the ON is X + 1?

_____

_____

Since the program prompts the user to select a number from 0 to 3, the numeric expression X + 1 will correctly index the four line numbers listed after the GOSUB.

Care must be taken whenever an arithmetic expression follows the ON. The arithmetic expression must generate a non negative number, or else an error will result.

11

Sequential File Processing

11.0 Introduction

The computer's primary memory is volatile; that is, data is lost when the power to the computer is turned off. There are many applications in which data must be permanently stored to be used at a later date or by another program. To permanently store data, nonvolatile storage devices are used, such as disks or magnetic tape. This chapter is an introduction to the storage of data on a diskette. Before reading on, it would be a good idea to first review Section 9.3 on fields and records.

11.1 Writing records to a sequential file

RULES FOR WRITING RECORDS TO A SEQUENTIAL FILE

1. Open the file
2. Advise the computer that it is about to write to a file
3. Actually write records to the file
4. Close the file.

The following algorithm transforms these rules into BASIC.

ALGORITHM X - WRITING RECORDS TO A FILE ON DISK

```
REM T$(I) ARE THE RECORDS THAT WILL BE SENT TO DISK
PRINT CHR$(4);"OPEN filename"
PRINT CHR$(4); "WRITE filename"
FOR I = 1 TO N
PRINT T$(I)
NEXT I
PRINT CHR$(4); "CLOSE filename"
```

EXPLANATION OF ALGORITHM X

PRINT CHR$(4);"OPEN filename"

The CHR$(4) is a special code that when used with a PRINT statement will direct commands to the Disk Operating System (DOS). OPEN filename is a command to DOS to open a disk file with the given name (Rule 1). If no file by that name exists, the file is created. (The CHR$(X) function is discussed further in Chapter 12.)

PRINT CHR$(4); "WRITE filename"

This command instructs the computer that all subsequent PRINT statements will print data to the disk file, not to the screen (Rule 2).

PRINT T$(I)

This PRINT statement will write each record T$(I) onto the disk into the given file name (Rule 3). Writing of these records is written sequentially starting with the first record.

PRINT CHR$(4); "CLOSE filename"

This statement will close the file and redirect PRINT statements to the CRT (Rule 4). IMPORTANT: Whenever you are finished writing to a file, it is imperative that you CLOSE the file. Otherwise, data could be lost. As data is written to a file it is temporarily stored in a "buffer" in the computer memory. Closing a file "flushes" the buffer and writes the data to the file.

APPLICATION

Consider the problem of permanently storing the names and ages of the residents of the Shady Lane Retirement Community. The module outline which solves this problem is the following:

MODULE OUTLINE

    I. ENTER NAMES AND AGES OF RESIDENTS INTO RECORDS
   II. WRITE THESE RECORDS TO A DISK FILE.

MODULE I

```
10 REM MODULE I - READ THE DATA FOR SHADY LANE
20 INPUT "TYPE NUMBER OF RESIDENTS: ";N
30 DIM T$(N)
35 LET B$ = "                    " : REM 15 SPACES IN B$
40 FOR I = 1 TO N
50 REM INPUT LAST NAME, FIRST NAME, AGE
60 INPUT "TYPE LAST NAME: ";L$
70 INPUT "TYPE FIRST NAME: ";F$
80 INPUT "TYPE AGE: ";A$
90 LET L$ = LEFT$(L$ + B$,15)
100 LET F$ = LEFT$(F$ + B$,10)
110 LET A$ = RIGHT$(B$ + A$,3)
```

115 LET T$(I) = L$ + F$ + A$
120 NEXT I
130 REM END OF MODULE

Module II that follows will store all of the records in the array T$ onto the disk under the file name SHADY LANE, using Algorithm X.

MODULE II

135 REM MODULE II - STORES THE RECORDS T$(I) OF
140 REM SHADY LANE ONTO THE DISK IN SEQUENTIAL ORDER
160 PRINT CHR$(4); "OPEN SHADY LANE"
170 PRINT CHR$(4); "WRITE SHADY LANE"
180 FOR I = 1 TO N
190 PRINT T$(I)
200 NEXT I
210 PRINT CHR$(4); "CLOSE SHADY LANE"
220 END

EXERCISES 11.1

1. Mr. Frank purchased a new Apple computer. Write a BASIC program that will store his personal telephone directory on disk where each record contains the following fields:

   Field 1: Last name
   Field 2: First name
   Field 3: Street address
   Field 4: City
   Field 5: Zip code
   Field 6: Telephone number

2. The Rent A Lemon auto rental company rents many different types of cars and trucks. The company has recently purchased an Apple computer. Write a BASIC program that stores on disk a file containing the following fields in each record.

   Field 1: Type of vehicle
   Field 2: Manufacturer
   Field 3: Body model
   Field 4: Year
   Field 5: Current mileage
   Field 6: Daily rental price
   Field 7: Mileage rental price

3. Mr. Jones, a Computer Science instructor, needs a BASIC program that will save the grades for each of his students. Write a program that will store on disk a file containing records made up of these fields:

   Field 1: Student last name
   Field 2: Student first name
   Field 3: Student identification number
   Field 4: First quiz
   Field 5: Second quiz
   Field 6: Third quiz
   Field 7: Final exam

11.2 Reading records from a sequential file

RULES FOR READING RECORDS FROM A SEQUENTIAL FILE

1. Open the file
2. Advise the computer that it is about to read from the file
3. Actually read records from the file
4. Close the file.

The following algorithm transforms these rules to BASIC.

ALGORITHM XI - READING RECORDS FROM A FILE ON DISK

```
        REM T$(I) WILL CONTAIN THE RECORDS FROM THE FILE
        ONERR GOTO lineB
        PRINT CHR$(4); "OPEN filename"
        PRINT CHR$(4); "READ filename"
        LET I = 0
lineA   LET I = I + 1
        INPUT T$(I)
        GOTO lineA
lineB   PRINT CHR$(4); "CLOSE filename"
        POKE 216,0
```

EXPLANATION OF ALGORITHM XI

ONERR GOTO lineB

This statement is an Applesoft instruction which causes a branch to a given line whenever an error occurs in the program. When all records in a data file have been read, the next attempt to read a record from the file causes an END OF DATA error. This error then causes the branch to the given line, lineB ,due to the ONERR statement. (There are other uses of the ONERR instruction. See the Applesoft II BASIC Programming Reference Manual.)

PRINT CHR$(4); "READ filename"

This instruction redirects all subsequent INPUT statements to accept data from the filename given (Rule 2).

INPUT T$(I)

This INPUT statement takes one record from the file on disk starting with the first record and assigns it to the variable T$(I).

POKE 216,0

This instruction cancels the ONERR statement so that subsequent errors do not cause branching to line lineB. (See Chapter 12 for further discussion of the POKE command.)

APPLICATION

In the previous program a file was created for the Shady Lane community. The following module outline will read this file from the disk back into the computer's main memory and will print the file onto the CRT.

MODULE OUTLINE

    I. READ THE SHADY LANE FILE FROM THE DISK.
   II. DISPLAY THE FILE ON THE CRT.

MODULE I

```
100 REM MODULE I - READ THE SHADY LANE FILE FROM THE DISK
105 DIM T$(100)
110 ONERR GOTO 170
120 PRINT CHR$(4); "OPEN SHADY LANE"
130 PRINT CHR$(4); "READ SHADY LANE"
135 LET I = 0
140 LET I = I + 1
150 INPUT T$(I)
160 GOTO 140
170 PRINT CHR$(4); "CLOSE SHADY LANE"
180 POKE 216,0
182 LET I = I - 1: REM I IS NO. OF RECORDS
185 REM END OF MODULE
```

Module II that follows will print the records T$(I) onto the CRT.

MODULE II

```
200 REM MODULE II - PRINT THE RECORDS
210 FOR K = 1 TO I
220 PRINT T$(K)
230 NEXT K
240 END
```

EXERCISES 11.2

1. Add a module between Modules I and II so that the records can be sorted by last name before printing to the CRT.

2. Write programs to read the data from the files created by the exercises in 11.1.

11.3 Storing data by fields

The Apple computer allows fields of a record to be stored directly onto the disk without the necessity of concatenating the fields together to form a record. Even though this method does not require fixed length fields, we shall still maintain appropriate field sizes. This is important when sorting and searching is to be performed on the file. The following program is the Shady Lane program redone so that fields are stored separately.

```
      10 REM MODULE I - ENTERING DATA
      20 INPUT "TYPE NUMBER OF RESIDENTS: ";N
      30 DIM T$(N,3)
      35 LET B$ = "                    " : REM 15 SPACES IN B$
      40 FOR I = 1 TO N
      50 REM ENTER LAST NAME, FIRST NAME, AND AGE
      60 INPUT "TYPE LAST NAME: ";L$
      70 INPUT "TYPE FIRST NAME: ";F$
      80 INPUT "TYPE AGE: ";A$
      85 REM PADDING FIELDS TO CORRECT LENGTHS
      90 LET T$(I,1) = LEFT$(L$ + B$,15)
      100 LET T$(I,2) = LEFT$(F$ + B$,10)
      110 LET T$(I,3) = RIGHT$(B$ + A$,3)
      120 NEXT I
      130 REM END OF MODULE I
      140 REM MODULE II - STORE ON DISK IN SEQUENTIAL ORDER
      160 PRINT CHR$(4);"OPEN SHADY LANE"
      170 PRINT CHR$(4);"WRITE SHADY LANE"
      180 FOR I = 1 TO N
      190 PRINT T$(I,1)
      200 PRINT T$(I,2)
      210 PRINT T$(I,3)
      215 NEXT I
      220 PRINT CHR$(4);"CLOSE SHADY LANE"
      230 END
```

The following program will now read the records from the file SHADY LANE three fields at a time and then print the data to the CRT.

```
100 REM PROGRAM TO READ RECORDS FROM SHADY LANE
125 DIM Q$(100)
130 ONERR GOTO 195
140 PRINT CHR$(4);"OPEN SHADY LANE"
150 PRINT CHR$(4);"READ SHADY LANE"
155 LET I = 0
160 LET I = I + 1
170 INPUT L$,F$,A$
180 LET Q$(I) = L$ + F$ + A$
190 GOTO 160
195 PRINT CHR$(4);"CLOSE SHADY LANE"
200 POKE 216,0
203 LET I = I - 1
205 FOR K = 1 TO I
210 PRINT Q$(K)
220 NEXT K
230 END
```

EXERCISES 11.3

1. Modify the programs written for the exercises in 11.1 using the method of storing fields separately.

11.4 Appending records to a file

Whenever a sequential file is opened by the OPEN statement, reading from the disk or writing to the disk ALWAYS starts at the FIRST record in the file. This section deals with the task of adding a record to the end of the file on disk.

RULES FOR APPENDING RECORDS TO A SEQUENTIAL FILE

1. Open the file in APPEND mode
2. Advise the computer that it is about to write to the file
3. Actually write records to the file
4. Close the file.

The following algorithm will transform these rules to BASIC.

ALGORITHM XII - APPENDING RECORDS TO A FILE

```
PRINT CHR$(4); "APPEND filename"
PRINT CHR$(4); "WRITE filename"
FOR I = 1 TO N
PRINT T$(I)
NEXT I
PRINT CHR$(4); "CLOSE filename"
```

EXPLANATION OF ALGORITHM XII

```
PRINT CHR$(4); "APPEND filename"
```

This instruction takes the place of the OPEN instruction. The file is opened but the addition of records will take place at the end of the file.

```
PRINT T$(I)
```

This PRINT instruction will write the record T$(I) to the end of the file.

APPLICATION

The following program will add additional records to the end of the SHADY LANE file.

```
100 REM MODULE I - ADDING ONE OR MORE NEW RESIDENTS
110 INPUT "HOW MANY NEW RESIDENTS DO YOU WISH TO ADD? ";N
120 DIM T$(N)
130 LET B$ = "               " : REM 15 SPACES IN B$
135 FOR I = 1 TO N
140 INPUT "TYPE LAST NAME: ";L$
150 INPUT "TYPE FIRST NAME: ";F$
160 INPUT "TYPE AGE: ";A$
170 LET L$ = LEFT$(L$ + B$,15)
180 LET F$ = LEFT$(F$ + B$,10)
190 LET A$ = RIGHT$(B$ + A$,3)
200 LET T$(I) = L$ + F$ + A$
210 NEXT I
220 MODULE II - APPENDS N RECORDS TO THE END OF FILE
230 PRINT CHR$(4); "APPEND SHADY LANE"
235 PRINT CHR$(4); "WRITE SHADY LANE"
```

```
240 FOR I = 1 TO N
250 PRINT T$(I)
260 NEXT I
270 PRINT CHR$(4); "CLOSE SHADY LANE"
280 END
```

EXERCISES 11.4

1. Write programs so that the user can append records to the files created by the exercises in 11.1.

11.5 Projects

1. A local bank has a need for a computer program that will perform the following tasks:

1. Creates a customer file on disk whose records contain the following fields:

   Field 1: Last name
   Field 2: First name
   Field 3: Address
   Field 4: Telephone number
   Field 5: Account number
   Field 6: Total amount in savings account

2. Updates Field 6 by adding the interest earned over a given period of time.
3. Prints the entire record of any customer when the customer's account number is entered.

2. Mrs. Smith owns shares of several stocks. Write a BASIC program for her that will perform the following tasks:

1. Stores on disk a file whose records are comprised of these fields:

   Field 1: Name of the stock
   Field 2: Number of shares owned
   Field 3: Price purchased
   Field 4: Total dividends received
   Field 5: Profits/loss when stock is sold.

2. Displays the file to the CRT.
3. Sorts the file along Field 1.
4. Computes the total profits gained from all stocks sold.

3. Professor Snodgrass needs a BASIC program that will store on disk a file containing the following information on the classes he teaches.

   subject
   room number
   student name
   student's quiz grades
   student's final exam grade
   student's final grade in the class

Write for him a menu-driven program that will perform the following tasks:

1. Creates the file
2. Prints the records of all students in a specified class
3. Searches the entire file for the records of any particular student and prints the records.

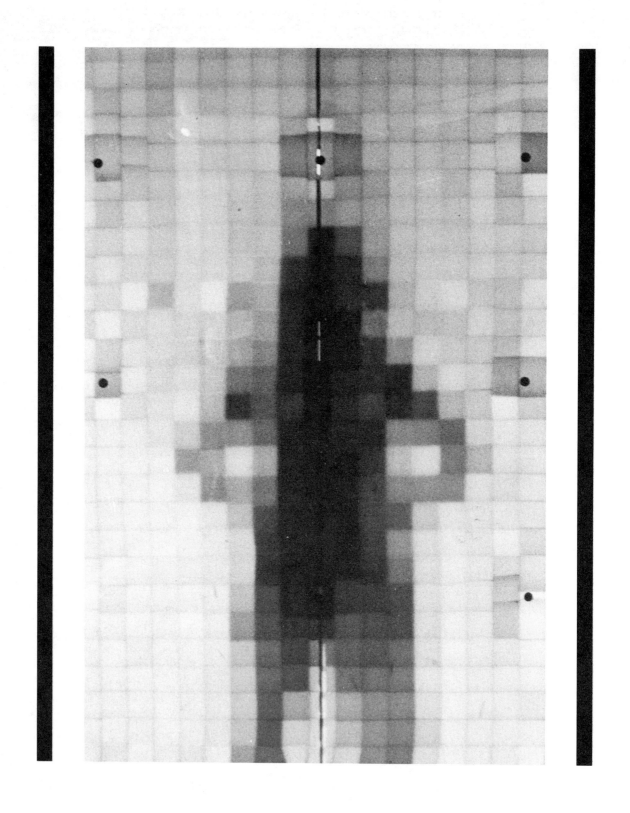

12

Special Features of Applesoft BASIC

12.0 Introduction

In this chapter we will discuss many of the features unique to Applesoft that make it such a powerful version of the BASIC language. These enhancements fall into five catagories:

(1) PEEK, POKE, and CALL
(2) Prettyprinting
(3) Graphics instructions
(4) Paddle and speaker control
(5) Miscellaneous topics.

12.1 PEEK, POKE, and CALL

The commands PEEK, POKE, and CALL are the windows to the unseen world of computer memory. The real importance of these commands will be seen in the section on prettyprinting, which you will certainly not want to miss.

Let's digress a moment to a short discussion on computer memory, which will help you understand the functions of PEEK and POKE.

A. A DIGRESSION TO DISCUSS COMPUTER MEMORY

Imagine a long line of boxes numbered in order beginning with zero. Computer memory is an electronic micro-miniaturized version of what you are now imagining. We can diagram it like this:

```
65535  ┌──────────┐
       │          │   "top of memory"
       └──────────┘
              .
              .
              .
       ┌──────────┐
   3   │          │
       ├──────────┤
   2   │          │
       ├──────────┤
   1   │          │
       ├──────────┤
   0   │          │   "bottom of memory"
       └──────────┘
```

Each box is called a *memory cell,* and the number to its left is called the *address* of that memory cell. The size of the microprocessor (the circuit which processes data on a microcomputer) determines the amount of memory that the computer may have. Most microcomputers, including the Apple II Plus, use an "8-bit" microprocessor and can have up to 65536 memory cells.

Each memory cell stores a pattern of eight electronic signals, called *bits.* Some of them are "on" and some of them are "off." These eight bits together are called a *byte.* They express a number in the binary number system. The pattern "00000000" represents the decimal number 0, while "11111111" equals 255 in the decimal system. It will not be necessary for you to understand binary numbers. Just remember that each memory cell holds a byte of information, and a byte is a decimal number from 0 to 255.

The memory we have been talking about comes in two varieties, ROM and RAM. ROM stands for *read only memory.* Information which must remain permanently in the computer is stored in ROM. In fact, Applesoft itself is stored in ROM, since the Apple must always know the Applesoft language. In the memory of the Apple II Plus, address 64708 is a ROM memory cell. It contains a 208. Nothing will ever change that, even if the power is turned off. On the Apple II Plus, ROM takes up over 14,000 memory cells.

RAM stands for *random access memory,* a name which really doesn't reveal what it's all about. RAM is memory which is changeable. It is called "volatile" memory for just that reason. Bytes stored in RAM memory cells are lost if the power is turned off or if new information overwrites the old. RAM memory is where your Applesoft programs are stored while they are being entered or run. On an Apple II Plus with all of the RAM it can have, about 48,000 addresses are devoted to RAM memory. This is often referred to as "48K," since "K" stands for "kilo," meaning 1000 in the metric system. To be accurate, "K" in computer jargon stands for 1024 rather than 1000.

B. THE PEEK(X) FUNCTION

Returning now from our "short" digression, let's discuss the purpose of PEEK in Applesoft BASIC. PEEK is actually a function like those in

Chapter 2. It requires an argument in parentheses. The PEEK(X) function returns the decimal number which is contained in memory cell X. For example:

LET A = PEEK(64708)

assigns to A the number 208, since 208 is the byte contained at address 64708, as mentioned above.

Example This program counts the number of memory cells between addresses 4000 and 5000 which contain zero:

```
100 LET S = 0
110 FOR K = 4000 TO 5000
120 IF PEEK(K) = 0 THEN LET S = S + 1
130 NEXT K
140 PRINT "THERE ARE ";S;" CELLS CONTAINING
       ZERO IN THAT RANGE."
150 END
```

C. THE POKE INSTRUCTION

As you might have guessed, the opposite of peeking is poking! That is, POKE is the instruction used for writing into a memory cell as opposed to reading from it. Since ROM memory is unchangeable, the POKE instruction is useful only with RAM. The instruction below writes the number 25 to the memory cell whose address is 5000:

POKE 5000,25

In general, therefore, the instruction takes the form

POKE ADDRESS,DATA

where ADDRESS is a RAM memory cell into which DATA is to be written.

Example Characters which appear on the CRT are actually stored as numbers in the computer's memory. All numbers that are stored in memory locations 1024 through 2047 appear as characters somewhere on the video screen. (To be accurate, there are 64 memory cells in that range which are not visible on the screen.) The screen, therefore, is a direct viewing window into memory locations 1024 through 2047.

Type in the command:

POKE 1468,193

You should see the letter "A" appear magically near the center of the screen. What you are doing is poking the special code which stands for the letter A directly into a memory cell which the Apple computer displays to the screen. (The number which corresponds to the letter A is equal to 128 plus the ASCII code for the letter A. See Section 12.5C.)

Example The following program fills all the cells whose addresses are 1024 to 2047 with the number 193. Since those are exactly the same addresses which the CRT displays, the effect is to fill the screen with the letter A.

```
100 FOR K = 1024 TO 2047
110 POKE K,193
120 NEXT K
130 END
```

D. THE CALL COMMAND

Sometimes a set of memory cells contains numbers which are actually instructions to the microprocessor. This set of numbers is known as a *machine language* program. Machine language programs are understood directly by the computer's microprocessor. (BASIC, on the other hand, must first be translated into machine language before it makes sense to the computer.)

There is one large machine language program contained in ROM memory known as the *monitor.* The monitor controls much of the activity of the computer which we take for granted. For example, how does the cursor know to move to the next line when forty characters have been typed? What causes the screen to scroll (move up one line) when the last line on the screen is filled? The answer is that the monitor program is "monitoring" the computer at all times. The monitor program contains machine language subroutines which can be used from within BASIC programs. The CALL instruction is the bridge between BASIC and machine language programs.

To run a machine language program from BASIC, type CALL ADDRESS, where ADDRESS is the starting address of the program. For instance, a routine which clears the screen starts at address 64600. It is part of the monitor program. To clear the screen, type:

CALL 64600

Example   This program will cause the entire screen to scroll up 10 lines. The monitor routine which scrolls one line starts at address 64624:

```
100 FOR K = 1 TO 10
110 CALL 64624
120 NEXT K
130 END
```

A final word about CALL before we move to applications in prettyprinting. Addresses high in memory are expressed as negative numbers in most books. For instance, the address 64600 is equivalent to -936. The computer understands either form. To find the corresponding negative number, subtract 65536 from the address. We will also use the negative number convention.

Example   CALL -936 is equivalent to CALL 64600

because 64600 - 65536 = -936.

CALL -912 is equivalent to CALL 64624
because 64624 - 65536 = -912.

12.2 Prettyprinting

In this section we will learn about many special Applesoft statements which will help you design nice looking screen displays. The instructions we will take up are

A. HOME
B. HTAB and VTAB
C. INVERSE, FLASH, and NORMAL
D. SPEED=
E. Text Windowing
F. Machine language CALLs.

These prettyprinting instructions are for screen displays only. Their effect on a printer is unpredictable.

A. HOME

The HOME instruction simply clears the screen and puts the cursor in the upper lefthand corner. HOME may be issued as an immediate mode command or used as a statement in a BASIC program. It is equivalent to CALL -936, discussed above.

B. HTAB and VTAB

With these two instructions, the cursor can be moved to any character position on the screen. HTAB stands for "horizontal tab," and the instruction

HTAB X

will move the cursor from its current position to column X of the current line. The number X should be in the range from 1 to 40. The "vertical tab" instruction

VTAB Y

moves the cursor to line Y from the top of the screen. The lines are numbered from 1 at the top to 24 at the bottom. Y should be in that range. VTAB Y will not affect the horizontal position of the cursor.

Example   This program prints the message contained in M$ at the center of the screen:

```
100 INPUT "TYPE A SHORT MESSAGE: ";M$
110 HOME
120 VTAB 12
130 HTAB INT((40-LEN(M$))/2)
140 PRINT M$
150 END
```

IMPORTANT: Notice that unlike the TAB(X) function, the HTAB and VTAB commands are NOT used from within a PRINT statement.

Example   This program draws the octagon pictured below. This could be a decorative border around a menu. (And, in fact, it will be in an example later on!)

```
100 HOME
110 REM DRAW TOP EDGE
120 VTAB 2 : HTAB 10: PRINT "**********************"
130 REM DRAW TOP SLANTED EDGES
140 FOR K = 3 TO 8
150 VTAB K : HTAB 12 - K : PRINT "*"
160 VTAB K : HTAB 29 + K : PRINT "*"
170 NEXT K
180 REM DRAW VERTICAL SIDES
190 FOR K = 9 TO 15
200 VTAB K : HTAB 4 : PRINT "*"
210 VTAB K : HTAB 37 : PRINT "*"
215 NEXT K
220 REM DRAW BOTTOM SLANTS
230 FOR K = 16 TO 21
240 VTAB K : HTAB K - 12 : PRINT "*"
250 VTAB K : HTAB 53 - K : PRINT "*"
260 NEXT K
270 REM DRAW BOTTOM EDGE
280 VTAB 22 : HTAB 10 : PRINT "********************"
290 END
```

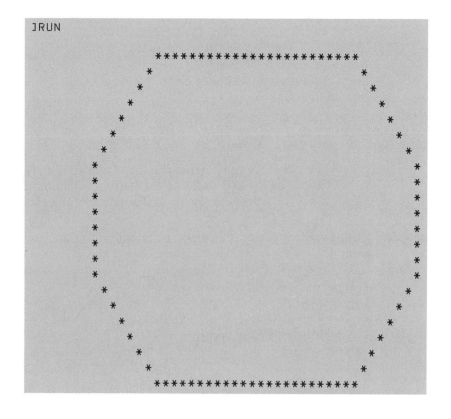

Example   The following is an interesting application of VTAB and HTAB. Two or more INPUT statements can be made to place their prompt messages on the same line. In this program, the user is asked to type his name and age. The messages "TYPE YOUR NAME:" and "AGE:" will appear on the same line.

```
100 HOME
110 VTAB 5
120 INPUT "TYPE YOUR NAME: ";N$
130 VTAB 5 : HTAB 30
140 INPUT "AGE: ";A
150 END
```

```
]RUN

TYPE YOUR NAME: JOHN DOE      AGE: 47
```

Of course the user, JOHN DOE, must press RETURN after typing his name in order for the second INPUT message to be displayed.

An improved alternative to the last example uses the PEEK function. Address 37 in memory stores the current vertical position of the cursor. Therefore, the instruction VTAB PEEK(37) will keep the cursor on the same line last written to on the screen. This eliminates the need to VTAB to a specific line on which the INPUT messages will appear. The program above can now be written this way:

```
100 INPUT "TYPE YOUR NAME: ";N$
110 VTAB PEEK(37) : HTAB 30
120 INPUT "AGE: ";A
130 END
```

The advantage is that the VTAB 5 instructions can be left out altogether.

C. INVERSE, FLASH, and NORMAL

The Apple usually displays text as white letters on a black background. This is the NORMAL mode. The instruction INVERSE changes the output to the screen so that characters are printed black on white background. The instruction FLASH prints characters which continually alternate between NORMAL and INVERSE, that is, they flash! The FLASH mode is particularly useful when the user's attention must be drawn to a certain message on the screen. NORMAL resets the output mode to normal. After an INVERSE, FLASH, or NORMAL instruction is executed, all subsequent output will be displayed in the mode chosen until one of the other two instructions is issued. Take note that when a mode is selected it only affects subsequent output. Text that is already on the screen will not be affected.

A word of advice: We find that if FLASH and INVERSE are overused, screen displays are often annoying and can cause eyestrain. Be conservative with their use.

Example   Here is a menu in which the title is printed in inverse and the input message is flashing. The menu choices are printed in normal mode:

```
290 REM APPEND THIS TO THE PROGRAM ABOVE
295 REM FOR A VERY NICE MENU DISPLAY
300 VTAB 8 : HTAB 11
310 INVERSE
320 PRINT "ELECTRONIC CHECKBOOK"
330 NORMAL
340 PRINT
350 HTAB 12 : PRINT "1. ENTER A CHECK"
360 HTAB 12 : PRINT "2. MAKE A DEPOSIT"
370 HTAB 12 : PRINT "3. SHOW BALANCE"
380 HTAB 12 : PRINT "4. QUIT"
390 PRINT
400 HTAB 11
410 FLASH
420 INPUT "YOUR CHOICE? ";C
430 NORMAL
...(program continues)...
```

Don't forget to set the mode back to NORMAL, as in lines 330 and 430.

D. SPEED =

You've probably noticed that the Apple prints text to the screen at an incredible rate of speed. In fact, at top speed the Apple can display about 1000 characters per second. If you could read that fast you would be reading at 12000 words per minute! Fortunately there is a way to adjust the rate at which text is written to the screen. The instruction is

SPEED = X

where X is any whole number from 0 to 255. The number 255 represents top speed (1000 cps). As the number decreases, so does the speed. When X is zero, the Apple is printing at a snail's pace, about six characters per second. That's a reading speed of about seventy-two words per minute.

The SPEED = instruction can be used in either the immediate or deferred mode.

Example   Try this out:

```
100 SPEED = 0
110 PRINT "THIS IS 6 CHARACTERS PER SECOND."
120 SPEED = 100
130 PRINT "THIS IS 16 CHARACTERS PER SECOND."
140 SPEED = 200
150 PRINT "THIS IS 100 CHARACTERS PER SECOND."
160 SPEED = 255
170 PRINT "THIS IS 1000 CHARACTERS PER SECOND."
180 END
```

Notice that doubling the number in the SPEED = instruction does NOT double the speed.

E. TEXT WINDOWING

A "text window" is a rectangular portion of the screen on which text can be displayed. The normal text window, of course, is the entire screen. It is twenty-four lines by forty columns. But it doesn't always have to be that way!

A text window smaller than the full screen gives the screen an interesting appearance. The portion of the screen lying outside of the window appears frozen while the normal printing activity takes place within the window. A typical use for this might be for displaying rules to a game or instructions to the user which must remain on the screen at all times. Or in another application, column headers can be frozen on the screen while data scrolls underneath them.

Changing the text window involves POKEing into memory four numbers. The four numbers define the new left margin, line width, top margin, and bottom margin of the window. These numbers go into addresses 32, 33, 34, and 35, respectively. Here are the details:

POKE 32, L

This sets the left margin of the text window to L, where L is between 0 and 39. A value of zero sets the margin to the far left of the screen, while a value of 39 sets the margin to the far right, with one column remaining for display. Think of L as the number of columns on the screen which lie frozen to the left of the text window. Caution: Don't change the left margin unless you also change the window width (see next).

POKE 33, W

This sets the width of the window to W, which must be a number from 1 to 40. If you are going to change the left margin of the text window, change the window width FIRST, so that the window will fit on the screen. For example, if you want to move the left margin of the text window so that there are five columns frozen to the left (POKE 32,5) then you must first change the width to 35 or less (POKE 33,35). Failure to do this may cause any BASIC program currently in memory to be lost.

POKE 34, T

This sets the top margin of the text window. The number T must be in the range from 0 to 23. Think of T as the number of lines which are frozen above the top of the window. A value of zero sets the top margin to the top line of the screen, while a value of 23 leaves one line at the bottom for display. Be sure that the top margin is set no lower than the bottom margin.

POKE 35, B

This sets the bottom margin of the text window to line B. The number B must be in the range from 0 to 24 where 24 is the bottom of the screen. Be sure to set the bottom margin to a value less than or equal to the top margin.

To reset the text window to the full screen, we could POKE the numbers 0, 40, 0, and 24 into addresses 32, 33, 34, and 35, respectively. But the instruction TEXT does this for us automatically. Use TEXT when your custom text window is no longer needed.

Example   This program displays a Fahrenheit to Celsius temperature conversion chart. The column headings are frozen at the top of the screen by lowering the top margin of the text window.

```
100 HOME
110 PRINT TAB(10);"FAHRENHEIT";TAB(25);"CELSIUS"
120 PRINT TAB(10);"----------      ";TAB(25);"-------"
125 REM THREE FROZEN LINES AT TOP
130 POKE 34,3
140 HOME : REM THIS PUTS US INTO THE NEW WINDOW
150 FOR F = 32 TO 212
160 LET C = 5/9 * (F - 32)
170 PRINT TAB(14);F;TAB(25);C
180 NEXT F
190 REM CHART IS DONE, RESET TO FULL WINDOW
200 TEXT
210 END
```

Example   Do you remember the earlier example which prints an octagon of asterisks? The following lines, when added to that program, change the text window to a rectangular region within the octagon. The octagon will then stay on the screen at all times.

```
290 REM CHANGE TOP MARGIN TO FREEZE FIVE
            LINES ABOVE THE WINDOW
300 POKE 34, 5
305 REM
310 REM CHANGE BOTTOM MARGIN TO FREEZE SIX
            LINES BELOW THE WINDOW
320 POKE 35, 18
325 REM
330 REM CHANGE WINDOW WIDTH TO 26 COLUMNS
340 POKE 33, 26
345 REM
350 REM MOVE LEFT MARGIN TO FREEZE 7 COLUMNS
            TO THE LEFT OF THE WINDOW
360 POKE 32, 7
365 REM
370 REM NOW MOVE TO THE INSIDE OF THE WINDOW
380 HOME
...(program continues)...
```

From the last two examples above, you have probably gathered that the HOME instruction can be used to jump into a window once it has been defined. It clears only that portion of the screen that lies within the window.

F. MACHINE LANGUAGE CALLS

In this final part of the prettyprinting section we discuss the built-in machine language routines that affect the appearance of the screen. These routines are part of the monitor program described earlier in this chapter. They can be executed from within your BASIC programs by using the instruction CALL X, where X is the starting address in memory. (Recall that when X is a negative number, it is equal to the actual memory address minus 65536.)

CALL -958

This instruction clears the text window from the current position of the cursor to the bottom margin. Characters to the left of the cursor and above remain on the screen.

CALL -868

This instruction clears the current line from the current position of the cursor to the end of the line.

CALL -912

As we saw earlier in this chapter, this instruction scrolls the text window by one line. Everything within the window is moved up one line.

Example   The program below asks the user to type a code number in the form XX-XXX. If the number typed is not of the correct length, or if the hyphen is missing, the input is rejected and the user must retype it. Study the program. What is the purpose of line 130?

```
100 PRINT "ENTER CODE NUMBER (XX-XXX)"
110 VTAB PEEK(37)
120 HTAB 30
130 CALL -868
140 INPUT "";C$
150 IF LEN(C$) <> 6 OR MID$(C$,3,1) <> "-"
        THEN GOTO 110
160 END
```

Here is an explanation. If the user types an incorrect code number, the IF-THEN statement at 150 sends control back to line 110. This does a vertical tab to the line last written on the screen. The cursor then moves to column 30. The CALL -868 instruction then clears the old bad input from the cursor's position to the end of the line. This leaves the user with a clean line on which to type the corrected code number.

12.3 Graphics

One of the most exciting features of the Apple II Plus is its ability to display color graphics. There are actually two graphics modes. They are called "low resolution" and "high resolution", usually referred to as "lo-res" and "hi-res" for short.

A. LOW RESOLUTION GRAPHICS

Using special commands unique to Applesoft BASIC, the Apple is able to light up small rectangles on the screen. In lo-res mode, the screen is divided into 1600 rectangles in a 40 by 40 grid. Each *pixel* (as these rectangles are called) can be displayed in any of sixteen colors. There are five lo-res instructions in Applesoft. They are GR, COLOR=, PLOT, HLIN, and VLIN. They may be used in either the immediate or deferred mode.

1. GR

This instruction puts the Apple into lo-res graphics mode. It converts the first 20 lines of the text screen into a 40-line graphics screen and clears it to black. Text will only be printed in the bottom four lines of the screen. To turn off this graphics mode, use the instruction TEXT.

2. COLOR =

This instruction sets the color for plotting, but no pixels are actually lighted until the PLOT instruction is given (below). There are sixteen colors numbered from 0 to 15. For example, the instruction

COLOR = 9

sets the color to orange for later plotting. Here is a complete list of the colors. (Yes, it is true there are two greys.) On a black-and-white TV set or video monitor, all colors are displayed as varying shades of grey.

0 black	4 dark green	8 brown	12 green
1 magenta	5 grey	9 orange	13 yellow
2 dark blue	6 medium blue	10 grey	14 aqua
3 purple	7 light blue	11 pink	15 white

3. PLOT C,R

The PLOT C,R instruction fills one pixel with the color chosen by the COLOR= instruction. The rectangle which is plotted is located at column C and row R of the graphics screen. There are forty columns numbered 0 to 39, with the zeroth column being at the far left of the screen. (Columns are vertical, rows are horizontal.) The forty rows are also numbered from 0 to 39. Row 0 is the row at the top of the screen.

Example   Type in these commands:

```
GR
COLOR=9
PLOT 0,0
PLOT 39,0
COLOR=13
PLOT 20,39
```

You should see an orange rectangle at the upper left-hand corner of the screen, another one in the upper righthand corner, and a yellow pixel at the center of the bottom line of the graphics screen (20 columns over, 39 rows down). Notice that the color remains fixed until changed with another COLOR= instruction.

Example   This program fills all 1600 pixels with randomly chosen colors:

```
100 REM PUT INTO GRAPHICS MODE
110 GR
120 REM THIS LOOP CHANGES THE COLUMN
130 FOR C = 0 TO 39
140 REM
150 REM THIS LOOP CHANGES THE ROW
160 FOR R = 0 TO 39
170 REM
180 REM ASSIGN A RANDOM COLOR FROM 0 TO 15
190 COLOR=INT(16*RND(1))
200 REM
210 REM PLOT AT THE CURRENT COLUMN AND ROW
220 PLOT C,R
230 REM
```

```
240 NEXT R
250 REM
260 NEXT C
270 END
```

4. HLIN C1,C2 AT R

HLIN stands for "horizontal line." The instruction HLIN C1,C2 AT R draws a horizontal line from column C1 to column C2 at row R. The number C1 must be less than or equal to C2. For example,

HLIN 0,39 AT 20

draws a line at the center of the graphics screen (row 20) from column 0 to column 39. The instruction

HLIN 31,36 AT 5

draws a short line (six pixels long) from the column 31 to the column 36 at row 5. This would be in the upper right portion of the screen.

5. VLIN R1,R2 AT C

This draws a vertical line from row R1 to row R2 at column C. The number R1 must be less than or equal to R2. For example,

VLIN 0,39 AT 20

draws a vertical line at the middle of the screen (column 20) from the top (row 0) to the bottom (row 39). (Strictly speaking there is no middle column in the lo-res screen, because there are an even number of columns. But 20 will do. Same goes for rows.)

Example   Here is a dazzling display. Try it out. It is an infinite loop so when you have had enough, either press the RESET key or type CTRL-C. Pressing the RESET key will cancel the graphics mode, while CTRL-C will not.

```
100 GR
110 FOR K = 0 TO 39
120 COLOR = INT(16*RND(1))
130 HLIN 0,39 AT K
140 VLIN 0,39 AT K
150 NEXT K
160 GOTO 110
170 END
```

Example   In this program, a bar graph is drawn which compares the monthly heating costs in a hypothetical household. The lengths of the vertical bars are all relative to the tallest one, which represents the largest monthly amount. The tallest bar is arbitrarily set to three-fourths of the total screen height.

```
100 REM FOLLOWING DATA ARE MONTHLY HEATING COSTS
110 REM FOR JANUARY THROUGH DECEMBER
120 DATA 105, 95, 85, 70, 40, 40, 35
130 DATA 30, 35, 48, 70, 90
140 REM
150 REM STORE DATA IN ARRAY
160 DIM C(12)
170 FOR K = 1 TO 12
```

```
180 READ C(K)
190 NEXT K
200 REM
210 REM FIND LARGEST VALUE
220 LET L = C(1)
230 FOR K = 2 TO 12
240 IF C(K) > L THEN LET L = C(K)
250 NEXT K
260 REM
270 REM NOW SET GRAPHICS MODE
280 REM AND PLOT A BAR FOR EACH MONTH.
290 REM THE LARGEST BAR IS 30 PIXELS TALL
300 REM AND ALL OTHER BARS ARE SCALED APPROPRIATELY.
305 GR
308 COLOR = 15
310 FOR K = 1 TO 12
315 REM SCALE C(K) TO WITHIN 30 SCREEN UNITS
320 LET H = C(K) / L * 30
321 REM ROUND H TO NEAREST INTEGER
322 LET H = INT(H + .5)
323 REM FROM ROW 40-H TO ROW 39 IS H PIXELS.
325 REM CHECK THAT H IS NOT ZERO, ELSE ERROR RESULTS.
330 IF H<>0 THEN VLIN 40-H,39 AT 3*K
340 NEXT K
350 REM PRINTS MONTH NUMBERS BELOW GRAPH
360 HOME
365 VTAB 21
370 FOR K = 1 TO 12
380 PRINT TAB(3*K + 1);K;
390 NEXT K
395 PRINT:PRINT
410 PRINT TAB(10);"MONTHLY HEATING COSTS";
420 REM FINAL SEMICOLON KEEPS TEXT FROM SCROLLING
430 REM ONE TOO MANY LINES WHEN PROGRAM ENDS.
440 END
```

B. HIGH RESOLUTION GRAPHICS

In the hi-res mode, the screen is divided into 280 columns and 160 rows, with four lines of text at the bottom. The text window may be optionally eliminated, which increases the number of rows to 192. This is a total of 53,760 pixels. Quite an improvement over lo-res! And to add to that, there are fewer graphics instructions to learn than in lo-res. They are HGR, HGR2, HCOLOR=, and HPLOT.

1. HGR and HGR2

Either instruction sets the graphics mode to high resolution and clears the hi-res screen to black. With HGR, four text lines remain at the bottom of the screen, as in lo-res graphics. HGR2 eliminates the text window and gives full screen graphics.

2. HCOLOR=

Colors with numbers 0 through 7 may be assigned with the HCOLOR= instruction. However, due to duplications of white and black, only six different colors are actually available in hi-res. They are

0 black	3 white	6 red
1 violet	4 black	7 white
2 green	5 blue	

3. HPLOT C,R and variations

To light a pixel on the hi-res screen, the instruction HPLOT C,R is used. C is a column number from 0 to 279. In full screen graphics (HGR2) the number R is a row number from 0 to 191. If a text window exists (HGR) then R should not exceed 159.

There are no special instructions to draw horizontal or vertical lines in the hi-res mode. Instead, a variation of the HPLOT instruction will draw a line between two given points. The instruction

HPLOT C1,R1 TO C2,R2

will cause a line to be drawn from point C1,R1 to point C2,R2. This is much more versatile than the lo-res HLIN and VLIN instructions.

Example   This program fills the full graphics screen with four vertical bands of color:

```
100 HGR2
110 HCOLOR = 1
120 FOR K = 0 TO 69
130 HPLOT K,0 TO K,191
140 NEXT K
150 HCOLOR = 2
160 FOR K = 70 TO 139
170 HPLOT K,0 TO K,191
180 NEXT K
190 HCOLOR = 5
200 FOR K = 140 TO 209
210 HPLOT K,0 TO K,191
220 NEXT K
230 HCOLOR = 6
240 FOR K = 210 TO 279
250 HPLOT K,0 TO K,191
260 NEXT K
270 END
```

To return to text mode, type TEXT.

Example   This program produces an interesting string art effect in the upper left-hand corner of the screen. Try it!

```
100 HGR
110 HCOLOR = 3
120 FOR K = 0 TO 159 STEP 7
130 HPLOT 0,159-K TO K,0
140 NEXT K
150 END
```

Another variation of the HPLOT instruction is useful. It looks like

HPLOT TO C,R

and causes a line to be drawn from the point last plotted to the point at column C, row R. This has many applications, such as charting the daily activity of fluctuating markets. (See next example.)

Example   This program charts the weekly price of gold per ounce over a period of twelve weeks. A horizontal line representing the average value of gold during the three-month period is also drawn. The chart is scaled so that the top of the screen represents the highest price of gold during that period, and the bottom of the screen represents the lowest. (Note: This data does not represent any actual twelve week period.)

```
100 REM STORE GOLD PRICES IN ARRAY
105 REM AND FIND THE AVERAGE PRICE
110 DATA 12 : REM NUMBER OF DATA POINTS
120 DATA 285, 300, 310, 308, 318, 313
130 DATA 310, 302, 320, 327, 333, 347
140 READ N
150 DIM G(N)
155 LET T = 0
160 FOR K = 1 TO N
170 READ G(K)
175 LET T = T + G(K)
180 NEXT K
185 LET AVE = T/N
190 REM
200 REM FIND LARGEST NUMBER AND SMALLEST NUMBER
210 LET L = G(1) : LET S = G(1)
220 FOR K = 1 TO N
230 IF G(K) > L THEN LET L = G(K)
240 IF G(K) < S THEN LET S = G(K)
250 NEXT K
260 REM
270 REM PLOT FIRST POINT, SCALED
272 HGR
275 HCOLOR = 3
280 LET Y = 159/(L-S) * (L-G(1))
290 HPLOT 0,Y
300 REM
310 REM NOW PLOT TO EVERY OTHER POINT
320 FOR K = 2 TO N
330 LET Y = 159/(L-S) * (L-G(K))
340 REM W IS HORIZONTAL SEPARATION OF DATA POINTS
345 LET W = 279/N
350 HPLOT TO W*K,Y
360 NEXT K
370 REM
430 REM DRAW LINE AT AVERAGE PRICE OF GOLD
440 LET Y = 159/(L-S) * (L-AVE)
450 HCOLOR = 6
460 HPLOT 0,Y TO 279,Y
470 REM
480 REM TEXT AT BOTTOM
490 HOME
```

500 VTAB 21
510 PRINT "TWELVE WEEK AVERAGE IS $";INT(AVE + .5); " PER OUNCE"
520 END

12.4 Paddle and speaker control

The game paddles and built-in speaker add a dimension to the Apple II Plus which sets it apart from many other microcomputers. The paddles are input devices, and the speaker is a unique output device. We will show you how you can easily use these features in your programs.

A. THE GAME PADDLES AND PUSHBUTTONS

Typically, a game paddle is a small plastic box with a circular knob that may be turned clockwise and counterclockwise. The position of the knob determines a number from zero to 255 which can be read by the computer. In addition, the paddle has from one to three buttons which act as on/off switches that the computer can also sense. A button is on only while it is being pushed. To read the game paddles from Applesoft, we use a built-in function called PDL(X). The buttons are read by PEEKing special memory locations.

Specifically, the function PDL(X) returns a number from 0 to 255 depending on the position of the knob on paddle X. There can be at most four paddles attached to the Apple at one time, and they are numbered 0, 1, 2, and 3. So X must be a number from 0 to 3. (Note: Most manufacturers of game paddles sell them in pairs. When plugged into the Apple, these are paddles 0 and 1. Because paddles 2 and 3 must be plugged into the same socket, they cannot be used if paddles 0 and 1 are already attached. Special adapters must be bought to allow all four paddles to be hooked up simultaneously.)

Example   This program displays the positions of paddles 0 and 1:

100 PRINT PDL(0),PDL(1)
110 GOTO 100
120 END

Try it. You will see a continuous stream of numbers being printed on the screen in two columns. Turn paddle 0 counterclockwise. The numbers in the first column will approach zero. Turn it clockwise. The numbers will approach 255. The same will be true of the numbers in the second column as you turn paddle 1. Stop the infinite loop with the RESET key or CTRL-C.

Example   This program turns the Apple into a low-resolution sketch pad. The paddles move a white square around the screen which leaves a trail as it moves:

100 GR
110 COLOR = 15
120 REM COLUMN NUMBER IS PADDLE 0,
130 REM SCALED TO A NUMBER FROM 0 TO 39.
140 LET C = INT(PDL(0)/255 * 39)
150 REM ROW NUMBER IS PADDLE 1, ALSO SCALED.

```
160 LET R = INT(PDL(1)/255 * 39)
170 PLOT C,R
180 GO TO 140
190 END
```

Again, this is an infinite loop, but we will see below how the pushbutton can be used to stop the program.

We will now incorporate the pushbuttons into the programs above. To see if button 0 is being pressed, PEEK at memory address -16287. The value stored there will be greater than 127 only if the button has been pushed. Addresses -16286 and -16285 do the same, but for buttons 1 and 2, respectively. For instance, the statement

IF PEEK(-16287) > 127 THEN PRINT "BUTTON 0 IS PRESSED"

will print the message only if button 0 is being pressed.

Example   This program will show the positions of the paddles and the state of the buttons.

```
100 TEXT : HOME
110 PRINT "PADDLE 0";TAB(12);"1";TAB(15);"BUTTON 0"; TAB(30);"1"
115 REM SET TOP OF WINDOW TO BELOW HEADER
120 POKE 34, 2
125 HOME : REM JUMP INSIDE WINDOW
130 LET P0 = PDL(0)
140 LET P1 = PDL(1)
150 LET B0$ = "OFF"
160 LET B1$ = "OFF"
170 IF PEEK(-16287) > 127 THEN B0$ = "ON"
180 IF PEEK(-16286) > 127 THEN B1$ = "ON"
190 PRINT TAB(8);P0;TAB(12);P1;TAB(22);B0$;TAB(30);B1$
200 GOTO 130
210 END
```

Example   The sketch pad program above can be improved by using one pushbutton to change colors and the other to stop the program. Here is the improved version:

```
100 GR
110 COLOR = 15
115 REM IF BUTTON 0 IS PRESSED CHOOSE A RANDOM COLOR
118 IF PEEK(-16287) > 127 THEN COLOR = INT(16*RND(1))
120 REM COLUMN NUMBER IS PADDLE 0,
130 REM SCALED TO A NUMBER FROM 0 TO 39.
140 LET C = INT(PDL(0)/255 * 39)
150 REM ROW NUMBER IS PADDLE 1, ALSO SCALED.
160 LET R = INT(PDL(1)/255 * 39)
170 PLOT C,R
180 REM IF BUTTON 1 IS PRESSED, STOP THE PROGRAM
190 IF PEEK(-16286) > 127 THEN GOTO 210
200 GO TO 115
210 END
```

B. USING THE SPEAKER

Memory location -16336 is the key to generating sounds from the Apple's speaker. PEEKing this address toggles the speaker once and produces a noticeable "click." At the most basic level, the speaker in the Apple can be made to generate tones by PEEKing this location at a rapid-fire pace. This short program produces a buzzing sound:

```
100 LET X = PEEK(-16336)
110 GOTO 100
120 END
```

To refine this sound, however, would take a "tighter" loop so that we PEEK at -16336 many more times per second. But the two line loop above is about the fastest we can get in BASIC. The solution to the problem is to write the loop in machine language, which executes many times faster than Applesoft.

Here is a subroutine that you can use in your programs. It POKEs into memory a machine language program which produces a tone of variable pitch and duration:

```
63997 POKE 770,173 : POKE 771,48 : POKE 772, 192 :
      POKE 773,136 : POKE 774,208 : POKE 775,4 :
      POKE 776,198 : POKE 777,1 : POKE 778,240

63998 POKE 779,8 : POKE 780,202 : POKE 781,208 :
      POKE 782,246 : POKE 783,166 : POKE 784,0 :
      POKE 785,76 : POKE 786,2 : POKE 787,3 :
      POKE 788, 96

63999 RETURN
```

To use the subroutine, type it into your program and insert the line

```
10 GOSUB 63997
```

Numbers between 1 and 255 represent the pitch and duration of a tone. Your program must POKE into addresses 0 and 1 the pitch and duration, respectively. Once that is done, the command CALL 770 runs the machine language routine which produces the tone.

Example   This little program allows you to type in pitch and duration numbers and to hear the sound which results. Stop the program by entering 0 for both numbers.

```
 10 GOSUB 63997
100 INPUT "DURATION? ";D
120 INPUT "PITCH? ";P
130 IF D=0 AND P=0 THEN GOTO 180
140 POKE 0,P
150 POKE 1,D
160 CALL 770
170 GOTO 100
180 END
```

```
63997 POKE 770,173 : POKE 771,48 : POKE 772, 192 :
      POKE 773,136 : POKE 774,208 : POKE 775,4 :
      POKE 776,198 : POKE 777,1 : POKE 778,240
63998 POKE 779,8 : POKE 780,202 : POKE 781,208 :
      POKE 782,246 : POKE 783,166 : POKE 784,0 :
      POKE 785,76 : POKE 786,2 : POKE 787,3 :
      POKE 788, 96
63999 RETURN
```

Example   Here is the beginning to "Twinkle, Twinkle, Little Star."

```
 10 GOSUB 63997
 20 REM EVERY TWO NUMBERS ARE PITCH AND DURATION
 30 DATA 120,100,120,100,80,100,80,100
 40 DATA 70,100,70,100,80,160,90,100,90,100
 50 DATA 95,100,95,100,106,100,106,100,120,160
 60 FOR K = 1 TO 14
 70 READ P,D
 80 POKE 0,P
 90 POKE 1,D
100 CALL 770
110 NEXT K
120 END
63997 POKE 770,173 : POKE 771,48 : POKE 772, 192 :
      POKE 773,136 : POKE 774,208 : POKE 775,4 :
      POKE 776,198 : POKE 777,1 : POKE 778,240
63998 POKE 779,8 : POKE 780,202 : POKE 781,208 :
      POKE 782,246 : POKE 783,166 : POKE 784,0 :
      POKE 785,76 : POKE 786,2 : POKE 787,3 :
      POKE 788, 96
63999 RETURN
```

There is probably a formula which relates the pitch numbers to the true pitch of the tone. But we can't find it! The pitch numbers for the little melody above were found by experimentation.

12.5 Miscellaneous topics

While your knowledge of Applesoft BASIC is now almost complete, there remain a few functions and statements which deserve your attention. For reasons of continuity and clarity, these topics were left out of earlier chapters, but they are by no means difficult. They include,

A. The DEF FN statement
B. The GET Statement
C. The ASC(X$) Function
D. The CHR$(X) Function.

A. THE DEF FN STATEMENT

As you know, the BASIC language is provided with a library of built-in arithmetic functions which perform special tasks, like generating a random number or finding a square root. In addition to these built-in functions, Applesoft provides a method for you, the programmer, to create your own functions. These are known as *user-defined functions*. User-defined functions can be designed to round off numbers, pick random whole numbers between 1 and 6, compute the tab offset to center a title, and so on.

The DEF FN statement is the key to making user-defined functions. Here is a typical example:

100 DEF FN C(X) = 5/9 * (X - 32)

You may recognize the expression on the right as the formula for converting Fahrenheit temperature to Celsius. Once this statement has been placed into a program, the expression FN C(X) returns the Celsius equivalent of X degrees Fahrenheit, as in this program:

100 DEF FN C(X) = 5/9 * (X - 32)
110 FOR F = 68 TO 86 STEP 9
120 PRINT F, FN C(F)
130 NEXT F
140 END

```
]RUN

68          20
77          25
86          30
```

The DEF FN statement requires a name and a formula for the function being defined. Any valid numeric variable name can be used as the name of a function. The name given to the function above is C, and the formula is 5/9 * (X - 32). Following the name must be a set of parentheses which contains a numeric variable, known as the "dummy" variable. This dummy variable is used only for the purpose of relating the formula to the function name, so that values may be "passed" to the formula. The dummy variable may be any numeric variable. For example, these three statements define the very same function:

100 DEF FN C(X) = 5/9 * (X - 32)

or

100 DEF FN C(A) = 5/9 * (A - 32)

or

100 DEF FN C(F) = 5/9 * (F - 32)

Once a function has been defined in a DEF FN statement, it is referenced in the program by FN, followed by the name and argument, as in FN C(5). IMPORTANT: The DEF FN statement must be executed before any reference to the function it defines is made.

Example   Here is a program which uses a user-defined function to round numbers to the nearest hundreth. Note that descriptive names can be given to the function, as long as the name contains no reserved words.

```
10 REM THIS PROGRAM SHOWS THE INTEREST EARNED
20 REM AND NEW PRINCIPAL AT THE END OF EACH YEAR
30 REM AS $1000 IS COMPOUNDED ANNUALLY AT
40 REM 8% PER YEAR FOR FIVE YEARS.
45 REM
50 DEF FN ROUND(X) = INT(100*X + .5)/100
55 REM PRINCIPAL STARTS AT $1000
60 LET P = 1000
65 PRINT "YEAR";TAB(10);"INTEREST";TAB(20);"PRINCIPAL"
70 FOR Y = 1 TO 5
75 REM COMPUTE INTEREST FOR ONE YEAR
80 LET I = .08 * P
85 REM COMPUTE NEW PRINCIPAL
90 LET P = P + I
100 REM PRINT RESULTS, ROUNDED TO CENTS
110 PRINT Y;TAB(10);FN ROUND(I);TAB(20);FN ROUND(P)
120 NEXT Y
130 END
```

```
]RUN

YEAR          INTEREST     PRINCIPAL
1             80           1080
2             86.4         1166.4
3             93.31        1259.71
4             100.78       1360.49
5             108.84       1469.33
```

Example   To generate random whole numbers from one to six, one could use this user-defined function:

```
10 DEF FN RDM(X) = INT(6*RND(1)) + 1
```

Notice that the formula on the right does not need a variable to define it. However, the dummy variable MUST appear in the definition of the function. When the function is used in the program, a numeric argument must appear in the parentheses of the function, although it is not used. For instance:

```
PRINT FN RDM(0)
```

```
PRINT FN RDM(12.2)
```

```
PRINT FN RDM(A)
```

will all print random numbers between one and six.

Example   This function will determine how far to tab so that a string will be centered on the screen:

```
100 DEF FN T(X) = INT(20 - LEN(A$)/2)
```

IMPORTANT: The dummy variable MUST be numeric; it cannot be a string variable. The only way this function can operate on strings is if the ACTUAL string variable containing the string to be centered is made part of the formula. This program centers the strings F$ and G$, which must be assigned to A$ before used by the function:

```
100 DEF FN T(X) = INT(20 - LEN(A$)/2)
110 LET F$ = "CHAPTER 12"
120 LET G$ = "SPECIAL FEATURES OF APPLESOFT BASIC"
130 REM
140 REM ASSIGN F$ TO A$ FOR USE IN THE FUNCTION
150 LET A$ = F$
160 PRINT TAB(FN T(0));A$
170 REM ASSIGN G$ TO A$
180 LET A$ = G$
190 PRINT TAB(FN T(0));A$
200 END
```

Notice again that the argument of the function is irrelevent, so we have used a zero.

B. THE GET STATEMENT

The GET statement is another form of an assignment statement which, like INPUT, waits for the user to type data on the keyboard. The instruction

GET A$

grabs the first key pressed and assigns it to A$. It does not require the RETURN key to be pressed, and it does not print the character which was typed.

Try running this little program:

```
100 PRINT "START TYPING, PRESS 'Q' TO QUIT"
110 GET A$
120 PRINT A$
130 IF A$="Q" THEN GOTO 150
140 GOTO 110
150 END
```

You will find that as you type, the letters instantly appear on the screen. There is no need to press RETURN. If you remove line 120 from the program, nothing will be displayed on the screen when the program is running. But the GET statement is still "getting" every key you type.

GET can be used with a numeric variable, as in

GET X

but we don't recommend it. If a letter is typed instead of a number, a SYNTAX ERROR results, and the program bombs. A better way to "get" numbers is:

```
10 GET X$
20 LET X = VAL(X$)
```

Then if X$ happens to be a character other than 0, 1, 2, ... , or 9, the VAL function will return a value of 0. The program will not bomb.

Example   In this program, the GET statement is used to accept the user's choice from a menu:

```
100 REM MENU OF CHOICES
110 PRINT "1. CHOICE ONE..."
120 PRINT "2. CHOICE TWO..."
130 PRINT "3. CHOICE THREE..."
140 PRINT "4. CHOICE FOUR..."
150 PRINT
160 PRINT "TYPE NUMBER, DON'T PRESS RETURN:";
170 GET N$
175 PRINT N$
180 LET N = VAL (N$)
190 ON N GOSUB 1000, 2000, 3000, 4000
200 GOTO 110
...(program continues)...
```

One disadvantage to using the GET function in menu selection is that the menu can have no more than nine choices, if they are numbered starting with 1. Also, to a user trained to hit the RETURN key after entering data, the GET statement can be frustrating.

The INPUT statement will not allow commas or colons to be accepted as part of a string being entered, unless the user precedes the string with a quotation mark. In the example which follows, a BASIC subroutine is written using the GET statement which overcomes the necessity of a leading quotation mark. The subroutine "gets" characters one at a time while they are being typed and concatenates them together to create a full line of input. Commas, colons, and even quotation marks will not be rejected.

Example   Study the subroutine beginning at line 1000 very carefully. Line 1040 uses the ASC function which we will discuss shortly. For now just understand that line 1040 is checking to see if the RETURN key was pressed.

```
100 REM THIS PROGRAM USES GET INSTEAD OF INPUT
110 REM IN ORDER TO ACCEPT COMMAS AND COLONS
120 REM AS PART OF THE INPUT
130 REM
140 PRINT "ENTER YOUR DATE OF BIRTH>> ";
150 GOSUB 1000
160 LET D$ = A$
170 PRINT "ENTER TIME OF BIRTH>> ";
175 GOSUB 1000
180 LET T$ = A$
190 PRINT
200 PRINT "YOU WERE BORN ON ";D$;" AT ";T$
210 GOTO 9999
220 REM
1000 REM SUBROUTINE TO GET INPUT
1005 REM FIRST INITIALIZE A$ TO THE NULL STRING
1010 LET A$ = ""
1015 REM GRAB KEY FROM KEYBOARD
1020 GET B$
1030 PRINT B$;
1040 REM IF KEY WAS RETURN KEY THEN FINISH UP
```

```
1050 IF ASC(B$) = 13 THEN GOTO 1090
1060 REM CHARACTER TYPED IS CONCATENATED TO A$
1070 LET A$ = A$ + B$
1080 GOTO 1020
1090 RETURN
9999 END
```

```
]RUN

ENTER YOUR DATE OF BIRTH>> MARCH 15, 1949
ENTER YOUR TIME OF BIRTH>> 6:45 AM

YOU WERE BORN ON MARCH 15, 1949 AT 6:45 AM
```

Remember, the underlined characters were typed by the user.

One shortcoming to the subroutine given in the example above is that it doesn't have an option for erasing characters if a wrong key is accidentally pressed. All characters, even the wrong ones, are concatenated to A$ at line 1070. We will fix this shortly.

C. THE ASC(X$) FUNCTION

Every character on the keyboard has a unique number assigned to it. When a key is pressed on the keyboard, the number associated with that character is stored in memory. The Apple computer, like most microcomputers, assigns numbers to characters according to the ASCII code. (ASCII stands for the American Standard Code for Information Interchange.) Under the ASCII code, for example, the letter A is assigned the code 65. In fact, all of the letters A through Z are given the codes 65 through 90, respectively. Even keys such as RETURN and the arrow keys are given codes. Here is a list of the ASCII codes for most of the characters on the Apple keyboard.

ASCII CHARACTER CODES

CHARACTER	CODE	CHARACTER	CODE
Bell (CTRL-G)	7	0	48
		1	49
Left Arrow	8	2	50
(backspace)		3	51
		4	52
RETURN	13	5	53
		6	54
Right Arrow	21	7	55
		8	56
Space	32	9	57
		:	58
!	33	;	59
"	34	<	60
#	35	=	61
$	36	>	62
%	37	?	63

CHARACTER	CODE	CHARACTER	CODE
&	38	@	64
'	39		
(	40	A	65
)	41	B	66
*	42	C	67
+	43	.	.
,	44	.	.
−	45	.	.
.	46	Y	89
/	47	Z	90

The ASC(X$) function returns the ASCII code of the first character of the string contained in X$. For example:

LET M = ASC("ABC")

assigns a 65 to M, since 65 is the ASCII code for the letter A.

Example   This program prints the ASCII code for keys pressed on the keyboard.

```
100 PRINT "START TYPING, PRESS 'Q' TO QUIT"
110 GET A$
120 PRINT A$,ASC(A$)
130 IF A$ = "Q" THEN GOTO 150
140 GOTO 110
150 END
```

Example   Here is the improvement of the subroutine in an earlier example which allows input with commas and colons. In this routine, keys pressed by accident may be erased using the left arrow key. Line 1080 checks the ASCII code of the key pressed to see if it is a left arrow.

```
 100 PRINT "TYPE SOMETHING."
 105 PRINT "USE LEFT ARROW TO CORRECT MISTAKES."
 110 GOSUB 1000
 120 PRINT "THIS IS WHAT YOU TYPED:"
 130 PRINT A$
 140 GOTO 9999
 150 REM
1000 REM SUBROUTINE TO GET INPUT
1010 REM FIRST INITIALIZE A$ TO THE NULL STRING
1020 LET A$ = ""
1030 REM GRAB KEY FROM KEYBOARD
1040 GET B$
1050 REM IF KEY WAS RETURN KEY THEN FINISH UP
1060 IF ASC(B$) = 13 THEN GOTO 1180
1070 REM IF KEY WAS LEFT ARROW THEN REMOVE LAST CHAR.
1080 IF ASC(B$) = 8 THEN GOTO 1120
1090 REM CHARACTER TYPED IS CONCATENATED TO A$
1100 LET A$ = A$ + B$
1110 GOTO 1160
```

```
1120 REM REMOVE ONE CHARACTER FROM A$
1130 REM UNLESS THERE ARE NO CHARACTERS TO REMOVE!
1140 IF LEN(A$) = 0 THEN GOTO 1040
1150 LET A$ = MID$(A$,1,LEN(A$)-1)
1160 PRINT B$;
1170 GOTO 1040
1180 PRINT
1190 RETURN
9999 END
```

D. THE CHR$(X) FUNCTION

In contrast to the ASC(X$) function which returns the ASCII code of its argument, CHR$(X) returns the character whose ASCII code is X. Thus:

PRINT CHR$(65)

would print an A on the screen.

You can use CHR$ to print special characters. For example:

PRINT CHR$(7);"WAKE UP!"

produces a beep from the Apple's speaker.

There are three characters that the Apple is capable of printing to the screen but for which there are no keys on the keyboard. They are the left bracket, "[", the backslash, "\", and the underline, "_". Their ASCII codes are 91, 92, and 95, respectively. This program prints the string APPLE][centered on the screen:

```
100 LET A$ = "APPLE ]" + CHR$(91)
110 LET T = INT(20 - LEN(A$)/2)
120 PRINT TAB(T);A$
130 END
```

By the way, the right bracket, "]", is a "shift-M" on the Apple keyboard. For some reason, this symbol was not printed on the key itself.

Appendix A

How to Operate the Apple II Plus

The Apple II Plus can be used in two modes -- with or without the Disk Operating System (affectionately known as "DOS"). DOS is a program written in machine language, not BASIC, which allows the computer to "talk to" the disk drive. If you want to save programs for use at a later date, or use programs that have been previously saved, then DOS is necessary. But when permanent storage isn't a requirement, DOS is not needed.

OPERATING THE APPLE WITHOUT DOS

This is the easiest mode. Sit down at the computer. At the left rear you will find a power switch. Flip on the power and you should see two lights come on. One is the power light at the lower left-hand corner of the keyboard. The other light is on the disk drive. It goes on whenever the disk drive is spinning, which it should be doing right now! Press the RESET key. The disk drive will stop and the red light will go out. Turn on the CRT (which is either a TV set or a video monitor). On the screen you should see the prompt, which is a right bracket (]), and the cursor, which is a flashing rectangle. You are now ready to program in Applesoft BASIC. Any programs that you write, however, cannot be saved on a diskette because we have no DOS.

OPERATING THE APPLE WITH DOS

Let's assume for the moment that you have in your hands an "initialized" diskette. Any initialized diskette will do. If you do not have an initialized diskette right now, keep reading. You will learn how to make one.

First a word about handling diskettes. They are pretty strong little buggers, but as the saying goes . . . don't fold, spindle, or mutilate! And especially don't wave magnets around them. You should also be aware that diskettes warp in the heat. So don't leave them on car dashboards or on top of overhead projectors. (We're guilty of both!!). Also, don't touch the magnetically coated plastic sheet that is sandwiched between the black cardboard.

Now where were we? Oh yes, you have an initialized diskette in hand. Open the door on the disk drive. With the label facing up and the oval opening away from you, insert the diskette and close the door. Now turn on the power as described above. This time the red light will go off all by itself after the disk spins for several seconds. What happens in these several seconds is that the DOS program is loaded from the diskette into the computer automatically. The expression we use to describe that process is *booting*. You have just *booted the system.* [NOTE: Occasionally the disk drive will keep spinning long after it should have stopped. Something is wrong. Press RESET and remove the diskette. It may be that (1) the diskette is not initialized, (2) it was initialized with an earlier revision of DOS, (3) the diskette wasn't seated properly in the disk drive, or (4) the disk drive needs repair. If you know that the diskette was initialized with the correct version of DOS (called DOS 3.3), then try booting the system again.]

After the red light goes off you should see the prompt and cursor. You are now ready to program in Applesoft. However, you are also able to access the disk drive and save or load programs. You should know a few of the most important DOS commands. They are INIT, CATALOG, LOAD, SAVE, and DELETE. Read on!

1. INIT

You will probably want to have a personal diskette on which you can keep your own programs. The diskettes are available at local computer stores for several dollars each. One will likely be enough for a semester's work, but you may want another to use as a back up for important programs. When you buy the diskette it is blank. Not only does it not contain any of your programs, but it also doesn't have DOS on it. To put DOS onto a blank diskette, you must initialize the diskette. Initializing the diskette automatically writes the DOS program onto it. Here's the procedure:

(a) First boot the system with an already initialized diskette.
(b) Remove the diskette and put your blank one in its place. Close the door on the disk drive.
(c) Type NEW to clear the working space, and press RETURN.
(d) Type in a short program such as

   10 HOME
   20 PRINT "THIS DISKETTE BELONGS TO JOHN Q. STUDENT"
   30 END

(e) With no line number in front of it, type

   INIT HELLO

   and press the RETURN key.

The disk will spin for about a minute and when it stops you're in business! You can use your diskette to boot the system from now on because your diskette has a copy of DOS on it. It also has one BASIC program on it called HELLO. You guessed it...the HELLO program is the one you typed in just before INITing the diskette. The HELLO program will run automatically every time you boot up. Try re-booting the system right now. Remember how? Just turn off the power and turn it back on with your initialized disk inserted in the drive. A WORD OF WARNING: If you INIT a diskette that isn't blank, you will lose all the information that is on it.

2. CATALOG

You can see which programs are stored on your diskette by typing CATALOG. Notice that the first program is called HELLO. Where did that come from?

A typical entry in the CATALOG might look like this:

A 006 BALANCING THE CHECKBOOK

The letter A means the program was written in Applesoft. The number 006 is a rough measure of how long the program is. The bigger the number, the longer the program. Finally, BALANCING THE CHECKBOOK is the name of the saved program.

3. LOAD

To bring a stored program back into the working space of the computer, type LOAD PROGRAM NAME, where PROGRAM NAME is the name of any Applesoft program found in the CATALOG. Once a program is LOADed, you can RUN it or work on it. By the way, if you just want to RUN the program you can type RUN PROGRAM NAME.

4. SAVE

Programs that you write can be saved to the diskette by typing SAVE PROGRAM NAME. The PROGRAM NAME can be any combination of up to thirty characters, it must start with a letter, and it cannot have commas in it. Spaces and other special characters are fine. You pick a name for your program only when you are ready to SAVE it, not when you begin writing it. WARNING: IF YOU SAVE YOUR PROGRAM USING THE NAME OF A PROGRAM ALREADY SAVED ON YOUR DISKETTE, THE PREVIOUSLY SAVED PROGRAM WILL BE ERASED.

5. DELETE

Unwanted programs can be removed from your diskette by typing DELETE PROGRAM NAME. You'll definitely want to remember the DELETE command if you ever get a DISK FULL error when you try to SAVE a program!

Well, that's about it! There's much more to learn, of course, but what you've just read covers all of the fundamentals. Refer to the "Disk Operating System Instructional and Reference Manual," the "Applesoft II BASIC Programming Reference Manual," and "The Applesoft Tutorial" for a more complete education.

Appendix B

Applesoft Reserved Words

In Chapter 1 you learned that no APPLESOFT variable name may contain a reserved word. Also, innocent combinations of valid variable names in certain APPLESOFT commands will inadvertently result in a reserved word. For example:

10 IF B<A THEN GOTO 100

lists as

10 IF B< AT HEN GOTO 100

The solution is to use parentheses:

10 IF (B<A) THEN GOTO 100

Here is a complete list of those combinations to stay away from.

ABS	AND	ASC	AT	ATN
CALL	CHR$	CLEAR	CONT	COS
DATA	DEF	DEL	DIM	DRAW
END	EXP	FLASH	FN	FOR
FRE	GET	GOSUB	GOTO	GR
HGR	HGR2	HLIN	HOME	HPLOT
HTAB	IF	INPUT	INT	INVERSE
LEFT$	LEN	LET	LIST	LOAD
LOG	MID$	NEW	NEXT	NORMAL
NOT	NOTRACE	ON	ONERR	OR
PDL	PEEK	PLOT	POKE	POP
POS	PRINT	READ	RECALL	REM
RESTORE	RESUME	RETURN	RIGHT$	RND
RUN	SAVE	SGN	SHLOAD	SIN
SQR	STEP	STOP	STORE	STR$
TAN	TEXT	THEN	TO	TRACE
USR	VAL	VLIN	VTAB	WAIT
XPLOT	XDRAW			

The following words may be used as long as they are not followed by an equals sign (" = "): SCALE, SPEED, and ROT.

The following words may be used as long as they are not followed by a left parenthesis ("("): SCRN, SPC, and TAB. This means they cannot be the last letters of an array name.

The words HIMEM and LOMEM may be used as long as they are not followed by a colon (":"). Since the colon is used in APPLESOFT to separate multiple statements on a line, it is possible that the HIMEM: and LOMEM: combinations could occur. It is best to avoid them altogether.

The words HCOLOR = and COLOR = are also reserved words, but the inclusion of OR within their names prevents their use anyway.

Finally, the words IN# and PR# are also reserved words. The # sign, however, makes these reserved words invalid within variable names.

Appendix C

Debugging With and Without Error Messages

Few people, even professional programmers, can write programs that run correctly the first time. Errors in computer programs are called "bugs" in computer jargon, and the process of finding them is called "debugging." Some bugs make themselves known through error messages which occur when the program is run. Other errors, such as mistakes in logical thinking, may produce faulty results but do not cause error messages. In this appendix we will discuss techniques for finding bugs in Applesoft programs with and without the help of error messages. Read Appendix D to learn how to edit program lines which are known to contain bugs.

A. DEBUGGING WITH THE HELP OF ERROR MESSAGES

What follows is a list of the most common error messages that occur and a description of the probable causes of the error.

1. SYNTAX ERROR

   This results when a statement is incorrectly constructed. It can be due to a number of things, typically a misspelled command, missing parentheses, reserved words in variable names, incorrect punctuation, etc.

2. UNDEF'D STATEMENT ERROR

   This error occurs when an attempt is made to branch to a line number which does not exist in the program.

3. BAD SUBSCRIPT ERROR

   This error results when a subscript exceeds the dimensions of an array, such as referring to A(16) when the array A has been dimensioned by DIM A(15). It can also occur if the number of dimensions is wrong, such as referring to A(16) when the array A has been dimensioned by DIM A(20,30). In a program which doesn't use arrays, the error can occur when the multiplication symbol "∗" is left out, as in

100 LET A = P(1 + R)^T

when

100 LET A = P∗(1 + R)^T

was intended. However, an error occurs only when the unintended "subscript" gets larger than 10.

4. ILLEGAL QUANTITY ERROR

This is an error that occurs when the argument of an arithmetic or string function is out of range, or when the subscript in an array variable is negative. For example, using SQR(-3) or LOG(0) in a program would result in an error, since they are mathematically impossible. The expression LEFT$(A$,0) would be in error because zero is out of the correct range for the LEFT$ function.

5. TYPE MISMATCH ERROR

This error is the result of attempting to use string data where numeric data was called for, or vice versa. Each of these statements would cause a TYPE MISMATCH error:

LET A$ = 14
LET C = B$
PRINT LEN(X)
IF G$ < P THEN GOTO 100

6. RETURN WITHOUT GOSUB ERROR

This error means that a RETURN statement was reached but there was no corresponding GOSUB statement to return to. Typically this is the result of not isolating subroutines from the main program. If the computer "falls" into a subroutine at the end of the main program, a RETURN WITHOUT GOSUB error will occur when the RETURN statement is encountered. A common solution is to put an END statement or a GOTO statement between the end of the main program and the beginning of the subroutines.

7. NEXT WITHOUT FOR ERROR

This error will occur if the NEXT statement shows an index variable which is different from the index in the FOR statement, such as

10 FOR J = 1 TO 10

         .

         .

         .

50 NEXT K

It will also occur if a NEXT statement exists when there is no FOR statement at all in the program. If you decide to remove a FOR statement in your program, delete the NEXT statement as well.

8. REDIM'D ARRAY ERROR

Once an array is dimensioned, it cannot be redimensioned. Doing so will result in a REDIM'D ARRAY error message. Here is an example:

```
10 LET A(5) = 8
20 DIM A(100)
```

Line 10 in this example caused the array A to be dimensioned to 10 automatically ("by default" in computer jargon), since it was the first reference to the array. Hence, line 20 is an attempt to redimension the array. If it is absolutely necessary to redimension an array, the CLEAR statement will make it possible to do so. (It could be placed at line 15 in the example above.) But be warned that CLEAR will erase the current values of ALL variables in your program.

9. OUT OF DATA ERROR

This error is the result of an attempt to assign data with a READ statement when all of the data in the DATA statements have already been assigned, or when there are no DATA statements at all.

10. UNDEF'D FUNCTION ERROR

This occurs when an attempt is made to use a user-defined function (see Chapter 12) which was not previously defined.

11. STRING TOO LONG ERROR

If the concatenation of strings results in a string longer than 255 characters, this error occurs.

12. OUT OF MEMORY ERROR

This error can occur for a number of reasons, but the most common is the nesting of GOSUBs more than twenty-four deep. It is not usually the intention of the programmer to have a subroutine call another subroutine which calls another subroutine, and so on, twenty-four times. But it can happen unintentionally when a GOTO statement instead of a RETURN statement causes a branch back to the main program. For example, this program will result in an OUT OF MEMORY error:

```
100 REM SUM THE NUMBERS FROM 1 TO 100
110 LET S=0
120 FOR I=1 TO 100
130 GOSUB 500
140 NEXT I
150 PRINT "THE SUM IS ";S
160 GOTO 999
500 REM SUBROUTINE TO ACCUMULATE THE NUMBERS
510 LET S=S+I
520 GOTO 140
999 END
```

Notice that line 520 sends control to line 140 not with a RETURN statement but with a GOTO statement. The subroutine is never "completed." Instead, it is called again, and then again, and so on, until the OUT OF MEMORY error interrupts the program on the twenty-fourth loop. Replacing line 520 with 520 RETURN will solve the problem. (This particular program would be better off without a subroutine at all, but we are not discussing style here.)

13. DIVISION BY ZERO ERROR

Attempting to divide by zero will cause this error. Division by zero is a mathematical impossibility.

B. DEBUGGING WITHOUT THE HELP OF ERROR MESSAGES

Programs can contain errors that do not produce error messages. This is usually caused by faulty logical reasoning on the part of the programmer. The appearance of unwanted or unexpected output is a clue that these kinds of errors exist. To help you track down these elusive errors, we offer two suggestions.

1. Place a few PRINT statements in various places in your program to show the current values of variables as the program is running. A variable which seems to have the wrong value can be tracked down this way.
2. The instruction STOP may be placed in your program. When a program is run, it will be interrupted and stop processing when it reaches the STOP statement. At that point you may use immediate mode commands, especially PRINT and LET, to display or change the values of any variables in the program. Typing CONT will start the program running again from the point at which it stopped.

```
        .
        .   (program lines)
        .
100 STOP
        .
        .   (program lines)
        .
```

```
]RUN

BREAK IN 100

]PRINT Z

14

]CONT

     (program continues running
      from line 100)
```

WARNING: Adding or changing any lines in the program will make CONT inoperable, and all variables will be cleared. A CAN'T CONTINUE error will result. Don't worry, however; just re-run the program.

Debugging is a skill that can only be learned with much practice. It is as much a part of producing a correct program as programming itself. The authors would like to offer this word of advice: Don't let others debug your programs for you or you will be missing a valuable learning experience!

Appendix D

Editing Program Lines Using Cursor Control

A program line which contains errors can always be corrected by retyping the line. However, there is another way. It is called "cursor control" and involves the use of special keys to move the cursor around the screen. (The "cursor" is the blinking rectangle which shows where the next character typed will occur.) Simply stated, to edit a program line using cursor control involves

1. LISTing the line,
2. Moving the cursor to the beginning of the line,
3. Tracing the line with the RIGHT-ARROW key,
4. Fixing the error when it is reached,
5. Tracing the remainder of the line, and
6. Pressing the RETURN key.

If you are like most people, chances are you will find that editing using cursor control is difficult at first. But you will also find it worthwhile learning, for once mastered it will save you a great deal of time.

A. THE SPECIAL KEYS FOR CONTROLLING THE CURSOR

There are certain keys which cause the cursor to move around the screen. You may want to read this while sitting at an Apple II Plus, so that you can see the effects for yourself.

The ESC key:

This key is pressed once. After pressing it, the I, J, K, and M keys are transformed into keys which move the cursor. Pressing any key other than I, J, K, or M will disable this cursor control feature. The relative locations of these keys on the keyboard and their functions are shown in this diagram:

(up)

I

(left) J   K (right)

M

(down)

In this mode, characters over which the cursor moves are NOT copied into the Apple's memory.

The RIGHT-ARROW key:

This key moves the cursor to the right. As the cursor traces over characters on the screen, those characters are copied into the Apple's memory, just as if they had been typed in from the keyboard. This is not the same as using ESC-K, since ESC-K does not copy characters into memory.

The LEFT-ARROW key:

This key moves the cursor to the left. If the cursor is tracing over characters in a program line, those characters are erased from the computer's memory. You have no doubt already used this key as a "backspace."

The REPT key:

A key can be made to automatically repeat itself if the REPT key is held down at the same time. This is a big time saver, since editing involves repeated use of the RIGHT-ARROW key.

B. AN ILLUSTRATED LESSON IN EDITING WITH CURSOR CONTROL

For the examples which follow, the underscore character "_" will be used to represent the cursor. IMPORTANT: If you make mistakes while editing the program line, press CTRL-X. This will cause any current edits to be abandoned. LIST the line again and start over.

Example 1   The program line

10 PRINT "DO YOU SEE AND ERRER?"

contains two errors. Let's work on changing ERRER to ERROR first.

1. LIST the line to the screen:

    ]LIST 10

    10 PRINT "DO YOU SEE AND ERRER?"

    ]_

    Notice the position of the cursor, which is below the zero in the line number.

2. Move the cursor up to the line. Do this by pressing ESC once. Then press the I key twice to move the cursor up two lines. The screen now looks like this:

    ]LIST 10

    1<u>0</u> PRINT "DO YOU SEE AND ERRER?"

    ]

3. Now move the cursor to the beginning of the line by pressing J once. This is important! Do NOT use the LEFT-ARROW key; it won't work here. Now we have

]LIST 10

<u>1</u>0 PRINT "DO YOU SEE AND ERRER?"

]

4. Using the RIGHT-ARROW key, move the cursor to the right, stopping on the letter to be changed:

]LIST 10

10 PRINT "DO YOU SEE AND ERR<u>E</u>R?"

]

5. Make the correction and continue with the RIGHT-ARROW key until you have traced the entire line:

]LIST 10

10 PRINT "DO YOU SEE AND ERROR?" _
]

6. Press the RETURN key, and the line will be entered into the program as corrected. LIST it to be sure:

]LIST 10

10 PRINT "DO YOU SEE AND ERROR?"

]_

Example 2   Let's work now on changing AND to AN.
　　　Do steps 1, 2, 3, and 4 to move the cursor to the letter D in AND. The screen should look like this:

]LIST 10

10 PRINT "DO YOU SEE AN<u>D</u> ERROR?"

]

Our object now is to skip over the letter D. Press the ESC key once. Press K and the cursor will move to the right one position WITHOUT copying the letter D into memory. Using the RIGHT-ARROW key continue tracing the line until you reach the end, and then press RETURN. Type LIST to see the corrected line.

]LIST 10

10 PRINT "DO YOU SEE AN ERROR?"

]_

This next example will show you how to insert characters into a line.

Example 3   Suppose the line

    10 IF X > 3 THEN GOTO 200

is part of your program. If after entering this line you decide that it should read

    10 IF X > 3 AND X < 8 THEN GOTO 200

you can insert the extra characters in this manner:

1. LIST the line and use the ESC, I, J, and RIGHT-ARROW keys to move the cursor to the space after the 3. (Remember to first back up to the beginning of the line using J before moving to the right with the RIGHT-ARROW.)

    ]LIST 10

    10 IF X > 3_THEN GOTO 200

    ]

2. Press the ESC key and then the I key to move the cursor up one line:

    ]LIST 10

    10 IF X > 3 ¯ THEN GOTO 200

    ]

3. Now type the characters to be inserted:

    ]LIST 10   AND X < 8_
    10 IF X > 3 THEN GOTO 200

    ]

4. Press ESC and then M to move the cursor down to the program line:

    ]LIST 10

            AND X < 8
    10 IF X > 3 THEN GOTO 200

    ]

5. Since the ESC key is still active, press J repeatedly to move the cursor back to the space after the 3.

    ]LIST 10
            AND X < 8
    10 IF X > 3_THEN GOTO 200

    ]

6. Now trace the remainder of the line using the RIGHT-ARROW key, and then press RETURN. LIST the line to see if it is correct:

    ]LIST 10

    10 IF X > 3 AND X < 8 THEN GOTO 200

    ]_

C. AN IMPORTANT NOTE ON EDITING LONG PROGRAM LINES

Program lines that take up two or more lines on the screen can also be edited using cursor control. However, it is advisable to type POKE 33,33 in immediate mode before listing the line to be edited. This changes the window width to thirty-three characters and has the additional desirable effect of removing unwanted spaces that are inserted automatically by the Apple. For example,

]LIST 50

```
50   PRINT "THIS IS AN EXAMPLE OF
        A RATHER LONG PROGRAM LINE.
         NOTICE THE EXTRA SPACES THE
        APPLE INSERTS AT THE BEGINN
        ING OF EACH LINE ON THE SCRE
        EN."
```

]POKE 33,33

]LIST 50

```
50 PRINT "THIS IS AN EXAMPLE OF
A RATHER LONG PROGRAM LINE. NOTI
CE THE EXTRA SPACES THE APPLE INS
ERTS AT THE BEGINNING OF EACH LIN
E ON THE SCREEN."
```

]TEXT

Using the RIGHT-ARROW key to trace over line 50 at the top will also copy the unwanted spaces into the program line. Without the embedded spaces, as in the bottom line 50, the RIGHT-ARROW key will copy only those characters which belong in the program line.

To return the screen to its normal forty character width, type TEXT in the immediate mode, as illustrated above.

Answers to chapter 1

Exercises 1.1

1. a, c, f
2. All of them are strings.
3. (a) 17   (b) 19   (c) 14   (d) 28

Exercises 1.3

1. a, b, c
2. a, c, d, f, h

Exercises 1.4

1. a, b, c, e
2. a, b, f

Exercises 1.5

1. (b) E$ is a string variable, so it cannot be assigned
        the numeric value contained in S.
    (c) Variables cannot begin with a number.
    (f) Can't assign a string value to a numeric variable.
    (h) M$ is a string variable but Y is a numeric variable.
    (i) F is a numeric variable but K$ is a string variable.

    The errors made in (b), (f), (h), and (i) are called
    TYPE MISMATCH errors.

2.

	T	R	R$	Q$	T$
	0	0			
LET T = 45	45	0			
LET R = 22.22	45	22.22			
LET T$ = "MICHELLE"	45	22.22			MICHELLE
LET Q$ = "WROTE"	45	22.22		WROTE	MICHELLE
LET R$ = "BEATLES"	45	22.22	BEATLES	WROTE	MICHELLE

3.

	A	B	C
	0	0	0
LET A = 3	3	0	0
LET B = 5	3	5	0
LET C = A	3	5	3
LET A = B	5	5	3
LET B = C	5	3	3

Exercises 1.6

1.

	F	G	X
	0	0	0
LET F = 3	3	0	0
LET G = 8	3	8	0
LET X = F	3	8	3
LET F = G	8	8	3
LET G = X	8	3	3

2.

	T	P	Z
	0	0	0
LET T = 7	7	0	0
LET P = 9	7	9	0
LET Z = P	7	9	9
LET P = T	7	7	9
LET T = Z	9	7	9

3.

	X$	Y$	Z1$	K$	P$
LET X$ = "SWEET"	SWEET				
LET Y$ = "GOOD"	SWEET	GOOD			
LET Z1$ = "PRINCE"	SWEET	GOOD	PRINCE		
LET K$ = "NIGHT"	SWEET	GOOD	PRINCE	NIGHT	
LET P$ = X$	SWEET	GOOD	PRINCE	NIGHT	SWEET
LET X$ = Y$	GOOD	GOOD	PRINCE	NIGHT	SWEET
LET Y$ = K$	GOOD	NIGHT	PRINCE	NIGHT	SWEET
LET K$ = Z1$	GOOD	NIGHT	PRINCE	PRINCE	SWEET
LET Z1$ = P$	GOOD	NIGHT	SWEET	PRINCE	SWEET
LET P$ = "!"	GOOD	NIGHT	SWEET	PRINCE	!

4.

	A	B	C	D
	0	0	0	0
LET A = 5	5	0	0	0
LET B = 4	5	4	0	0
LET C = 3	5	4	3	0
LET D = C	5	4	3	3
LET C = B	5	4	4	3
LET B = A	5	5	4	3
LET A = D	3	5	4	3

5.

	R$	Q$	T$	K$
LET R$ = "MARY"	MARY			
LET Q$ = "JOHN"	MARY	JOHN		
LET T$ = "LOVES"	MARY	JOHN	LOVES	
LET K$ = R$	MARY	JOHN	LOVES	MARY
LET R$ = Q$	JOHN	JOHN	LOVES	MARY
LET Q$ = T$	JOHN	LOVES	LOVES	MARY
LET T$ = K$	JOHN	LOVES	MARY	MARY

Exercises 1.7

1.

	V	S	R$	CRT
	0	0		
PRINT V	0	0		0
LET V = 17	17	0		
PRINT V	17	0		17
LET S = 42	17	42		

(continued)

	V	S	R$	CRT
PRINT S	17	42		42
LET V = S	42	42		
PRINT "V IS NOW"	42	42		V IS NOW
PRINT V	42	42		42
LET R$ = "THAT'S FUN"	42	42	THAT'S FUN	
PRINT R$	42	42	THAT'S FUN	THAT'S FUN
PRINT "THE END"	42	42	THAT'S FUN	THE END

Exercises 1.8

1.

	X	A	C3
	0	0	0
LET X = 4	4	0	0
LET A = X − 2	4	2	0
LET C3 = A*X	4	2	8
LET X = C3^A	64	2	8

2.

	E	F
	0	0
LET E = 3	3	0
LET F = E*E	3	9
LET F = F − E	3	6
LET F = F − E	3	3
LET E = F^E	27	3

3.

	A	CRT
	0	
LET A = 6	6	
PRINT A*3 + 2	6	20
PRINT A/3*2	6	4
LET A = (A − 4)^2	4	
PRINT A − A/4	4	3
PRINT (A − A)/4	4	0
LET A = A*A − A + A/A	13	
PRINT "A*A − A + A/A"	13	A*A − A + A/A

4.

	X	K	F	CRT
	0	0	0	
LET K = 5	0	5	0	
LET X = K/K	1	5	0	
LET F = K − X	1	5	4	
PRINT K + F	1	5	4	9
LET X = K + K	10	5	4	
LET K = (K − F)/K	10	0.2	4	
PRINT X*(X − K)	10	0.2	4	98

5.

	P	R	A	CRT
	0	0	0	
LET P = 2500	2500	0	0	
LET R = .15	2500	.15	0	
LET A = P*(1 + R)	2500	.15	2875	
PRINT A	2500	.15	2875	2875

6. LET P = 2500
   LET R = .15
   LET N = 5
   LET A = P*(1 + R)^N
   PRINT A

7.

	X1	X2	X3	X4	X5	CRT
	0	0	0	0	0	
LET X1 = 1	1	0	0	0	0	
LET X2 = 2*X1	1	2	0	0	0	
LET X3 = 3*X2	1	2	6	0	0	
LET X4 = 4*X3	1	2	6	24	0	
LET X5 = 5*X4	1	2	6	24	120	
PRINT X1	1	2	6	24	120	1
PRINT X2	1	2	6	24	120	2
PRINT X3	1	2	6	24	120	6
PRINT X4	1	2	6	24	120	24
PRINT X5	1	2	6	24	120	120

8. (continued from the Box Diagram in the exercise)

	X	Y	CRT
LET Y = Y + 1	6	4	
LET X = X*Y	24	4	
PRINT X	24	4	24
LET Y = Y + 1	24	5	
LET X = X*Y	120	5	
PRINT X	120	5	120

9.

	S	C1	T1	C2	T2	P	CRT
	0	0	0	0	0	0	
LET S = 250	250	0	0	0	0	0	
LET C1 = 76.25	250	76.25	0	0	0	0	
LET T1 = S*C1	250	76.25	19062.5	0	0	0	
PRINT T1	250	76.25	19062.5	0	0	0	19062.5
LET C2 = 81.5	250	76.25	19062.5	81.5	0	0	

(continued)	S	C1	T1	C2	T2	P	CRT
LET T2 = S*C2	250	76.25	19062.5	81.5	20375	0	
LET P = T2 − T1	250	76.25	19062.5	81.5	20375	1312.5	
PRINT P	250	76.25	19062.5	81.5	20375	1312.5	1312.5

10. Before the PRINT P command add the commands:

LET D = 4.5*S
LET P = P + D

11. Before the PRINT P command add the commands:

LET B1 = .05*T1
LET B2 = .07*T2
LET P = P − B1 − B2

Answers to chapter 2

Exercises 2.1

1. (a) PRINT SQR(X + Y)
   Computer gives 2.64575131
   (b) PRINT SQR(X*Y)
   Computer gives 3.46410162
   (c) PRINT SQR(X + SQR((X + 4*Y)/3))
   Computer gives 2.34874679
   (d) PRINT SQR(X − Y)
   Computer gives an ILLEGAL QUANTITY ERROR because you can't take the square root of a negative number.
2. LET K = 3.4
   LET X1 = SQR(K)
   LET X2 = −SQR(K)
   PRINT X1
   PRINT X2
   Computer displays 1.84390889 and −1.84390889.
   LET K = 7
   LET X1 = SQR(K)
   LET X2 = −SQR(K)
   PRINT X1
   PRINT X2
   Computer displays 2.64575131 and −2.64575131.
   LET K = 150
   LET X1 = SQR(K)
   LET X2 = −SQR(K)
   PRINT X1
   PRINT X2
   Computer displays 12.2474487 and −12.2474487.
3. LET A = 1300
   LET P = 1000
   LET R = SQR(A/P) − 1
   PRINT R
   Computer displays .140175425. That is, about 14%.
4. LET A = 1
   LET B = −7
   LET C = −11
   LET X1 = (−B + SQR(B^2 − 4*A*C))/(2*A)
   LET X2 = (−B − SQR(B^2 − 4*A*C))/(2*A)
   PRINT X1
   PRINT X2
   Computer displays 8.32182538 and −1.32182538.
   LET A = 5
   LET B = −1
   LET C = −5

LET X1 = (−B + SQR(B^2 − 4*A*C))/(2*A)
LET X2 = (−B − SQR(B^2 − 4*A*C))/(2*A)
PRINT X1
PRINT X2
   Computer displays 1.10498756 and −.904987562.
LET A = 14
LET B = 111
LET C = −2
LET X1 = (−B + SQR(B^2 − 4*A*C))/(2*A)
LET X2 = (−B − SQR(B^2 − 4*A*C))/(2*A)
PRINT X1
PRINT X2
   Computer displays .0179772586 and −7.94654869.
5. LET S = (X + Y − ABS(X − Y))/2
6. LET A = INT(10*A + .5)/10
7. LET A = INT(.01*A + .5)/.01
   or   LET A = INT(A/100 + .5)*100
8. PRINT INT(20*RND(1)) + 1
   PRINT INT(20*RND(1)) + 1
   PRINT INT(20*RND(1)) + 1
   PRINT INT(20*RND(1)) + 1
   PRINT INT(20*RND(1)) + 1
9. PRINT INT(10*RND(1)) + 6
   PRINT INT(10*RND(1)) + 6
   PRINT INT(10*RND(1)) + 6
   PRINT INT(10*RND(1)) + 6
   PRINT INT(10*RND(1)) + 6
10. LET P1 = 179000000
    LET P2 = 203000000
    LET T2 = 1970 − 1960
    LET K = (LOG(P2) − LOG(P1))/T2
    LET T1 = 2000 − 1960
    LET Q = P1*EXP(K*T1)
    PRINT Q
       Computer displays 296090896.
11. LET A = 1.732
    LET B = 1
    LET C = 2
    LET CS = (B^2 + C^2 − A^2)/(2*B*C)
    PRINT CS
       Computer displays .500044

Note: We cannot write LET COS(A1) = (B^2 + C^2 − A^2)/(2*B*C) because only variables may appear on the left side of a LET statement. The expression COS(A1) is not a variable; it is a function.

Exercises 2.2

1. (a) 21   (b) RING (c) L   (d) ITH MID (e) 7
   (f) MID (g) STR (h) TH (i) N
2. (a) Missing $ after MID
   (b) Argument must be numeric
   (c) Argument must be a string.

(d) Number of characters to be selected must be greater than zero.
(e) Quotes needed around the string DOUGHNUT.
(f) Argument must be a string only.

Answers to chapter 3

Exercises 3.4

1 and 2 combined.

(a)

Line	W	CRT
	0	
100 LET W = 126	126	
110 PRINT "A PERSON WEIGHING"	126	A PERSON WEIGHING
120 PRINT W	126	126
130 PRINT "POUNDS ON EARTH"	126	POUNDS ON EARTH
140 PRINT "WOULD WEIGH"	126	WOULD WEIGH
150 PRINT W/6	126	21
160 PRINT "POUNDS ON THE MOON"	126	POUNDS ON THE MOON
170 END	126	

(b)

Line	T1	T2	T3	A	CRT
	0	0	0	0	
10 LET T1 = 80	80	0	0	0	
20 LET T2 = 85	80	85	0	0	
30 LET T3 = 93	80	85	93	0	
40 LET A = (T1 + T2 + T3)/3	80	85	93	86	
50 PRINT "MY TEST AVERAGE"	80	85	93	86	MY TEST AVERAGE
60 PRINT A	80	85	93	86	86
70 END	80	85	93	86	

3. (a)
```
10 LET X = 23
20 LET Q = 2
30 LET L = X − Q
40 LET X = X + Q
50 PRINT X + Q
60 END
```

(b)
```
100 LET E1 = −6
110 LET T = 1
120 LET R$ = "SMART"
130 LET E1 = E1*E1
140 PRINT R$
150 END
```

4.

Line	B	D	C	S	CRT
	0	0	0	0	
100 LET B = 458.65	458.85	0	0	0	
110 LET D = 125.50	458.85	125.5	0	0	
120 LET C = 45.76	458.85	125.5	45.76	0	

(continued)

	B	D	C	S	CRT
130 LET S=B+D−C	458.85	125.5	45.76	538.59	
140 PRINT S	458.85	125.5	45.76	538.59	538.59
150 END	458.85	125.5	45.76	538.59	

5.

	B	D	C	S	CRT
	0	0	0	0	
100 LET S=B+D−C	0	0	0	0	
110 LET D=125.50	0	125.5	0	0	
120 LET C=45.76	0	125.5	45.76	0	
130 LET B=458.65	458.65	125.5	45.76	0	
140 PRINT S	458.65	125.5	45.76	0	0
150 END	458.65	125.5	45.76	0	

This program doesn't find the correct ending balance S, because B, D, and C have not been assigned values at the time S is computed.

6.

	B	C	A	CRT
	0	0	0	
100 LET B=34	34	0	0	
110 LET C=110	34	110	0	
120 LET A=180−B−C	34	110	36	
130 PRINT A	34	110	36	36
140 END	34	110	36	

7.

	B	C	A	CRT
	0	0	0	
100 LET A=180−B−C	0	0	180	
110 LET C=110	0	110	180	
120 LET B=34	34	110	180	
130 PRINT A	34	110	180	180
140 END	34	110	180	

By interchanging lines 100 and 120, the variable A is assigned while B and C still contain zero.

8.
```
20 LET C=90
30 LET A=26.72
40 LET B=180−A−C
50 PRINT B
60 END
```

9.

	P	D	R	I	CRT
	0	0	0	0	
100 LET P=6000	6000	0	0	0	
110 LET D=1000	6000	1000	0	0	
120 LET R=.015	6000	1000	.015	0	

130 LET I = (P − D) * R	6000	1000	.015	75	
140 PRINT I	6000	1000	.015	75	(75)
150 END	6000	1000	.015	75	

10.
```
100 LET P = 6000
110 LET D = 1000
120 LET R = .015
130 LET I = (P − D)*R
140 PRINT "FIRST MONTH'S INTEREST OWED"
150 PRINT I
160 LET B = P − D + I − 250
170 PRINT "AMOUNT STILL OWED"
180 PRINT B
190 END
```

11.

	P	R	I	CRT
	0	0	0	
5 LET P = 5000	5000	0	0	
10 LET R = .015	5000	.015	0	
15 LET I = P*R	5000	.015	75	
20 LET P = P + I	5075	.015	75	
25 PRINT "INTEREST EARNED"	5075	.015	75	INTEREST EARNED
30 PRINT I	5075	.015	75	75
35 PRINT "AMOUNT IN ACCOUNT AFTER ONE MONTH"	5075	.015	75	AMOUNT IN ACCOUNT AFTER ONE MONTH
40 PRINT P	5075	.015	75	5075
45 END	5075	.015	75	

12. Change lines 5 and 10 to:

```
5 LET P = 4800
10 LET R = .02
```

13.
```
5 LET P = 4800
10 LET R = .02
20 LET I = P*R
40 LET P = P + I
50 PRINT "INTEREST EARNED FOR FIRST MONTH IS"
60 PRINT I
70 PRINT "PRINCIPAL AT THE END OF FIRST MONTH IS"
80 PRINT P
90 LET I = P*R
100 LET P = P + I
110 PRINT "INTEREST EARNED FOR THE SECOND MONTH IS"
120 PRINT I
130 PRINT "PRINCIPAL AT THE END OF THE SECOND MONTH IS"
140 PRINT P
150 END
```

```
]RUN

INTEREST EARNED FOR FIRST MONTH IS
-96
PRINCIPAL AT THE END OF THE FIRST MONTH IS
4896
INTEREST EARNED FOR THE SECOND MONTH IS
97.92
PRINCIPAL AT THE END OF THE SECOND MONTH IS
4993.92
```

14.

	IBM	P1	ITT	P2	T	CRT
	0	0	0	0	0	
100 LET IBM = 120	120	0	0	0	0	
200 LET P1 = 76.75	120	76.75	0	0	0	
300 LET ITT = 76	120	76.75	76	0	0	
500 LET P2 = 23.50	120	76.75	76	23.5	0	
550 LET T = IBM*P1 + ITT*P2	120	76.75	76	23.5	10996	
575 PRINT "MR. JONES' TOTAL INVESTMENT IS"	120	76.75	76	23.5	10996	MR. JONES' TOTAL INVESTMENT IS
600 PRINT T	120	76.75	76	23.5	10996	10996
800 END	120	76.75	76	23.5	10996	

15. Add the following BASIC lines to the program:

```
510 LET FM = 250
520 LET P3 = 65.25
550 LET T = IBM*P1 + ITT*P2 + FM*P3
```

Exercises 3.5

1.

	Y	D	H	M	CRT
	0	0	0	0	
70 LET Y = 5	5	0	0	0	
80 LET D = 365*Y	5	1825	0	0	
90 LET H = 24*D	5	1825	43800	0	
120 LET M = 60*H	5	1825	43800	2628000	
130 PRINT "THE NUMBER OF MINUTES EQUALS"	5	1825	43800	2628000	THE NUMBER OF MINUTES EQUALS
140 PRINT M	5	1825	43800	2628000	2628000
150 END	5	1825	43800	2628000	

2.
```
10 REM M IS THE NUMBER OF MINUTES
20 REM H IS THE NUMBER OF HOURS
30 REM D IS THE NUMBER OF DAYS
40 REM Y IS THE NUMBER OF YEARS
50 LET M = 2628000
60 LET H = M/60
70 LET D = H/24
80 LET Y = D/365
90 PRINT "THE NUMBER OF YEARS IS"
100 PRINT Y
110 END
```

Exercises 3.7

1. (a)
```
20 REM ASSIGNMENT MODULE       80 REM OUTPUT MODULE
30 LET X = 24                  90 PRINT X
40 LET Y = -4                  95 PRINT Z
50 REM COMPUTE MODULE          100 PRINT T
60 LET Z = X+Y                 110 END
70 LET T = 2*X - Y^3
```

(b)
```
10 REM ASSIGNMENT MODULE          70 PRINT Q$
20 LET Q$ = "MY"                  80 PRINT R$
30 LET R$ = "NAME"                90 PRINT E1$
40 LET E1$ = "IS"                100 PRINT W$
50 LET W$ = "MOZART"             110 PRINT "!"
60 REM OUTPUT MODULE             120 END
```

Answers to chapter 4

Exercises 4.2

1. (a) 25   5   625
        255625
        25 5 625
   (b) MR. TALKER'S PHONE NUMBER IS 555-8324
   (c) ANTIDISESTABLISHMENTARIANISM HAS 28 LETTERS.

Answers to chapter 5

Exercises 5.1

1. (a)

	A	D	F1	H	CRT
	0	0	0	0	
200 READ A,D,F1	5	6	−2	0	
210 LET H = 2*A − D/2*F1	5	6	−2	16	
220 PRINT H	5	6	−2	16	16
230 DATA 5,6, − 2	5	6	−2	16	
240 END	5	6	−2	16	

(b)

	R$	T	E	F$	CRT
		0	0		
30 READ R$,T,E,F$	TEA	4	2	?	
35 PRINT R$,T,E;	TEA	4	2	?	TEA 4 2
40 PRINT F$	TEA	4	2	?	TEA 4 2?
50 DATA "TEA"	TEA	4	2	?	
60 DATA 4,2	TEA	4	2	?	
70 DATA "?"	TEA	4	2	?	
80 END	TEA	4	2	?	

(c)

	X	Y	Z	CRT
10 DATA 2,3,4	0	0	0	
20 READ X,Y,Z	2	3	4	
30 LET Z = X+Y+Z	2	3	9	
40 PRINT Z	2	3	9	9
50 END	2	3	9	

2. (a) Won't run. T, a numeric variable, is being assigned the string "WELL".
   (b) Won't run. Not enough data for the variables in the READ statement.
   (c) Output: MOZART   4

(d) Won't run. No DATA statement for the READ statement.

(e) Output: 7   7   7

(f) Output: 3   5

3. (a) 100 REM BALANCING THE CHECKBOOK
       110 READ B,D,C
       120 LET S = B + D − C
       130 PRINT S
       140 DATA 458.65, 125.50, 45.76
       150 END

   (b) 100 REM SOLVING FOR AN ANGLE
       110 READ B,C
       120 LET A = 180 − B − C
       130 PRINT A
       140 DATA 34,110
       150 END

   (c) 100 REM INTEREST CHARGES
       110 READ P,D,R
       120 LET I = (P − D)∗R
       130 PRINT I
       140 DATA 6000,1000,.015
       150 END

   (d) 100 REM STOCK MARKET ANALYSIS
       110 READ IBM, P1, ITT, P2
       120 LET T = IBM∗P1 + ITT∗P2
       130 PRINT "MR. JONES' TOTAL INVESTMENT IS"
       140 PRINT T
       150 DATA 120, 76.75, 75, 23.50
       160 END

Exercises 5.2

1. 100 REM COMPUTES THE AVERAGE AGE OF THE GIRLS ONLY
   110 LET S = 0
   120 READ N$,A
   130 READ N$,A
   135 PRINT N$;" IS ";A;" YEARS OLD."
   140 LET S = S + A
   150 READ N$,A
   155 PRINT N$;" IS ";A;" YEARS OLD."
   160 LET S = S + A
   170 READ N$,A
   180 READ N$,A
   185 PRINT N$;" IS ";A;" YEARS OLD."
   190 LET S = S + A
   200 LET M = S/3
   210 PRINT "THE AVERAGE AGE OF THE GIRLS IS ";M
   220 DATA "ERIC",6,"KRISTIN",8,"MELANIE",10
   230 DATA "ROY",12,"KIM",13,"PAUL",18
   240 END

```
JRUN

10.3333333
```

Exercise 5.3

1. 110 REM STUDENT TEST AVERAGES
   120 READ A,B,C
   130 PRINT "DENNIS'S AVERAGE SCORE IS "; (A + B + C)/3
   140 READ A,B,C
   150 PRINT "ALAN'S AVERAGE SCORE IS "; (A + B + C)/3
   160 READ A,B,C
   170 PRINT "TOM'S AVERAGE SCORE IS "; (A + B + C)/3
   180 READ A,B,C
   190 PRINT "ANDY'S AVERAGE SCORE IS "; (A + B + C)/3
   200 RESTORE
   210 REM COMPUTE CLASS AVERAGE FOR EACH TEST
   220 LET S1 = 0 : REM ACCUMULATOR FOR TEST 1 SCORES
   230 LET S2 = 0 : REM ACCUMULATOR FOR TEST 2 SCORES

```
240 LET S3 = 0 : REM ACCUMULATOR FOR TEST 3 SCORES
250 READ A,B,C
260 LET S1 = S1 + A
270 LET S2 = S2 + B
280 LET S3 = S3 + C
290 READ A,B,C
300 LET S1 = S1 + A
310 LET S2 = S2 + B
320 LET S3 = S3 + C
330 READ A,B,C
340 LET S1 = S1 + A
350 LET S2 = S2 + B
360 LET S3 = S3 + C
370 READ A,B,C
380 LET S1 = S1 + A
390 LET S2 = S2 + B
400 LET S3 = S3 + C
410 PRINT "TEST 1 AVERAGE = ";S1/4
420 PRINT "TEST 2 AVERAGE = ";S2/4
430 PRINT "TEST 3 AVERAGE = ";S3/4
440 REM
450 DATA 78,89,56,56,66,89,81,55,99,66,78,80
460 END
```

Exercises 5.4

```
1. 100 REM STOCK ANALYSIS FOR ARBITRARY VALUES
   110 REM
   115 REM ASSIGNMENT MODULE
   120 INPUT "HOW MANY SHARES OF IBM? ";S1
   130 INPUT "HOW MUCH PER SHARE? ";D1
   140 INPUT "HOW MANY SHARES OF SONY? ";S2
   150 INPUT "HOW MUCH PER SHARE? ";D2
   160 INPUT "HOW MANY SHARES OF ITT? ";S3
   170 INPUT "HOW MUCH PER SHARE? ";D3
   180 REM COMPUTE MODULE
   190 LET I1 = S1*D1
   200 LET I2 = S2*D2
   210 LET I3 = S3*D3
   220 LET T = I1 + I2 + I3
   230 REM
   240 REM OUTPUT MODULE
   260 PRINT
   270 PRINT "YOUR INVESTMENT IN IBM IS $";I1
   280 PRINT "YOUR INVESTMENT IN SONY IS $";I2
   290 PRINT "YOUR INVESTMENT IN ITT IS $";I3
   300 PRINT "YOUR TOTAL INVESTMENT IS $";T
   310 END
2.   5 INPUT "WHAT IS THE PRINCIPAL INVESTMENT? ";P
    10 INPUT "WHAT IS THE MONTHLY INTEREST RATE? ";R
    20 LET I = P*R
    30 LET P = P + I
    40 PRINT "INTEREST EARNED: ";I
    50 PRINT "AMOUNT IN ACCOUNT AFTER ONE MONTH: ";P
    60 END
```

Answers to chapter 6

Exercises 6.1

1. (a) FALSE   (b) TRUE   (c) TRUE   (d) FALSE
2. (a) The numeric value 2 cannot be compared with
       the string variable X$.
   (b) The string "4" cannot be compared with numeric
       variable B.
   (c) PRINT R is not a condition.
   (d) Condition cannot follow THEN.

3.

	X	X1$	T	Z$	CRT
	0		0		
100 LET X = 2	2		0		
110 LET X1$ = "HELLO"	2	HELLO	0		
120 LET T = 4	2	HELLO	4		
130 LET Z$ = "SO LONG"	2	HELLO	4	SO LONG	
140 IF X + 1<>2 THEN LET T = 0	2	HELLO	0	SO LONG	
150 IF T = 0 THEN PRINT X	2	HELLO	0	SO LONG	2
160 IF X1$<Z$ THEN LET Z$ = "TOMORROW"	2	HELLO	0	TOMORROW	
170 IF T>X + 6 THEN LET T = 5	2	HELLO	0	TOMORROW	
180 END	2	HELLO	0	TOMORROW	

4. (a)

	R	V1	K$
	0	0	
100 LET R = 2	2	0	
110 LET V1 = 45	2	45	
120 LET K$ = "HE"	2	45	HE
130 IF K$>"SHE" OR V1 = 100 THEN LET R = R + 1	2	45	HE
140 IF K$<"SHE" OR V1 = 100 THEN LET R = R − 2	0	45	HE
150 IF K$<"SHE" AND V1<>100 THEN LET R = R − 2	− 2	45	HE
160 END	− 2	45	HE

(b)

	G3$	T$	R	Y
			0	0
10 LET G3$ = "CAT"	CAT		0	0
20 LET T$ = "DOG"	CAT	DOG	0	0
30 LET R = 3	CAT	DOG	3	0
40 IF G3$<>"KITTY" AND R<2 THEN LET Y = Y + R∗2	CAT	DOG	3	0
50 IF G3$<>"KITTY" OR R<2 THEN LET Y = Y + R∗2	CAT	DOG	3	6
60 IF (R = 5 AND T$ = "DOG") OR T$<>"POOCH" THEN LET T$ = "CHOW"	CAT	CHOW	3	6
70 IF (R = 5 OR T$ = "PUPPY") AND T$<>"POOCH" THEN LET T$ = "BONE"	CAT	CHOW	3	6
80 END	CAT	CHOW	3	6

5. (a)

	X	Y	L	CRT
	0	0	0	
10 INPUT X,Y	35	72	0	? 35,72
20 LET L=X	35	72	35	
30 IF Y>L THEN LET L=Y	35	72	72	
40 PRINT "THE LARGER ONE IS ";L	35	72	72	THE LARGER ONE IS 72
50 END	35	72	72	

(b) Change to the following lines:

```
30 IF Y<L THEN LET L=Y
40 PRINT "THE SMALLER ONE IS ";L
```

(c)
```
10 INPUT X,Y
20 LET L=X
30 IF Y>L THEN LET L=Y
40 IF X<>Y THEN PRINT "THE LARGER ONE IS ";L
50 IF X=Y THEN PRINT "THEY ARE EQUAL"
60 END
```

(d)
```
10 INPUT X,Y
20 IF X>Y THEN PRINT "THE LARGER ONE IS ";X
30 IF X<Y THEN PRINT "THE LARGER ONE IS ";Y
40 END
```

6. (a)

	X	Y	Z	L	CRT
	0	0	0	0	
120 INPUT X,Y,Z	5	23	17	0	? 5,23,17
130 LET L=X	5	23	17	5	
140 IF L<Y THEN LET L=Y	5	23	17	23	
150 IF L<Z THEN LET L=Z	5	23	17	23	
160 PRINT "THE LARGEST IS" ;L	5	23	17	23	THE LARGEST IS 23
170 END	5	23	17	23	

(b) The variable L is always assumed to hold the largest number. When another number is found to be larger, it is placed in L.

(c)
```
100 REM FINDS THE SMALLEST OF FOUR NUMBERS
120 INPUT X,Y,Z,W
130 LET L=X
140 IF L>Y THEN LET L=Y
150 IF L>Z THEN LET L=Z
160 IF L>W THEN LET L=W
170 PRINT "THE SMALLEST IS ";L
180 END
```

7. (a) If something other than PEANUTS, WALNUTS, or CASHEWS is typed in, the value of X will remain zero. Line 130 will detect this, print a message, and end the program. Good programs will check for unexpected input.

(b) Delete lines 110 to 200 and include these lines instead:

```
110 INPUT "HOW MANY POUNDS DO YOU WANT OF PEANUTS? ";P
120 INPUT "HOW MANY POUNDS DO YOU WANT OF WALNUTS? ";W
130 INPUT "HOW MANY POUNDS DO YOU WANT OF CASHEWS? ";C
140 LET Q=1.85*P + 2.34*W + 4.85*C
150 PRINT "THE TOTAL PRICE IS ";Q
160 END
```

(c) Make these changes to the original program:

    155 READ A1,A2,A3
    160 IF N$ = "PEANUTS" THEN LET Q = P∗A1
    170 IF N$ = "WALNUTS" THEN LET Q = P∗A2
    180 IF N$ = "CASHEWS" THEN LET Q = P∗A3
    200 DATA 1.85,2.34,4.85
    210 END

(d) So that the input will be on the same line as the question.

(e) Change and add the following lines

    120 IF N$ = "PEANUTS" THEN LET X = 1
    122 IF N$ = "WALNUTS" THEN LET X = 1
    125 IF N$ = "CASHEWS" THEN LET X = 1

Exercises 6. 2

1. No difference, IF the user types only YES or NO. (See #2)

2. It forces the user to type YES to terminate the program. Anything else will start the program over again. In a good program, "drastic" decisions, such as ending the program should require a specific response. All other responses should cause the least harm, which in this case means starting the program over again.

   If line 50 is replaced with 50 IF D$ = "NO" THEN GOTO 20 , then an unexpected input will end the program . This is not desirable.

3. 110 REM ASSIGNMENT MODULE
   115 LET S = 0
   120 LET A = 3
   125 REM COMPUTE MODULE
   130 LET S = S + A
   140 IF A = 1001 THEN GOTO 180
   160 LET A = A + 2
   170 GOTO 130
   175 REM OUTPUT MODULE
   180 PRINT "THE SUM IS ";S
   190 END

4. 140 REM ASSIGNMENT MODULE
   150 LET S = 0
   160 LET D = 1
   170 REM COMPUTE MODULE
   190 LET S = S + (1/D)^2
   200 LET D = D + 1
   210 IF D<51 THEN GOTO 190
   220 REM OUTPUT MODULE
   230 PRINT "THE SUM IS ";S
   240 END

5. An OUT OF DATA error would occur if there were only one asterisk at the end of the data list. Actually, the second asterisk may be any string. It is read into Y$ but not used.

6. Assume the same data statements are used (lines 20-45).

   50 INPUT "TYPE TELEPHONE NUMBER ";N$
   60 READ X$,Y$
   70 IF Y$ = "∗" THEN PRINT "THE TELEPHONE # DOES NOT EXIST": GOTO 100
   80 IF Y$<>N$ THEN GOTO 60
   90 PRINT "FOR THE PHONE NUMBER ";N$;" THE NAME IS ";X$
   100 END

7. Change these lines:

   20 DATA "JOE'S BUTCHER SHOP","24 HOG ST.", "234-5678" (etc.)
   40 DATA "CALIFORNIA BANK","13 MAPLE ST","445-5678"
   45 DATA "∗","∗","∗"
   60 READ X$,Y$,Z$
   100 PRINT N$;" 'S NUMBER IS ";Z$
   105 PRINT "THE ADDRESS IS ";Y$

8. Whether or not a deposit is to be made, the variable
   D is reset to zero. Then, if no deposit is made, the
   formula in line 150 will still work.
9. 110 INPUT "ENTER THE CURRENT BALANCE ";B
   120 INPUT "DO YOU WISH TO MAKE A DEPOSIT? ";A$
   125 LET D = 0
   130 IF A$ = "YES" THEN INPUT "TYPE DEPOSIT: ";D
   135 LET B = B + D
   140 INPUT "ENTER CHECK'S VALUE (TYPE 0 WHEN FINISHED) ";C
   150 IF C = 0 THEN GOTO 190
   160 LET B = B – C
   165 GOTO 140
   190 INPUT "DO YOU WISH TO MAKE ANOTHER ENTRY?";A$
   200 IF A$ = "YES" THEN GOTO 125
   210 PRINT "YOUR NEW BALANCE IS ";B
   220 END

Answers to chapter 7

Exercises 7.1

1.

	Q	R$	CRT
110 FOR Q = 1 TO 3	1		
FIRST LOOP			
120 READ R$	1	CHINA	
130 PRINT R$	1	CHINA	CHINA
140 NEXT Q	2	CHINA	
SECOND LOOP			
120 READ R$	2	2	
130 PRINT R$	2	2	2
140 NEXT Q	3	2	
THIRD LOOP			
120 READ R$	3	EUROPE	
130 PRINT R$	3	EUROPE	EUROPE
140 NEXT Q	4	EUROPE	
150 END	4	EUROPE	

2.

	I	K	CRT
20 FOR I = 1 TO 10	1	0	
FIRST LOOP			
30 LET K = 2*I	1	2	
40 IF K>4 THEN GOTO 60	1	2	
50 NEXT I	2	2	
SECOND LOOP			
30 LET K = 2*I	2	4	
40 IF K>4 THEN GOTO 60	2	4	
50 NEXT I	3	4	

(continued)   I   K   CRT

THIRD LOOP

   30 LET K = 2*I   [3]   [6]

   40 IF K>4 THEN GOTO 60   [3]   [6]

LOOP FINISHED

   60 PRINT "THAT'S ALL FOLKS"   [3]   [6]   (THAT'S ALL FOLKS)

   70 END   [3]   [6]

3. 100 FOR I = 3 TO 6
   110 LET P = 2*I − 5
   115 PRINT P
   120 NEXT I
   130 END

4. (a) 1.2   (b) 3.5   12.25   (c) 3   (d) 8
       1.4   3   9   6
       1.6   2.5   6.25
       1.8   2   4
       2   1.5   2.25
       2.2   1   1
       2.4   .5   .25
       2.6   0   0

Exercises 7.2

1. 20 REM ASSIGNMENT MODULE
    30 INPUT "WHAT IS THE INITIAL INVESTMENT? ";P
    40 INPUT "WHAT IS THE INTEREST RATE? ";R
    50 INPUT "FOR HOW MANY YEARS? "; N
    55 PRINT
    60 REM COMPUTE AND OUTPUT MODULES
    65 REM THE FOLLOWING LINE CONVERTS AN INTEREST RATE SUCH
    68 REM AS 15 PERCENT TO .15
    70 IF R>1 THEN LET R = R/100
    80 FOR I = 1 TO N
    90 LET P = P + P*R
    100 PRINT "AMOUNT AFTER ";I;" YEARS IS $";P
    110 NEXT I
    120 END

```
]RUN
WHAT IS THE INITIAL INVESTMENT? 1000
WHAT IS THE INTEREST RATE? 6.5
FOR HOW MANY YEARS? 10

AMOUNT AFTER 1 YEARS IS 1065
AMOUNT AFTER 2 YEARS IS 1134.225
AMOUNT AFTER 3 YEARS IS 1207.94963
AMOUNT AFTER 4 YEARS IS 1286.46635
AMOUNT AFTER 5 YEARS IS 1370.08666
AMOUNT AFTER 6 YEARS IS 1459.1423
AMOUNT AFTER 7 YEARS IS 1553.98655
AMOUNT AFTER 8 YEARS IS 1654.99567
AMOUNT AFTER 9 YEARS IS 1762.57039
AMOUNT AFTER 10 YEARS IS 1877.13747
```

2. Add the following statements:
       85 LET V = P*R + V
      115 PRINT "TOTAL INTEREST EARNED IS $";V
3. 10 INPUT "HOW MANY TERMS? ";M
      20 LET S = 0
      30 FOR K = 1 TO M
      40 LET S = S + 1/(K*(K+1)*(K+2))

```
50 NEXT K
60 PRINT "THE SUM OF   ";M;"   TERMS IS   ";S
70 END
```

```
]RUN
HOW MANY TERMS? 10
THE SUM OF 10 TERMS IS .246212121
```

```
]RUN
HOW MANY TERMS? 100
THE SUM OF 100 TERMS IS .249951466
```

```
]RUN
HOW MANY TERMS? 1000
THE SUM OF 1000 TERMS IS .249999501
```

4.
```
100 REM FIND SUM OF NUMBERS IN DATA LIST
105 LET S = 0
110 FOR I = 1 TO 10
120 READ X
130 LET S = S + X
140 NEXT I
150 REM COMPUTE AVERAGE
160 LET A = S/10
170 RESTORE
180 REM FINDS AND PRINTS ALL NUMBERS LESS THAN AVERAGE
190 FOR I = 1 TO 10
200 READ X
210 IF A> = X THEN PRINT X
220 NEXT I
230 DATA 567,45,668,3322, − 234,44,6789, − 34,67,77
240 END
```

```
]RUN
567
45
668
-234
44
-34
67
77
```

5.
```
100 LET S = 0
110 FOR I = 1 TO 50
120 LET X = INT(RND(1)*100) + 1
130 LET S = S + X
140 NEXT I
145 LET S = S/50
150 PRINT "THE AVERAGE OF THE FIFTY RANDOM NUMBERS IS ";S
160 END
```

6. Using the same DATA statements the program could be written

```
(110 − 140 as before)
150 INPUT "WHAT IS THE TELEPHONE NUMBER? ";T$
160 FOR I = 1 TO 5
170 READ X$,Y$
180 IF Y$<>T$ THEN GOTO 215
190 PRINT "THE NAME IS ";X$
200 LET E = 1
210 LET I = 5
215 NEXT I
220 IF E = 1 THEN GOTO 240
230 PRINT "SORRY, NO SUCH TELEPHONE NUMBER"
240 END
```

```
]RUN
WHAT IS THE TELEPHONE NUMBER? 235-6666
THE NAME IS MARY JONES
```

7. Change and add the following lines:

    102 REM THE FOLLOWING DATA STATEMENT TELLS THE NUMBER OF
    105 REM NAMES IN THE DIRECTORY
    107 DATA 5
    145 READ N
    160 FOR I = 1 TO N

Exercises 7. 3

1. The empty PRINT statement disables the last semicolon, so that the next row of numbers appears on a new line.
2. 100 FOR I = 1 TO 4
    110 FOR J = 1 TO 5
    120 PRINT I;" + ";J;" = ";I + J;"   ";
    140 NEXT J
    145 PRINT
    150 NEXT I
    160 END

Answers to chapter 8

Exercises 8.1

1.

Line	I	C(1)	C(2)	C(3)	S	CRT
	0	0	0	0	0	
110 FOR I = 1 TO 3	1	0	0	0	0	
120 INPUT "TYPE A NUMBER: ";C(I)	1	23	0	0	0	TYPE A NUMBER: 23
130 NEXT I	2	23	0	0	0	
120 INPUT "TYPE A NUMBER: ";C(I)	2	23	5	0	0	TYPE A NUMBER: 5
130 NEXT I	3	23	5	0	0	
120 INPUT "TYPE A NUMBER: ";C(I)	3	23	5	− 22	0	TYPE A NUMBER: − 22
130 NEXT I	4	23	5	− 22	0	
140 LET S = 0	4	23	5	− 22	0	
150 FOR I = 1 TO 3	1	23	5	− 22	0	
160 LET S = S + C(I)	1	23	5	− 22	23	
170 NEXT I	2	23	5	− 22	23	
160 LET S = S + C(I)	2	23	5	− 22	28	
170 NEXT I	3	23	5	− 22	28	
160 LET S = S + C(I)	3	23	5	− 22	6	
170 NEXT I	4	23	5	− 22	6	
190 PRINT "SUM IS ";S	4	23	5	− 22	6	SUM IS 6

200 END

2. Here is one of many solutions:

    LET A(1) = (A(4) − A(2))/A(2)   LET A(3) = A(4) + A(2)
    LET A(2) = A(1) + A(1)   LET A(2) = A(2) − A(2)
    LET A(4) = A(2) + A(2) + A(4)

3.

	K	I	G(1)	G(2)	G(3)
10 DATA 3,2	0	0	0	0	0
15 READ I,K	2	3	0	0	0
20 LET G(I) = 10	2	3	0	0	10
25 LET G(K) = 4	2	3	0	4	10
30 LET G(I − K) = 5*G(I)	2	3	50	4	10
35 RESTORE	2	3	50	4	10
40 READ G(K),K	2	3	50	3	10
45 LET G(K − 1) = G(G(K))	2	3	10	3	10

4.
```
 90 REM ASSIGNMENT MODULE
100 FOR K = 1 TO 10
110 INPUT "TYPE A NUMBER "; B(K)
120 NEXT K
125 REM COMPUTATION MODULE
130 LET S = 0
140 FOR K = 1 TO 10
150 LET S = S + B(K)
160 NEXT K
170 LET A = S/10
175 REM OUTPUT MODULE
180 PRINT "THE FOLLOWING NUMBERS ARE GREATER THAN ";A
185 FOR I = 1 TO 10
190 IF A<B(I) THEN PRINT B(I)
200 NEXT I
205 PRINT
210 PRINT "THE FOLLOWING NUMBERS ARE LESS THAN OR EQUAL TO ";A
220 FOR I = 1 TO 10
230 IF A> = B(I) THEN PRINT B(I)
240 NEXT I
250 END
```

Exercises 8.2

1.
```
100 DIM A(30),E1(30),E2(30),E3(30)
110 REM STORES GRADES AND THE AVERAGE FOR EACH STUDENT
120 FOR I = 1 TO 30
130 PRINT "STUDENT NUMBER ";I
140 INPUT "WHAT ARE THE GRADES? ";E1(I),E2(I),E3(I)
145 LET A(I) = (E1(I) + E2(I) + E3(I))/3
150 PRINT
160 NEXT I
170 REM PRINTS STUDENT NUMBERS OF THOSE WHOSE TEST
180 REM AVERAGE IS GREATER THAN 80.
190 PRINT "THE FOLLOWING STUDENT NUMBERS HAVE AN AVERAGE
         GRADE GREATER THAN 80"
200 FOR I = 1 TO 30
210 IF A(I)>80 THEN PRINT I
220 NEXT I
230 END
```

2. Without the parentheses, the computer would associate the letter A with the T in THEN and consider it as the reserved word AT. This would cause a SYNTAX ERROR.

3.
```
100 REM STORES N RANDOM NUMBERS BETWEEN 1 AND 100
110 INPUT "HOW MANY RANDOM NUMBERS ARE TO BE COMPUTED? ";N
120 DIM R(N)
125 REM ASSIGNMENT MODULE
130 FOR I = 1 TO N
140 LET R(I) = INT(RND(1)*100) + 1
150 NEXT I
160 REM COMPUTES THE AVERAGE OF THE N NUMBERS
165 LET S = 0
```

```
170 REM COMPUTATION MODULE
180 FOR I = 1 TO N
190 LET S = S + R(I)
200 NEXT I
210 LET A = S/N
220 REM OUTPUT MODULE
230 REM PRINTS ALL NUMBERS LARGER THAN THE AVERAGE
235 PRINT "THE FOLLOWING ARE ALL NUMBERS LARGER THAN ";A
240 FOR I = 1 TO N
250 IF A<R(I) THEN PRINT R(I)
260 NEXT I
270 REM PRINTS ALL OF THE EVEN NUMBERS
280 PRINT "THE FOLLOWING ARE ALL EVEN NUMBERS: "
290 FOR I = 1 TO N
300 IF INT(R(I)/2) = R(I)/2 THEN PRINT R(I)
310 NEXT I
320 END
```

4.
```
100 REM STORING AND AVERAGING N RANDOM NUMBERS
105 INPUT "HOW MANY RANDOM NUMBERS TO BE AVERAGED? ";N
110 DIM W(N)
120 LET S = 0
130 LET C = 0
140 FOR K = 1 TO N
150 LET W(K) = RND(1)
160 LET S = S + W(K)
170 NEXT K
180 LET A = S/N
190 PRINT "THE AVERAGE IS "; A
200 FOR K = 1 TO N
210 IF (W(K)>A) THEN PRINT W(K): LET C = C + 1
220 NEXT K
230 PRINT C;" NUMBERS ARE LARGER THAN THE AVERAGE."
240 END
```

5.
```
100 INPUT "HOW MANY NUMBERS TO BE USED IN COMPUTING THE
        STANDARD DEVIATION? ";N
105 DIM A(N),B(N)
110 REM ENTER N NUMBERS INTO THE ARRAY A
120 FOR I = 1 TO N
130 INPUT A(I)
140 NEXT I
150 REM PERFORM STEP (A)
155 LET S = 0
160 FOR I = 1 TO N
170 LET S = S + A(I)
180 NEXT I
190 REM WE USE A FOR AVERAGE. THE SIMPLE VARIABLE A IS
200 REM DIFFERENT THAN THE ARRAY A.
210 LET A = S/N
220 REM PERFORM STEP (B)
230 FOR J = 1 TO N
240 LET B(J) = A(J) − A
250 NEXT J
260 REM PERFORM STEP (C)
270 FOR J = 1 TO N
280 LET B(J) = B(J)^2
290 NEXT J
300 REM PERFORM STEP (D)
310 LET S = 0
320 FOR I = 1 TO N
330 LET S = S + B(I)
340 NEXT I
350 LET S = S/N
360 REM COMPLETE STEP (E)
370 LET S = SQR(S)
380 REM OUTPUT THE STANDARD DEVIATION
390 PRINT S
400 END
```

Exercises 8.3

1. Five passes are necessary to sort six numbers. N − 1 passes are necessary to sort N numbers.

2. 100 REM BUBBLE SORT, DESCENDING ORDER
   115 DIM A(10)
   120 DATA 23, − 56,100,45,56,34,444,67,0,45
   130 FOR I = 1 TO 10
   140 READ A(I)
   150 NEXT I
   160 FOR K = 1 TO 9
   170 FOR J = 1 TO 9
   190 IF A(J)<A(J + 1) THEN LET L = A(J) : LET A(J) = A(J + 1) :
       LET A(J + 1) = L
   230 NEXT J
   240 NEXT K
   250 REM SORTING IS DONE, NOW PRINT ARRAY
   260 FOR I = 1 TO 10
   270 PRINT A(I);"   ";
   280 NEXT I
   300 END

3. The program would only make one pass on the numbers resulting in the largest number of the array being moved to location A(4) of the array A.

4. 100 REM BUBBLE SORT, ASCENDING ORDER
   110 REM FOR AN ARBITRARY NUMBER OF NUMBERS
   120 INPUT "HOW MANY NUMBERS ARE YOU ENTERING? ";N
   125 DIM A(N)
   130 FOR I = 1 TO N
   140 INPUT "TYPE A NUMBER: ";A(I)
   150 NEXT I
   160 REM SORT THE NUMBERS
   170 FOR K = 1 TO N − 1
   180 FOR J = 1 TO N − 1
   190 IF A(J)>A(J + 1) THEN LET L = A(J) : LET A(J) = A(J + 1) :
       LET A(J + 1) = L
   200 NEXT J
   210 NEXT K
   220 REM SORTING IS DONE, PRINT ARRAY
   230 FOR I = 1 TO N
   240 PRINT A(I);" ";
   250 NEXT I
   260 END

5. In program for problem 4 above, change line 180 to:

   180 FOR J = 1 TO N − K

Exercises 8.4

1.

	N	I	R(1)	R(2)	R(3)	K	CRT
125 LET I = 0	0	0	0	0	0	0	
130 INPUT "TYPE A DECIMAL NUMBER: ";N	6	0	0	0	0	0	TYPE A DECIMAL NUMBER: 6
140 LET I = I + 1	6	1	0	0	0	0	
150 LET R(I) = N − 2* INT(N/2)	6	1	0	0	0	0	
160 LET N = INT(N/2)	3	1	0	0	0	0	
140 LET I = I + 1	3	2	0	0	0	0	

(continued)

	N	I	R(1)	R(2)	R(3)	K	CRT
150 LET R(I)=N-2* INT(N/2)	3	2	0	1	0	0	
160 LET N=INT(N/2)	1	2	0	1	0	0	
140 LET I=I+1	1	3	0	1	0	0	
150 LET R(I)=N-2* INT(N/2)	1	3	0	1	1	0	
160 LET N=INT(N/2)	0	3	0	1	1	0	
190 FOR K=I TO 1 STEP -1	0	3	0	1	1	3	
200 PRINT R(K);	0	3	0	1	1	3	1
210 NEXT K	0	3	0	1	1	2	
200 PRINT R(K);	0	3	0	1	1	2	11
210 NEXT K	0	3	0	1	1	3	
200 PRINT R(K);	0	3	0	1	1	3	110
210 NEXT K	0	3	0	1	1	4	
220 END	0	3	0	1	1	4	

2.
```
100 REM CONVERTS N FROM DECIMAL TO THE BASE EIGHT
115 DIM R(100)
120 REM ASSIGNMENT MODULE
125 LET I=0
130 INPUT "TYPE A DECIMAL NUMBER: ";N
140 LET I=I+1
145 REM COMPUTE MODULE
150 LET R(I)=N-8*INT(N/8)
160 LET N=INT(N/8)
170 IF N>0 THEN GOTO 140
180 REM OUTPUT MODULE
190 FOR K=I TO 1 STEP -1
200 PRINT R(K);
210 NEXT K
220 END
```

3.
```
100 REM CONVERTS N FROM DECIMAL TO BASE 5 OR 7
115 DIM R(100)
120 REM ASSIGNMENT MODULE
125 LET I=0
130 INPUT "TYPE A DECIMAL NUMBER: ";N
135 PRINT "DO YOU WANT THE NUMBER ";N;" CONVERTED TO BASE
       5 OR 7?"
138 INPUT B
140 LET I=I+1
145 REM COMPUTE MODULE
150 LET R(I)=N-B*INT(N/B)
160 LET N=INT(N/B)
170 IF N>0 THEN GOTO 140
180 REM OUTPUT MODULE
190 FOR K=I TO 1 STEP -1
200 PRINT R(K);
210 NEXT K
220 END
```

4. Change line 160 to the following:

   160 IF (S(I)<=6.5) OR (Y(I)>70) THEN GOTO 170

5.
```
100 DATA 6, 67, 6.5, 72, 5.75, 80, 9, 55
110 DATA 8.5, 62, 5, 81, 6, 70, 9, 50
```

```
120 DIM S(8),Y(8)
130 FOR K = 1 TO 8
140 READ S(K), Y(K)
150 NEXT K
155 LET A = 0 : LET C = 0
160 REM SCAN ARRAY Y
170 FOR I = 1 TO 8
180 IF Y(I)>65 THEN PRINT S(I),Y(I):LET A = A + S(I):LET C = C + 1
190 NEXT I
200 PRINT "THE AVERAGE SLEEPING TIME FOR THOSE WHO LIVED
        OVER 65 YEARS IS ";A/C
210 END
```

6.
```
10 DIM R(50)
20 FOR I = 1 TO 50
30 LET R(I) = INT(RND(1)*20) + 1
40 NEXT I
50 LET A = 0 : REM A STORES NUMBER OF FIVES
55 LET B = 0 : REM B STORES NUMBER OF TENS
60 FOR I = 1 TO 50
70 IF R(I) = 5 THEN LET A = A + 1
80 IF R(I) = 10 THEN LET B = B + 1
90 NEXT I
100 PRINT "THE TOTAL NUMBER OF FIVES IS ";A
110 PRINT "THE TOTAL NUMBER OF TENS IS ";B
120 END
```

7.
```
10 DATA 34, 67, 345, 35, 678
20 DIM A(5)
30 FOR I = 1 TO 5
40 READ A(I)
50 NEXT I
60 FOR K = 1 TO 30
65 PRINT "SAMPLE NUMBER ";K
70 FOR I = 1 TO 3
80 LET R = INT(5*RND(1)) + 1
90 PRINT A(R);"   ";
100 NEXT I
110 PRINT
120 NEXT K
130 END
```

8.
```
110 REM PICK 30 RANDOM NUMBERS FROM 1 TO 365
115 REM SIGNAL IF ANY NUMBER IS PICKED TWICE
120 DIM A(365)
125 REM INITIALIZE ARRAY, JUST TO BE SURE
130 FOR J = 1 TO 365
140 LET A(J) = 0
150 NEXT J
160 REM NOW PICK RANDOM NUMBERS
180 FOR K = 1 TO 30
190 LET R = INT(365*RND(1)) + 1
200 LET A(R) = A(R) + 1
210 NEXT K
220 REM CHECK FOR A NUMBER PICKED MORE THAN ONCE.
223 REM FIRST SET FLAG FOR FAILURE
225 LET F = 0
230 FOR J = 1 TO 365
240 IF A(J)< = 1 THEN GOTO 270
245 REM SUCCESS PRINTED ONLY IF A(J)>1
250 PRINT "SUCCESS"
251 REM SET FLAG FOR SUCCESS
252 LET F = 1
255 REM SET J TO UPPER LIMIT TO FINISH LOOP
260 LET J = 365
270 NEXT J
280 IF F = 0 THEN PRINT "FAILURE"
290 END
```

9.
```
100 REM TEST THE BIRTHDAY PROBLEM
110 REM DO 100 TRAILS OF PROGRAM IN PROBLEM 9.
115 DIM A(365)
```

```
120 LET S = 0
122 REM BEGIN 100 PASSES
123 FOR P = 1 TO 100
125 REM INITIALIZE ARRAY . . . NECESSARY NOW.
130 FOR J = 1 TO 365
140 LET A(J) = 0
150 NEXT J
160 REM NOW PICK RANDOM NUMBERS
170 REM EXAMPLE: IF 253 IS PICKED, ADD ONE TO CELL 253
180 FOR K = 1 TO 30
190 LET R = INT(365*RND(1)) + 1
200 LET A(R) = A(R) + 1
210 NEXT K
220 REM CHECK FOR A NUMBER PICKED MORE THAN ONCE
223 REM FIRST SET FLAG FOR FAILURE
225 LET F = 0
230 FOR J = 1 TO 365
240 IF A(J) < = 1 THEN GOTO 270
245 REM SUCCESS PRINTED ONLY IF A(J)>1
250 PRINT "SUCCESS"
251 REM SET FLAG FOR SUCCESS
252 LET F = 1
253 REM COUNT NUMBER OF SUCCESSES
254 LET S = S + 1
255 REM SET J TO UPPER LIMIT TO FINISH LOOP
260 LET J = 365
270 NEXT J
280 IF F = 0 THEN PRINT "FAILURE"
282 REM GO BACK FOR NEXT PASS
283 NEXT P
285 PRINT "THERE WERE ";S; " SUCCESSES IN 100 TRIALS."
290 END
```

10. This is a simulation of the game of Keno.

```
100 DIM N(80)
110 FOR I = 1 TO 80
120 LET N(I) = I
130 NEXT I
140 FOR I =  1 TO 20
150 LET R = INT(80*RND(1)) + 1
160 IF N(R) = 0 THEN GOTO 150
170 PRINT N(R)
180 LET N(R) = 0
190 NEXT I
200 END
```

Exercises 8.5

1. The two-dimensional array P will look like this:

	col 1	col 2
row 1	45	56
row 2	2	5

2.
```
210 PRINT "CALCULATE YEARLY UTILITY BILL FOR:"
220 PRINT "1 ELECTRIC BILL"
230 PRINT "2 GAS BILL"
240 PRINT "3 PHONE BILL"
250 INPUT "TYPE NUMBER DESIRED";N
260 FOR I = 1 TO 12
270 LET S = S + U(N,I)
280 NEXT I
290 END
```

3.
```
300 INPUT ""LIST ALL GAS BILLS EXCEEDING WHAT AMOUNT? ";X
310 FOR I = 1 TO 12
320 IF X<U(2,I) THEN PRINT U(2,I);" FOR MONTH ";I
330 NEXT I
340 END
```

4.
```
300 PRINT "1 ELECTRIC BILL"
310 PRINT "2 GAS BILL"
320 PRINT "3 PHONE BILL"
330 INPUT "TYPE NUMBER DESIRED: ";N
340 IF N = 1 THEN LET Q$ = "ELECTRIC BILLS"
350 IF N = 2 THEN LET Q$ = "GAS BILLS"
360 IF N = 3 THEN LET Q$ = "PHONE BILLS"
370 PRINT "LIST ALL ";Q$;" EXCEEDING WHAT AMOUNT";
380 INPUT X
390 FOR I = 1 TO 12
400 IF X<U(N,I) THEN PRINT U(N,I);" FOR MONTH ";I
410 NEXT I
420 END
```

5. Add this to the program:

```
190 REM COMPUTE EACH STUDENT'S QUIZ AVERAGE
200 FOR I = 1 TO N
210 LET S = 0
220 FOR J = 1 TO M
230 LET S = S + A(I,J)
240 NEXT J
250 PRINT "AVERAGE GRADE FOR STUDENT ";I;" IS "; S/M
260 NEXT I
270 REM COMPUTE CLASS AVERAGE FOR EACH QUIZ
280 FOR J = 1 TO M
290 LET S = 0
300 FOR I = 1 TO N
310 LET S = S + A(I,J)
320 NEXT I
330 PRINT "AVERAGE FOR QUIZ ";J; " IS ";S/N
340 NEXT J
350 END
```

Exercises 8.6

1.
```
100 DATA "DALLAS", "CHICAGO", "MIAMI", "BRONX"
105 DIM C$(4)
110 FOR I = 1 TO 4
120 READ C$(I)
130 NEXT I
150 REM USE THE BUBBLE SORT
160 FOR I = 1 TO 3
170 FOR J = 1 TO 3
180 IF C$(J)>C$(J + 1) THEN LET L$ = C$(J) : LET C$(J) = C$(J + 1) :
    LET C$(J + 1) = L$
190 NEXT J
200 NEXT I
210 FOR I = 1 TO 4
220 PRINT C$(I)
230 NEXT I
240 END
```

2.
```
100 REM THIS PROGRAM ACCEPTS STRINGS TYPED BY THE USER
110 REM AND SORTS THE STRINGS.
120 INPUT"HOW MANY STRINGS WILL YOU BE ENTERING? ";N
130 DIM A$(N)
140 FOR I = 1 TO N
150 INPUT "TYPE A STRING: ";A$(I)
160 NEXT I
170 REM BUBBLE SORT ON THE ARRAY
180 FOR I = 1 TO N - 1
190 FOR J = 1 TO N - 1
200 IF A$(J)>A$(J + 1) THEN LET L$ = A$(J) : LET A$(J) = A$(J + 1) :
    LET A$(J + 1) = L$
210 NEXT J
220 NEXT I
230 REM PRINT THE SORTED ARRAY
240 FOR I = 1 TO N
250 PRINT A$(I)
260 NEXT I
270 END
```

3. 200 INPUT "ENTER NAME (FIRST FEW LETTERS WILL DO): ";N$
    220 IF N$ = LEFT$(K$(I,1),LEN(N$)) THEN PRINT K$(I,1),K$(I,2)

4. 100 REM RANDOM SELECTION OF 11 PLAYERS FROM A TEAM OF 14
    120 DATA "SALLY", "MARY LOU", "FRANKIE", "CONNIE", "GAIL"
    125 DATA "MARSHA", "JANE", "BETTY", "TAMY", "MAY", "APRIL"
    130 DATA "JUDY", "JOAN", "MARY ANN"
    150 DIM P$(14)
    160 FOR J = 1 TO 14
    170 READ P$(J)
    180 NEXT J
    185 FOR I = 1 TO 11
    190 LET L = INT(14*RND(1)) + 1
    210 IF P$(L) = "ALREADY CHOSEN" THEN GOTO 190
    220 PRINT P$(L)
    230 LET P$(L) = "ALREADY CHOSEN"
    240 NEXT I
    250 END

5. Add to the program:

    260 REM COMPUTE TOTAL CUSTOMER DEPOSITS
    270 LET T = 0
    280 FOR I = 1 TO K
    290 LET T = T + VAL(R$(I,5))
    300 NEXT I
    310 PRINT "TOTAL DEPOSITS EQUAL $";T
    400 END

6. Add this to the program:

    400 REM FIND NAMES OF CUSTOMERS WHOSE
    410 REM DEPOSITS ARE BETWEEN $100 AND $200
    420 FOR I = 1 TO K
    430 IF VAL(R$(I,5))> = 100 AND VAL(R$(I,5))< = 200 THEN
            PRINT R$(I,1);" 'S DEPOSIT WAS $";R$(I,5)
    440 NEXT I
    500 END

7. Add this to the program:

    500 REM FIND CUSTOMER FROM CAR'S SERIAL NUMBER
    510 INPUT "ENTER THE CAR'S SERIAL NUMBER (OR ZERO TO QUIT)";SN$
    515 IF SN$ = "0" THEN GOTO 610
    520 FOR I = 1 TO K
    530 IF SN$<> R$(I,4) THEN GOTO 590
    540 PRINT "THAT CAR WAS LEASED TO . . ."
    550 PRINT "NAME: ";R$(I,1)
    560 PRINT "ADDRESS: ";R$(I,2)
    570 PRINT "PHONE #: ";R$(I,3)
    580 PRINT "DEPOSIT: ";R$(I,5) : LET I = K
    590 NEXT I
    600 GOTO 510
    610 END

Answers to chapter 9

Exercises 9.1

1. The affect would be to cause names like "ACEHEARTS" instead of "ACE OF HEARTS" to
    be stored in the C$ array.

2. 100 REM FIRST NAMES
    110 DATA "MADELINE","KRISTIN","KYMBERLY","CHARLOTTE"
    120 REM MIDDLE NAMES
    130 DATA "MAY","DANIELLE","ERIN","MICHELLE"
    140 REM
    150 DIM F$(4), M$(4), N$(16)
    160 REM   ASSIGNMENT MODULE
    170 FOR K = 1 TO 4

```
180 READ F$(K)
190 NEXT K
200 FOR K = 1 TO 4
210 READ M$(K)
220 NEXT K
230 REM
240 REM          COMPUTE MODULE
245 LET  C = 0
250 FOR J = 1 TO 4
260 FOR K = 1 TO 4
265 LET C = C + 1
270 LET N$(C) = F$(J) + " " + M$(K) + " " + "DAMOISELLE"
280 NEXT K
290 NEXT J
300 REM
310 REM          OUTPUT MODULE
320 FOR K = 1 TO 16
330 PRINT N$(K)
340 NEXT K
350 END
```

```
]RUN

MADELINE MAY DAMOISELLE
MADELINE DANIELLE DAMOISELLE
MADELINE ERIN DAMOISELLE
MADELINE MICHELLE DAMOISELLE
KRISTIN MAY DAMOISELLE
KRISTIN DANIELLE DAMOISELLE
KRISTIN ERIN DAMOISELLE
KRISTIN MICHELLE DAMOISELLE
KYMBERLY MAY DAMOISELLE
KYMBERLY DANIELLE DAMOISELLE
KYMBERLY ERIN DAMOISELLE
KYMBERLY MICHELLE DAMOISELLE
CHARLOTTE MAY DAMOISELLE
CHARLOTTE DANIELLE DAMOISELLE
CHARLOTTE ERIN DAMOISELLE
CHARLOTTE MICHELLE DAMOISELLE
```

3.
```
100 REM          ASSIGNMENT MODULE
110 REM
120 INPUT "TYPE IN A WORD: ";W$
130 REM
140 REM          COMPUTE MODULE
150 LET A$ = LEFT$(W$,1)
160 LET B$ = MID$(W$,2)
170 LET W$ = B$ + A$ + "AY"
180 REM
190 REM          OUTPUT MODULE
200 REM
210 PRINT "THAT WORD IN PIGLATIN IS ";W$
220 END
```

4.
```
100 REM          ASSIGNMENT MODULE
110 REM
120 PRINT "ENTER FIRST AND LAST NAME."
130 INPUT "SEPARATE THEM WITH A SPACE: ";N$
140 REM
150 REM          COMPUTE MODULE
160 REM FIND THE SPACE CHARACTER
170 FOR K = 1 TO LEN(N$)
180 IF MID$(N$,K,1) = " " THEN GOTO 210
190 NEXT K
200 PRINT "NO SPACE, TRY AGAIN." : GOTO 120
210 REM
220 REM SEPARATE NAMES AND REATTACH BACKWARDS
230 LET F$ = LEFT$(N$,K - 1)
240 LET L$ = MID$(N$,K + 1)
250 LET N$ = L$ + " " + F$
260 REM
270 REM          OUTPUT MODULE
280 PRINT "YOUR NAME, LAST NAME FIRST, IS ";N$
290 END
```

Exercises 9.2

```
1.    10 INPUT "WHAT IS THE NUMBER? ";N
      20 REM
      30 REM STEPS 1 AND 2 COMBINED
      40 LET N1$ = "00" + STR$(INT(100*N + .5))
      50 REM
      60 REM STEPS 3, 4, 5, AND 6 COMBINED
      70 LET N$ = STR$(VAL(LEFT$(N1$,LEN(N1$) − 2))) + "." +
            RIGHT$(N1$,2)
      80 REM
      90 PRINT "HERE'S THE NUMBER IN DOLLARS & CENTS: $";N$
     100 END
```

Exercises 9.3

```
1.    10 REM          ASSIGNMENT MODULE
      20 INPUT "HOW MANY PEOPLE? ";N
      30 DIM R$(N)
      40 LET B$ = "            "
      50 FOR I = 1 TO N
      60 PRINT
      70 INPUT "TYPE LAST NAME: ";L$
      80 INPUT "TYPE FIRST NAME: ";F$
      90 INPUT "TYPE TELEPHONE NUMBER: ";T$
      95 INPUT "TYPE MONTHLY SALARY: ";S$
     100 LET L$ = LEFT$(L$ + B$,10)
     110 LET F$ = LEFT$(F$ + B$,9)
     120 LET T$ = LEFT$(T$ + B$,8)
     125 LET S$ = RIGHT$(B$ + S$,5)
     130 LET R$(I) = L$ + F$ + T$ + S$
     140 NEXT I
     150 REM          COMPUTE MODULE, SORT ON SALARY
     160 FOR J = 1 TO N − 1
     170 FOR K = 1 TO N − 1
     180 REM SALARY FIELD STARTS AT POSITION 28 IN RECORD
     190 IF MID$(R$(K),28,5) > MID$(R$(K + 1),28,5) THEN
            LET X$ = R$(K) : LET R$(K) = R$(K + 1) : LET R$(K + 1) = X$
     200 NEXT K
     210 NEXT J
     220 REM          OUTPUT MODULE
     230 PRINT
     240 FOR I = 1 TO N
     250 PRINT R$(I)
     260 NEXT I
     270 END
```

```
2.   100 REM        ASSIGNMENT MODULE
     110 REM
     120 INPUT "HOW MANY INTEGERS TO SORT? ";N
     130 DIM A$(N)
     140 FOR K = 1 TO N
     150 PRINT "TYPE IN NUMBER ";K;": ";
     160 INPUT " ";NUM
     170 REM RIGHT JUSTIFY NUM IN A FIELD OF 10 CHAR'S.
     180 LET N$ = RIGHT$("          " + STR$(NUM),10)
     190 LET A$(K) = N$
     200 NEXT K
     210 REM
     220 REM        SORTING MODULE
     230 FOR P = 1 TO N − 1
     240 FOR C = 1 TO N − 1
     250 IF A$(C) > A$(C + 1) LET T$ = A$(C) :
            LET A$(C) = A$(C + 1) : LET A$(C + 1) = T$
     260 NEXT C
     270 NEXT P
     280 REM
     290 REM        OUTPUT MODULE
     300 FOR K = 1 TO N
     310 PRINT A$(K)
     320 NEXT K
     330 END
```

```
]RUN
HOW MANY INTEGERS TO SORT? 5
TYPE IN NUMBER 1: 0342
TYPE IN NUMBER 2: 00013
TYPE IN NUMBER 3: 24
TYPE IN NUMBER 4: 92142
TYPE IN NUMBER 5: 1
        1
       13
       24
      342
    92142
```

3.
```
100 REM      ASSIGNMENT MODULE
110 REM
120 INPUT "HOW MANY WORDS TO SORT? ";N
130 DIM A$(N)
140 FOR K = 1 TO N
150 PRINT "TYPE IN WORD ";K;": ";
160 INPUT "";W$
170 REM LEFT JUSTIFY W$ IN A FIELD OF 15 CHAR'S.
180 LET W$ = LEFT$(W$+"                ",15)
190 LET A$(K) = W$
200 NEXT K
210 REM
220 REM      SORTING MODULE
230 FOR P = 1 TO N−1
240 FOR C = 1 TO N−1
250 IF A$(C) > A$(C+1) THEN LET T$ = A$(C) :
    LET A$(C) = A$(C+1) : LET A$(C+1) = T$
260 NEXT C
270 NEXT P
280 REM
290 REM      OUTPUT MODULE
300 PRINT
310 PRINT "HERE THEY ARE SORTED AND LEFT − JUSTIFIED:"
320 FOR K = 1 TO N
330 PRINT A$(K)
340 NEXT K
350 END
```

```
]RUN
HOW MANY WORDS TO SORT? 4
TYPE IN WORD 1: ROCKET
TYPE IN WORD 2: GUARD
TYPE IN WORD 3: HAMLET
TYPE IN WORD 4: MISSISSIPPI

HERE THEY ARE SORTED AND LEFT-JUSTIFIED:
GUARD
HAMLET
MISSISSIPPI
ROCKET
```

4. Just change lines 180 and 310 to read

```
180 LET W$ = RIGHT$("                " + W$,15)
```

```
310 PRINT "HERE THEY ARE SORTED AND RIGHT − JUSTIFIED:"
```

The rest of the program is the same.

Answers to chapter 10

Exercises 10.1

1.
```
REM A$(N,M) IS A STRING ARRAY
REM N IS THE NUMBER OF ROWS
REM M IS THE NUMBER OF COLUMNS
FOR I = 1 TO N
FOR J = 1 TO M
```

```
      INPUT "ENTER A STRING "; A$(I,J)
      NEXT J
      NEXT I
```

2.
```
   REM A(N,M) IS THE ARRAY
   REM N IS THE NUMBER OF ROWS
   REM M IS THE NUMBER OF COLUMNS
   REM S( ) IS THE ARRAY CONTAINING THE SUMS OF EACH COLUMN
   FOR I = 1 TO M
   LET S(I) = 0
   FOR J = 1 TO N
   LET S(I) = S(I) + A(J,I)
   NEXT J
   NEXT I
```

3.
```
   255 REM THE FOLLOWING LINES ARE A CONTINUATION
   260 REM OF THE YELLOW STONE TAXI PROGRAM
   270 DIM S(Q),T(Q)
   280 FOR I = 1 TO Q
   290 LET S(I) = S(I) + VAL(MID$(R$(I),38,4))
   300 LET T(I) = T(I) + VAL(RIGHT$(R$(I),4))
   400 NEXT I
```

4.
```
   10 INPUT "TYPE THE NUMBER OF CUSTOMERS
             IN THE MAILING LIST ";N
   20 DIM R$(N)
   30 FOR I = 1 TO N
   40 LET B$ = "                              "
   50 INPUT "TYPE LAST NAME "; F1$
   60 INPUT "TYPE FIRST NAME ";F2$
   70 INPUT "TYPE STREET ADDRESS ";F3$
   80 INPUT "TYPE CITY ";F4$
   90 INPUT "TYPE ZIP CODE ";F5$
   100 INPUT "TYPE TELEPHONE NUMBER ";F6$
   110 LET F1$ = LEFT$(F$+B$,30)
   120 LET F2$ = LEFT$(F$+B$,15)
   130 LET F3$ = LEFT$(F$+B$,30)
   140 LET F4$ = LEFT$(F$+B$,20)
   150 LET F5$ = LEFT$(F$+B$,14)
   160 LET F6$ = LEFT$(F$+B$,5)
   170 LET R$(I)=F1$ + F2$ + F3$ + F4$ + F5$ + F6$
   180 NEXT I
```

5.
```
   FOR I = 1 TO Q
   INPUT "ENTER FIELD 1: ";F1$
   INPUT "ENTER FIELD 2: ";F2$
       :
   etc.
       :
   LET F1$=RIGHT$(B$+F1$,A1)
   LET F2$=RIGHT$(B$+F2$,A2)
       :
   etc.
       :
   LET R$(I)=F1$ + F2$ + . . . etc . . .
   NEXT I
```

6.
```
   REM BUBBLE SORT IN DESCENDING ORDER
   REM N IS THE NUMBER OF ITEMS TO BE SORTED
   FOR K = 1 TO N-1
   FOR J = 1 TO N-K
   IF A(J) < A(J+1) THEN LET L = A(J) :
       LET A(J) = A(J+1) : LET A(J+1) = L
   NEXT J
   NEXT K
```

7.
```
   260 REM SORTING ALONG THE LEFTMOST FIELD
   270 FOR K=1 TO Q-1
   280 FOR J=1 TO Q-K
   290 IF LEFT$(R$(J),25)>LEFT$(R$(J+1),25) THEN LET L$=R$(J):
       LET R$(J)=R$(J+1) : LET R$(J+1)=L$
   300 NEXT J
   310 NEXT K
```

8. 180 REM CONTINUATION OF PROGRAM IN PROBLEM 4
    190 PRINT "1 SORT ON LAST NAME"
    200 PRINT "2 SORT ON FIRST NAME"
    210 PRINT "3 SORT ON STREET ADDRESS"
    220 PRINT "4 SORT ON CITY"
    230 PRINT "5 SORT ON ZIP CODE"
    240 PRINT "6 SORT ON TELEPHONE NUMBER"
    250 INPUT "TYPE NUMBER DESIRED ";W
    260 IF W = 1 THEN LET C = 1: D = 30
    270 IF W = 2 THEN LET C = 31: D = 15
    280 IF W = 3 THEN LET C = 46: D = 30
    290 IF W = 4 THEN LET C = 76: D = 20
    300 IF W = 5 THEN LET C = 96: D = 5
    310 IF W = 6 THEN LET C = 101:D = 14
    320 REM SORT ON THE INDICATED FIELD
    330 FOR I = 1 TO N − 1
    335 FOR J = 1 TO N − I
    340 IF MID$(R$(J),C,D) < MID$(R$(J + 1),C,D) THEN
            LET L$ = R$(J): LET R$(J) = R$(J + 1) :
            LET R$(J + 1) = L$
    350 NEXT J
    360 NEXT I

9. REM R$(N,M) IS A TWO-DIMENSIONAL ARRAY
    REM A IS THE ROW TO BE SEARCHED
    REM S$ IS THE STRING SEARCHED FOR
    LET L = 0
    FOR I = 1 TO N
    IF S$ = R$(A,I) THEN LET L = I : LET I = N
    NEXT I
    IF L = 0 THEN (instruction)

10. The following changes will work:

    270 INPUT "ENTER TELEPHONE NUMBER TO BE SEARCHED FOR ";S$
    280 LET S$ = LEFT$(S$ + B$,8)
    320 IF S$ = RIGHT$(R$(I),8) THEN LET L = I : LET I = N

Exercises 10. 2

1. Algorithm V.

2. Algorithm II.

3. Replace Modules IV and V in the Shady Lane program with the following modules.

    270 REM MODULE TO SORT BY AGE
    280 FOR I = 1 TO N − 1
    290 FOR J = 1 TO N − I
    300 IF MID$(T$(J),26,3)>MID$(T$(J + 1),26,3) THEN
            LET L$ = T$(J) : LET T$(J) = T$(J + 1) : LET T$(J + 1) = L$
    310 NEXT J
    320 NEXT I
    325 REM
    330 REM MODULE TO PRINT REPORT
    340 PRINT "LAST NAME";TAB(17);"FIRST NAME";TAB(35);"AGE"
    350 FOR I = 1 TO N
    360 PRINT LEFT$(T$(I),15);TAB(17);MID$(T$(I),16,10);
            TAB(35);MID$(T$(I),26)
    370 NEXT I
    375 REM
    380 REM   MODULE TO SORT BY FIRST NAME
    390 FOR I = 1 TO N − 1
    400 FOR J = 1 TO N − I
    410 IF MID$(T$(J),16,10) > MID$(T$(J + 1),16,10) THEN
            LET L$ = T$(J) : LET T$(J) = T$(J + 1) : LET T$(J + 1) = L$
    420 NEXT J
    430 NEXT I
    440 REM
    450 REM MODULE TO PRINT REPORT
    460 PRINT "LAST NAME";TAB(17);"FIRST NAME";TAB(35);"AGE"
    470 FOR I = 1 TO N
    480 PRINT LEFT$(T$(I),15);TAB(17);MID$(T$(I),16,10);
            TAB(35);MID$(T$(I),26)

```
490 NEXT I
500 END
```

4. Just replace Module IV in the Shady Lane program with:

```
270 REM MODULE IV - SORT ON AGE FIRST, LAST NAME SECOND
280 FOR I = 1 TO N-1
290 FOR J = 1 TO N-I
300 LET H1$ = MID$(T$(J),26,3) + LEFT$(T$(J),15)
310 LET H2$ = MID$(T$(J+1),26,3) + LEFT$(T$(J+1),15)
320 IF H1$ > H2$ THEN LET L$ = T$(J) : LET T$(J) = T$(J+1):
        LET T$(J+1) = L$
330 NEXT J
340 NEXT I
350 REM END OF MODULE IV
```

5.
```
10 REM MODULE I - CREATE RECORDS
20 INPUT "HOW MANY BOOKS ARE THERE? ";N
30 DIM G$(N)
40 LET B$ = "                          "
45 FOR I = 1 TO N
50 INPUT "TYPE AUTHOR'S LAST NAME: ";L$
60 INPUT "TYPE AUTHOR'S FIRST NAME: ";F$
70 INPUT "TYPE TITLE OF BOOK: ";T$
80 INPUT "TYPE PUBLISHING COMPANY: ";P$
90 INPUT "TYPE PRICE PAID: ";V$
100 LET G$(I) = LEFT$(L$+B$,25) + LEFT$(F$+B$,15) +
        LEFT$(T$+B$,30) + LEFT$(P$+B$,25) + RIGHT$(B$+V$,3)
110 NEXT I
120 REM MODULE II - SORT AND PRINT REPORTS
125 REM FIRST SORT ON LAST NAME
130 FOR I = 1 TO N-1
140 FOR J = 1 TO N-I
150 IF LEFT$(G$(J),25) > LEFT$(G$(J+1),25) THEN
        LET L$ = G$(J) : LET G$(J) = G$(J+1) : LET G$(J+1) = L$
160 NEXT J
170 NEXT I
180 PRINT "SORTED BY AUTHOR'S LAST NAME"
190 PRINT
200 FOR I = 1 TO N
210 PRINT G$(I)
220 NEXT I
225 REM NOW SORT ON TITLE
230 FOR I = 1 TO N-1
240 FOR J = 1 TO N-I
250 IF MID$(G$(J),41,30) > MID$(G$(J+1),41,30) THEN
        LET L$ = G$(J) : LET G$(J) = G$(J+1) : LET G$(J+1) = L$
260 NEXT J
270 NEXT I
280 PRINT "SORTED BY TITLE"
290 PRINT
300 FOR I = 1 TO N
310 PRINT G$(I)
320 NEXT I
330 REM MODULE III - COMPARE PRICES
340 INPUT "ENTER A PRICE FOR COMPARISON: ";X
350 FOR I = 1 TO N
360 IF X > VAL(RIGHT$(G$(I),3)) THEN PRINT G$(I)
370 NEXT I
380 END
```

6. Replace Module III in the Daytime Soap Opera program with:

```
160 REM MODULE III - FIND NUMBER OF LINES AND COST
165 LET N = INT(L/35)
170 LET C = 55*N
175 IF L = 35*N THEN GOTO 190
180 IF L-35*N <= 17 THEN LET C = C+28
185 IF L-35*N > 17 THEN LET C = C+55
190 REM END OF MODULE III
```

7. Replace Module III with this:

```
160 REM MODULE III
165 LET N = INT(L/44)
170 IF L = 44*N THEN LET S = N
175 IF L>44*N THEN LET S = N + 1
185 IF S>4 THEN LET C = 55*4 + 45*(S – 4) : GOTO 195
190 LET C = 55*S
195 REM END OF MODULE III
```

Exercises 10.3

1. Change line 240 in Module II to read

```
240 LET Q = 25
```

Exercises 10.4

1. Add these lines:

```
 70 ON K GOSUB 90,190,260,400
190 MODULE II – SEARCH BY STUDENT NUMBER
200 INPUT "ENTER A STUDENT NUMBER: ";Q$
210 LET K = 1
220 GOSUB 330
230 RETURN
250 REM
260 REM MODULE III – SEARCH BY LAST NAME
270 INPUT "ENTER STUDENT'S LAST NAME: ";Q$
280 LET K = 2
290 GOSUB 330
295 RETURN
330 REM SUBROUTINE FOR SEARCHING
340 LET L = 0
350 FOR I = 1 TO N
360 IF Q$ = S$(I,K) THEN LET L = I
370 NEXT I
380 IF L <> 0 THEN PRINTS$ (L,1),S$(L,2),S$(L,3),S$(L,4)
390 RETURN
400 END
```

2. Change line 290 in Module III on page 192 to read

```
290 IF Q$ = S$(I,2) THEN PRINT S$(L,1),S$(L,2),S$(L,3),S$(L,4)
```

and delete line 310.

Answers to chapter 11

Exercises 11.1

1.
```
 10 REM MODULE I – ENTER DATA INTO MEMORY
 20 INPUT "HOW MANY NAMES ARE YOU ENTERING? ";N
 30 DIM T$(N)
 35 LET B$ = "                                              "
 40 FOR I = 1 TO N
 45 INPUT "ENTER LAST NAME: ";L$
 50 INPUT "FIRST NAME: ";F$
 60 INPUT "STREET ADDRESS: ";A$
 70 INPUT "CITY: ";C$
 80 INPUT "ZIP: ";Z$
 90 INPUT "TELEPHONE NO.: ";P$
100 LET L$ = LEFTS(L$ + B$,15)
110 LET F$ = LEFTS(F$ + B$,10)
120 LET A$ = LEFTS(A$ + B$,35)
130 LET C$ = LEFTS(C$ + B$,15)
140 LET Z$ = LEFTS(Z$ + B$,5)
150 LET P$ = LEFTS(P$ + B$,14)
160 LET T$(I) = L$ + F$ + A$ + C$ + Z$ + P$
170 NEXT I
```

```
180 REM MODULE II – STORE ON DISK IN A FILE
190 PRINT CHR$(4);"OPEN DIRECTORY"
200 PRINT CHR$(4);"WRITE DIRECTORY"
210 FOR I = 1 TO N
220 PRINT T$(I)
230 NEXT I
240 PRINT CHR$(4);"CLOSE DIRECTORY"
250 END
```

2.
```
100 REM MODULE I
110 INPUT "HOW MANY VEHICLES ARE THERE? ";N
120 DIM C$(N)
130 LET B$ = "                    "
140 FOR I = 1 TO N
150 INPUT "TYPE OF VEHICLE: ";V$
160 INPUT "MANUFACTURER: ";M$
170 INPUT "BODY MODEL: ";K$
180 INPUT "YEAR: ";Y$
190 INPUT "CURRENT MILEAGE: ";I$
200 INPUT "DAILY RENTAL PRICE: ";P$
210 INPUT "MILEAGE RENTAL PRICE: ";A$
220 LET V$ = LEFT$(V$ + B$,15)
230 LET M$ = LEFT$(M$ + B$,15)
240 LET K$ = LEFT$(K$ + B$,15)
250 LET Y$ = LEFT$(Y$ + B$,4)
260 LET I$ = RIGHT$(B$ + I$,6)
270 LET P$ = RIGHT$(B$ + P$,5)
280 LET A$ = RIGHT$(B$ + A$,5)
290 LET C$(I) = V$ + M$ + K$ + Y$ + I$ + P$ + A$
300 NEXT I
310 REM MODULE II
320 PRINT CHR$(4);"OPEN LEMON AUTO"
330 PRINT CHR$(4);"WRITE LEMON AUTO"
340 FOR I = 1 TO N
350 PRINT C$(I)
360 NEXT I
370 PRINT CHR$(4);"CLOSE LEMON AUTO"
380 END
```

3.
```
100 REM MODULE I
110 INPUT "HOW MANY STUDENTS ARE THERE? ";N
120 DIM S$(N)
130 LET B$ = "                    "
140 FOR I = 1 TO N
150 PRINT "ENTERING STUDENT ";I
160 INPUT "STUDENT'S LAST NAME: ";L$
170 INPUT "STUDENT'S FIRST NAME: ";F$
180 INPUT "STUDENT'S IDENTIFICATION NO. ";I$
190 INPUT "FIRST QUIZ GRADE: ";G1$
200 INPUT "SECOND QUIZ GRADE: ";G2$
210 INPUT "THIRD QUIZ GRADE: ";G3$
220 INPUT "FINAL EXAM GRADE: ";E$
230 LET L$ = LEFT$(L$ + B$,15)
240 LET F$ = LEFT$(F$ + B$,10)
250 LET I$ = RIGHT$(B$ + I$,7)
260 LET G1$ = RIGHT$(B$ + G1$,3)
270 LET G2$ = RIGHT$(B$ + G2$,3)
280 LET G3$ = RIGHT$(B$ + G3$,3)
290 LET E$ = RIGHT$(B$ + E$,3)
300 LET S$(I) = L$ + F$ + I$ + G1$ + G2$ + G3$ + E$
310 NEXT I
320 REM MODULE II
330 PRINT CHR$(4);"OPEN GRADES"
340 PRINT CHR$(4);"WRITE GRADES"
350 FOR I = 1 TO N
360 PRINT S$(I)
370 NEXT I
380 PRINT CHR$(4);"CLOSE GRADES"
390 END
```

Exercises 11.2

1. 190 REM MODULE TO SORT RECORDS BY LAST NAME
   192 FOR J = 1 TO I − 1
   194 FOR K = 1 TO I − J
   196 IF LEFT$(T$(K),15) > LEFT$(T$(K + 1),15) THEN
       LET L$ = T$(K) : LET T$(K) = T$(K + 1) : LET T$(K + 1) = L$
   197 NEXT K
   198 NEXT J

2. (a) 100 REM READ THE TELEPHONE DIRECTORY FROM DISK
       110 DIM T$(100) : REM THIS ASSUMES 100 OR FEWER NAMES
       120 ONERR GOTO 190
       130 PRINT CHR$(4);"OPEN DIRECTORY"
       140 PRINT CHR$(4);"READ DIRECTORY"
       150 LET N = 0
       160 LET N = N + 1
       170 INPUT T$(N)
       180 GOTO 160
       190 PRINT CHR$(4);"CLOSE DIRECTORY"
       195 POKE 216,0
       200 LET N = N − 1 : REM N IS NUMBER OF RECORDS IN FILE
       210 END

   If the number of records is known, the program can be written this way:

       100 INPUT "HOW MANY RECORDS ARE ON FILE? ";N
       110 DIM T$(N)
       120 PRINT CHR$(4);"OPEN DIRECTORY"
       130 PRINT CHR$(4);"READ DIRECTORY"
       140 FOR I = 1 TO N
       150 INPUT T$(I)
       160 NEXT I
       170 PRINT CHR$(4);"CLOSE DIRECTORY"
       180 END

   (b) 100 REM READ THE LEMON AUTO FILE
       110 DIM C$(100) : REM THIS ASSUMES 100 OR FEWER VEHICLES
       120 ONERR GOTO 190
       130 PRINT CHR$(4);"OPEN LEMON AUTO"
       140 PRINT CHR$(4);"READ LEMON AUTO"
       150 LET N = 0
       160 LET N = N + 1
       170 INPUT C$(N)
       180 GOTO 160
       190 PRINT CHR$(4);"CLOSE LEMON AUTO"
       195 POKE 216,0
       200 LET N = N − 1 : REM N IS NUMBER OF RECORDS IN FILE
       210 END

   (c) 100 REM READ THE GRADE FILE
       110 DIM S$(100) : REM THIS ASSUMES 100 OR FEWER STUDENTS
       120 ONERR GOTO 190
       130 PRINT CHR$(4);"OPEN GRADES"
       140 PRINT CHR$(4);"READ GRADES"
       150 LET N = 0
       160 LET N = N + 1
       170 INPUT S$(N)
       180 GOTO 160
       190 PRINT CHR$(4);"CLOSE GRADES"
       195 POKE 216,0
       200 LET N = N − 1 : REM N IS NUMBER OF RECORDS IN FILE
       210 END

Exercises 11.3

1. (a) 10 REM MODULE I − ENTER DATA INTO MEMORY
       20 INPUT "HOW MANY NAMES ARE YOU ENTERING? ";N
       30 DIM T$(N,6)
       35 LET B$ = "   "
       40 FOR I = 1 TO N
       45 INPUT "ENTER LAST NAME: ";L$
       50 INPUT "FIRST NAME: ";F$
       60 INPUT "STREET ADDRESS: ";A$
       70 INPUT "CITY: ";C$

```
  80 INPUT "ZIP: ";Z$
  90 INPUT "TELEPHONE NO.: ";P$
 100 LET T$(I,1)=LEFT$(L$+B$,15)
 110 LET T$(I,2)=LEFT$(F$+B$,10)
 120 LET T$(I,3)=LEFT$(A$+B$,35)
 130 LET T$(I,4)=LEFT$(C$+B$,15)
 140 LET T$(I,5)=LEFT$(Z$+B$,5)
 150 LET T$(I,6)=LEFT$(P$+B$,14)
 170 NEXT I
 180 REM MODULE II − STORE ON DISK IN A FILE
 190 PRINT CHR$(4);"OPEN DIRECTORY"
 200 PRINT CHR$(4);"WRITE DIRECTORY"
 210 FOR I = 1 TO N
 215 FOR K = 1 TO 6
 220 PRINT T$(I,K)
 225 NEXT K
 230 NEXT I
 240 PRINT CHR$(4);"CLOSE DIRECTORY"
 250 END
```

(b)
```
 100 REM MODULE I
 110 INPUT "HOW MANY VEHICLES ARE THERE? ";N
 120 DIM C$(N,7)
 130 LET B$ = "                   "
 140 FOR I = 1 TO N
 150 INPUT "TYPE OF VEHICLE: ";V$
 160 INPUT "MANUFACTURER: ";M$
 170 INPUT "BODY MODEL: ";K$
 180 INPUT "YEAR: ";Y$
 190 INPUT "CURRENT MILEAGE: ";I$
 200 INPUT "DAILY RENTAL PRICE: ";P$
 210 INPUT "MILEAGE RENTAL PRICE: ";A$
 220 LET C$(I,1)=LEFT$(V$+B$,15)
 230 LET C$(I,2)=LEFT$(M$+B$,15)
 240 LET C$(I,3)=LEFT$(K$+B$,15)
 250 LET C$(I,4)=LEFT$(Y$+B$,4)
 260 LET C$(I,5)=RIGHT$(B$+I$,6)
 270 LET C$(I,6)=RIGHT$(B$+P$,5)
 280 LET C$(I,7)=RIGHT$(B$+A$,5)
 300 NEXT I
 310 REM MODULE II
 320 PRINT CHR$(4);"OPEN LEMON AUTO"
 330 PRINT CHR$(4);"WRITE LEMON AUTO"
 340 FOR I = 1 TO N
 345 FOR K = 1 TO 7
 350 PRINT C$(I,K)
 355 NEXT K
 360 NEXT I
 370 PRINT CHR$(4);"CLOSE LEMON AUTO"
 380 END
```

(c)
```
 100 REM MODULE I
 110 INPUT "HOW MANY STUDENTS ARE THERE? ";N
 120 DIM S$(N,7)
 130 LET B$ = "                 "
 140 FOR I = 1 TO N
 150 PRINT "ENTERING STUDENT ";I
 160 INPUT "STUDENT'S LAST NAME: ";L$
 170 INPUT "STUDENT'S FIRST NAME: ";F$
 180 INPUT "STUDENT'S IDENTIFICATION NO. ";I$
 190 INPUT "FIRST QUIZ GRADE: ";G1$
 200 INPUT "SECOND QUIZ GRADE: ";G2$
 210 INPUT "THIRD QUIZ GRADE: ";G3$
 220 INPUT "FINAL EXAM GRADE: ";E$
 230 LET S$(I,1)=LEFT$(L$+B$,15)
 240 LET S$(I,2)=LEFT$(F$+B$,10)
 250 LET S$(I,3)=RIGHT$(B$+I$,7)
 260 LET S$(I,4)=RIGHT$(B$+G1$,3)
 270 LET S$(I,5)=RIGHT$(B$+G2$,3)
 280 LET S$(I,6)=RIGHT$(B$+G3$,3)
 290 LET S$(I,7)=RIGHT$(B$+E$,3)
 310 NEXT I
```

```
320 REM MODULE II
330 PRINT CHR$(4);"OPEN GRADES"
340 PRINT CHR$(4);"WRITE GRADES"
350 FOR I = 1 TO N
355 FOR K = 1 TO 7
360 PRINT S$(I,K)
365 NEXT K
370 NEXT I
380 PRINT CHR$(4);"CLOSE GRADES"
390 END
```

Exercises 11.4

1. To change the programs written in Exercises 11.1
   so that new records may be appended to the file,
   just modify these two lines in each program:

   (a) 20 INPUT "HOW MANY NEW NAMES ARE YOU ENTERING? ";N
        190 PRINT CHR$(4);"APPEND DIRECTORY"

   (b) 110 INPUT "HOW MANY NEW VEHICLES ARE THERE? ";N
        320 PRINT CHR$(4);"APPEND LEMON AUTO"

   (c) 110 INPUT "HOW MANY NEW STUDENTS ARE THERE? ";N
        330 PRINT CHR$(4);"APPEND GRADES"

Index